# THE APPRENTICESHIP OF ERNEST HEMINGWAY

EDITED BY CHARLES A. FENTON

*The Best Short Stories of World War II*

# THE
# *APPRENTICESHIP*
## OF
# *ERNEST*
# *HEMINGWAY*

## THE EARLY YEARS

BY

## CHARLES A. FENTON

## THE VIKING PRESS
### NEW YORK

VIKING COMPASS EDITION

ISSUED IN 1958 BY THE VIKING PRESS, INC.

625 MADISON AVENUE, NEW YORK, N.Y. 10022

DISTRIBUTED IN CANADA BY

THE MACMILLAN COMPANY OF CANADA LIMITED

FIFTH PRINTING NOVEMBER 1968

*The author is grateful to the editors of the* American Quarterly, New World Writing, *and the* Atlantic *for permission to reprint sections of this book which first appeared in somewhat different form in their publications.*

*The material written by Ernest Hemingway for the Toronto Daily Star and the Toronto Star Weekly is copyright 1920, 1921, 1922, 1923, and 1924 by Ernest Hemingway.*

THIS EDITION PUBLISHED BY ARRANGEMENT WITH

FARRAR, STRAUS AND CUDAHY, INC.

PRINTED IN U.S.A. BY THE COLONIAL PRESS INC.

TO

DANIEL H. FENTON

# *CONTENTS*

# CONTENTS

# PREFACE AND ACKNOWLEDGMENTS

This book is a definition of the process by which Ernest Hemingway transposed a conventional talent into an artistic skill. It is based on the premise that his extraordinary position—"Hemingway is the bronze god of the whole contemporary literary experience in America," said Alfred Kazin in 1942—warrants close investigation of a period that lasted no more than half a dozen years. That the apprenticeship was a vital element is verified by the almost immediate assumption of Hemingway's importance—by critics, public, and, above all, by other writers—as soon as his work began to appear in the United States in 1925, and by the durability of his creative life.

The principal instrument of his literary apprenticeship was journalism. Hemingway was a working newspaperman, both intermittently and for long intervals, during the years between October, 1916, and December, 1923. Other factors contributed to the nature and importance of this apprenticeship, including war, travel, sport, and a variety of vocational and literary associations. Hemingway's apprenticeship was extensive, sustained, and purposeful, involving influence which have been overlooked or misunderstood. It was a powerful force in the formation of the style and attitudes which have been generally regarded as characteristic of his mature work. It was also, in terms of journalism itself, and in terms of his first expatriate fiction in 1922 and 1923, a period of achievement as well as development.

ix

In a very real sense Hemingway's apprenticeship has never ended. This too has contributed to his durability. It is also additional verification of the importance of the 1916-1923 apprenticeship, which established his professional principles and habits. He has continued to impose upon himself a demanding growth and a rigid discipline. "I'm apprenticed out at it," he told a friend in 1949, "until I die. Dopes can say you mastered it. But I know nobody ever mastered it, nor could not have done better." This is the story of his first apprenticeship.

It is a story to which many people have contributed their memories and judgment. No more than its outlines could have been detected without the help of more individuals than I care to remember. I have inadequately acknowledged my immense debts in the Notes to individual chapters. Some of these debts require additional acknowledgment: either geographical availability, or their own patience, and in certain cases a fatal combination of the two, made the following individuals particularly vulnerable to my persistence. I am deeply grateful to Archibald S. Alexander; Professor Carlos Baker; Morley Callaghan; Gregory Clark; the late J. Herbert Cranston; J. Charles Edgar; John Gehlmann; the late Henry J. Haskell; William D. Horne, Jr.; Mrs. Guy Hickok; Wilson Hicks; Chester Kerr; Clifford Knight; David Randall; Mary Lowry Ross; William B. Smith; Y. K. Smith; Frederick W. Spiegel; Arthur L. Thexton; Professor Edward Wagenknecht; and Donald M. Wright.

Part of the story, too, was to be found in libraries. I was the beneficiary not only of James T. Babb, Librarian, Sterling Memorial Library, Yale University, and his resourceful staff, but also of the Kansas City (Mo.) Public Library, and in particular Miss Grace Berger, Reference Chief; Stanley Pargellis and The Newberry Library; John D. Gordon, Curator, Berg Collection, New York Public Library; Miss Elsie McKay, Librarian, Oak Park (Ill.) Public Library; Miss Laura E. Loeber, Reference Librarian, Toronto Public Library; and The Toronto Star Reference Library. I am grateful on many counts to Donald C. Gallup, Curator, Yale Collection of American Literature.

Mr. Hemingway generously answered a number of troublesome questions at the beginning of the investigation, but I am even more indebted to him for the grace with which he endured the invasions of a project that held little appeal and considerable irritation for him. Like everyone who serves with and near Benjamin C. Nangle, I owe him more than I can say; I owe more than most, since he was compelled to teach me a great deal while allowing me to pose as his colleague. I have cited one aspect of my obligation to Norman Holmes Pearson in the Notes to Chapter Seven, but it is a debt whose many aspects cannot be properly catalogued. The debt was compounded by the part he played in the version of this book which was originally presented as a dissertation for the degree of Doctor of Philosophy at Yale University. To my wife, for whom the project represented even more of an invasion than for its subject, I offer not only my thanks but also, again, my apologies.

Yale University                                      C.A.F.

7 March 1954

THE  APPRENTICESHIP  OF  ERNEST  HEMINGWAY

# OAK PARK

"What does one learn about writing in
high school? You are lucky if you're
not taught to write badly."[1]

*I.*

Ernest Hemingway has always been acutely aware of
Oak Park, Illinois, where he was born in July, 1899 and
lived continuously until 1917. The fact that he has rarely
written directly of his boyhood there is misleading as a
measure of his response to the community. By conscious
design he substituted other experiences for his absorption in
that particular world.

A number of unpleasant things happened to Hemingway
in Oak Park. He was never wholly at ease with its rather
special milieu, nor it with him. Oak Park, however, has
always been a fundamental element in his attitudes. It conditioned certain of his values in a way that is almost a parody
of popular concepts about the importance of heredity and
environment. Even in middle age, thirty-five years after he
graduated from its high school and left its physical boundaries, he still thought of Oak Park with creative regret. "I
had a wonderful novel to write about Oak Park," Hemingway said in 1952, "and would never do it because I did not
want to hurt living people."

Had he written such a novel, or should he ever write one
in the future, it would be intensely discussed, if not actually
read, in Oak Park; its interest in him has been even greater,

and far less charitable, than his in the community. The town is vastly changed today, bigger, shabbier, less genteel and spacious, but Hemingway's legend is an explosive one among those of his generation who have remained there. Older residents take a perverse pride in his achievement and his fame. They invariably preface their discussions of his work by hastily disclaiming any actual acquaintanceship with it. Their principal concern is directed at what they understand to be its general tone.

"The wonder to me," said one of his teachers many years after Hemingway's departure, "and to a lot of other Oak Parkers, is how a boy brought up in Christian and Puritan nurture should know and write so well of the devil and the underworld." Most of the community shares the pious bewilderment of that older group. "It is a puzzle," another native declared in 1952, "and, too, an amazement to Oak Park that Ernest should have written the kind of books that he did."

Those comments, although they were made at midcentury, are in the authentic idiom of pre-World War I Oak Park. The community was more than respectable. It was respectable and prosperous. It was also Protestant and middle class. It exulted in all these characteristics. For Oak Park there was nothing ludicrous in its qualities. Its citizens experienced the same sense of community membership as occurs in such suburbs as Brookline, Massachusetts; they thought of themselves as specifically living in Oak Park rather than Chicago, just as one lives in Brookline rather than Boston. "Oak Park," a contemporary of Hemingway once said, without satire, "has prided itself on being the largest village in the world."

As was only natural, though not apparent to most residents of Oak Park, such a structure had flaws as well as virtues. If Oak Park could boast that it had successfully resisted incorporation into the politics and corruption of nearby Chicago, thus retaining a mild town-meeting flavor in its management, it was also heir to the provincialism of village life. One's neighbors were scrutinized with New England severity. If one happened to be, like Ernest Hemingway, the oldest son of a union between two such locally prominent families as the Hemingways and the Halls, the scrutiny was merely the more intense. It was an atmosphere calculated both to irritate and attract a boy who was proud, competitive, and intelligent, particularly if his intelligence were of a satiric and inquiring kind.

It was also a rather limited world in the superficial sense of not presenting a variety of types or scenes. The forthcoming shock of contact with the ugliness of, for example, journalism and war, would be intense and memorable for a young man raised in such a relatively sheltered world. There is a pleasant sameness to the streets of the older part of Oak Park, north of Washington Boulevard, which documents the local boast that this was the middle-class capital of the world. The houses have become seedy rather than charming in their antiquity, for fashionable suburbia has moved northward along the Lake. Now there are boarding houses along North Kenilworth Avenue, but the burgher solidity of forty years ago is still detectable.

It was a world far more homogeneous, socially and economically, than exists today in similar American residential districts. Oak Parkers, trying to communicate the flavor of their childhoods, stress the fact that there was no other side of the tracks; their memories err, as it happens, but the deeply cherished illusion is even more revealing through being inaccurate.[2] Some fathers were clearly more successful than others, and there were delicate gradations within the social equality of Oak Park, but in the vision of the average Oak Park child there was neither poverty nor ostentation. There were no saloons, for the town was righteously dry; the wide-open streets of nearby Cicero were an unknown excitement for most Oak Park adolescents. The center of social life, even for the most sophisticated, was the school and the family church. The boundary between Chicago and Oak Park, in fact, was defined by the irreverent as the point where the saloons ended and the churches began.

In such a community education was as important as religion, and equally earnest. Like most Midwesterners of their class and period, Oak Parkers had a real hostility toward the eastern private schools to which many of them might well have sent their children. They therefore established for the local school system, and particularly in the secondary field, standards that were genuinely impressive. Few of the graduates of Oak Park High had any difficulty with the admission requirements of Williams, Mount Holyoke, Wellesley, Yale, Amherst, or the fashionable and more regionally attractive Beloit. Oak Park candidates dominated the competitive exams for the ten scholarships the University of Chicago awarded annually to area students. Teaching salaries were well above the average. The academic plant was first-class in every way. Those graduates who later attended college—the percentage was generally as high as two-thirds of a senior class, exceptional for the period— frequently discovered that Oak Park teaching was superior to their later instruction. Residents of the town were likely to maintain, with justification, that four years at Oak Park High were the equivalent of two years of college.

The school's curriculum, quite naturally, was built around the liberal arts. The English Department, to which Hemingway responded most fully, and in whose classes his contemporaries remembered him most clearly, was large and efficient. English was required during each of the four years. For all classes, from English I through English IV, there was an emphasis on the fundamentals of language. "I think the level of instruction in Oak Park was high," said Janet Lewis, a 1916 graduate who became both a poet and university teacher, "because we learned to spell, and to write coherently."

Even in freshman year, however, there were also intensive reading assignments. The backbone of the syllabus was the literary achievement of the past, to such a degree, in fact, that the University of Chicago once criticized the English Department for the predominance of classics in its courses. In their first year of English the Oak Park students read a widely used text of the period, H. A. Guerber's *Myths of Greece and Rome*. The stories were "narrated," Guerber pointed out in his subtitle, "with special reference to literature and art." Guerber's presentation of the myths themselves was in a conventionally literary idiom, but his narrative style was lively and entertaining.

There was, in fact, an emphasis on narrative in English I, where Hemingway's section was taught by Frank J. Platt, the department chairman. Two of the supplementary texts were Rhodes' *Old Testament Narratives* and *One Hundred Narrative Poems*. The fiction that was read in class, novels such as *Ivanhoe*, was material of the same emphatic story content. There was also a great deal of outside reading. Some of it was in "good current literature"—H. G. Wells, for example, and Owen Wister—but the popular novels of the era were virtually outlawed.

It was nonetheless as sound a reading background as one could ask of a freshman English course, and superior to the average curriculum. It becomes less lugubrious in terms of Hemingway's mature work when we recall that he subsequently said, "that's how I learned to write—by reading the Bible," adding that by the Bible he meant particularly the Old Testament.[3] The concern with the substantial work of the past continued in English II, part of whose assignments and classroom discussions included a survey of American literature. English III was primarily public speaking and essay writing. In senior year the emphasis returned to the classics. Here, in English IV, Oak Park seniors encountered a study of English literature so thorough that one of Hemingway's classmates later found that an advanced English survey at the University of Chicago was a duplication of his high school course. The discipline of intensive drill which had begun in English I was thus continued in the fourth year, save that now it revolved around the study and memorization of long passages of verse, particularly Chaucer and Shakespeare.

By senior year, however, Hemingway was writing as well as reading. His instructor in English I, in fact, who remembered him as a "bright scholar," gifted in "the communicative arts," later maintained that even in his freshman themes Hemingway wrote "with an avid interest in realistic adventure." Several contemporaries from Mr. Platt's section had the same memories. They also remembered that Hemingway's work was highly individual. "I can recall," said one of them, who was for a time a close friend and neighbor, "that his writings in this class were different to the extent that it seemed to me they might not be acceptable as the assignment."

It was after freshman year, however, that Hemingway worked under what he himself cited as his significant teachers. Questioned many years later about the English faculty in general, Hemingway mentioned only two teachers. "In High School," he said in 1951, "I had two teachers of English: Miss Fannie Biggs and Miss Dixon. I think they were the two advisers on the *Tabula* [the school literary magazine] and they were both very nice and especially nice to me because I had to try to be an athlete as well as try to learn to write English." Miss Biggs' and Miss Dixon's principal teaching assignments were in the upperclass courses that stressed composition and public speaking. Hemingway's interest in writing was stimulated both by the nature of the curriculum and by the particular gifts of these two teachers.

"I think Ernie started seriously to write soon after 1915," said an older student who saw a good deal of him at this time. "He had a typewriter on the third floor, well away from his family. By that time he was writing for the fun of it and apparently felt that he was developing ability along that line. He would read to me some of the things he was writing and was quite enthusiastic." It was about this time too, however, as he became heavy enough for the varsity squads, that athletics began to interfere with his writing. "It was not like Scott [Fitzgerald] wanting to be an athlete," Hemingway once explained. "I had no ambition nor choice. At Oak Park if you could play football you had to play it." Miss Dixon and Miss Biggs relieved some of the frustration.

They were exceptional as teachers and as individuals. Their quality is eagerly documented by the testimony of colleagues and students. Margaret Dixon expressed in her classes the vigor and conviction of an articulate, positive woman. She was gifted in and interested by verbal narrative. "At an evening social or party among friends," the chairman of her department remembered, "she would be the center of attraction, as she regaled her listeners with details of some lively experience." A classmate of Hemingway, who later became a teacher himself, remembered her with startling clarity. Edward Wagenknecht studied under her for two successive years, and "knew her very well." He could recall both her personality and her classes.

"Margaret Dixon," said Wagenknecht in 1951, "was a very frank, straightforward, honest, down-to-earth person, though within the standards of decorous respectability that were favored in Oak Park. She had a temper, and her class was never a dull place. She was an outspoken liberal. Again and again, she expressed in the classroom her admiration for

Woodrow Wilson and her utter contempt for Theodore Roosevelt. She was also more interested in movies than most high school teachers admitted they were in those days."

Miss Dixon's friends in Oak Park often heard her describe Hemingway with enthusiasm, speaking of him as the most brilliant student she ever had; they realized too that a woman of her hard integrity would be incapable of altering the past to fit the achievement of Hemingway's maturity. In her teaching, according to a classmate who worked with Hemingway on the school paper and sat near him in class, Miss Dixon "pushed the creative side, and urged us to use our imagination and dare to try putting into writing our original and interesting thoughts." Miss Dixon was a blunt critic. "She was salty in her criticism, proud and full of praise for our efforts and quite ready to rip at what was not good."

Margaret Dixon's importance to Hemingway was in this area of temperament and attitude. Her blunt honesty and mild iconoclasm were valuable antidotes to the smug complacence of Oak Park. "Her economic and social ideas," one of her personal friends recalled drily, "were somewhat at variance with the very conservative school and community." American high schools have been blessed with many Miss Dixons; she was not professionally unique, nor was her relationship with Hemingway an unusual one, but it was a piece of extreme good fortune that she was available to Hemingway. "She was always trying to get us to write stories and essays," another classmate of Hemingway testified. "I don't believe I ever had any professors at Dartmouth or Illinois who were better instructors and I majored in English."

Fannie Biggs, the other English teacher whom Hemingway described as "very nice and especially nice to me," was the ideal complement for Miss Dixon. "She was a kind of genius," according to one of her colleagues, "a frail but wiry little woman, with a well-read mind, with exacting requirements, and with a fine sense of humor." Her associates defined the two women by comparing them to one another. "Miss Dixon's work," said another member of the department, "was a clarification in whatever the assignment might be. Miss Biggs, out of much more temperamental disposition, would flourish more in the field of imagination."

Fannie Biggs' interest in Hemingway was somewhat more personal than Miss Dixon's. She responded not only to his potential as a student, but to his problems as an individual. She observed his difficulties, most of them common to all adolescent boys, a few of them peculiar to his particular position, and did what she could, in the most tentative way, to soften them. Hemingway was at ease with her, in a manner that was neither odd nor excessive. Occasionally he spoke to her in a peripheral fashion about something that was troubling him. A year after he graduated from high school, and with seven months of Kansas City newspaper work completed, it was to Fannie Biggs that Hemingway boasted mildly about his journalistic triumphs, just before he left in May, 1918 for the war in Italy. Years later, when he recalled the one teacher as Miss Dixon, he remembered the other as Fannie Biggs. There was a difference.

The difference came as much as anything from the fact that while Miss Dixon was interested in writing, Fannie Biggs was devoted to it. It was Fannie Biggs who was the principal force in the Story Club, a picked class which was selected by competition at the end of junior year and which met once a week under her leadership during the next year. These seniors, usually a group of twenty-five, read their stories aloud and discussed them critically. "I remember," one of those young writers declared, "that she was always particularly pleased when Ernest would come up with something definitely unusual." Other classmates had the same recollections. "She was very much interested in Ernest and his evident ability and love of writing. I have clearly remembered and mentioned many times her picking out themes of Ernest's and reading them to the class as outstanding examples of whatever it was she had requested."

Oak Park regarded Fannie Biggs as the creative member of the English Department. Her students could always recall the energy of her vision, and one of them remembered that when she helped him on his commencement address, in the spring of 1917, she reshaped his heavy paragraphs into "a poetic approach whose meaning I scarcely understood at the time and have come to value later." The title toward which she led young Edward Willcox's oratory indicates the nature of her temperament. His commencement address for the class of 1917 was "A Plea for Pan."

*II.*

It would be a distortion, however, to conceive of Hemingway as a predominantly bookish or literary high school student. In the accumulation of extracurricular posts and memberships Hemingway was spectacularly well-rounded. It required eight lines to list his achievements in the Class Book. Only the class president and one of its star athletes exceeded him in the length of their paragraphs.

Hemingway was chosen to write the Class Prophecy, which automatically admitted him to the elite group of Class Day Speakers. He was a member of the orchestra during his first three years. In senior year he played Richard Brinsley Sheridan in the class play, Fitch's *Beau Brummell*. As a junior he was a reporter for the weekly newspaper, the *Trapeze;* the next year he became one of its six editors. During both those years he contributed stories and poems to the literary magazine. In his last two years he belonged to a trio of debating and self-improvement groups. The

Hanna Club met at regular intervals to listen to prominent businessmen and local civic leaders; the Burke Club was an exercise in oratory and parliamentary procedure, and the Boys' High School Club offered its members a series of addresses "on efficiency, Christianity and such things that are desirable to the life of a boy."[4] Hemingway was in the Athletic Association as a freshman, sophomore, and senior. He played junior varsity football in his second and third years; in his senior year he was on the championship first team. He was track manager, too, that year, and a member of the swimming team. He was captain of water basketball. During his first three years, according to the Class Book, he belonged to the Boys' Rifle Club.

That particular membership became part of the class legend, for the Boys' Rifle Club was in reality a desperate inspiration which Hemingway devised as editor of the *Trapeze*, during a week when he was confronted by an empty column and no material with which to fill it. He hastily created the mythical organization, stimulated by the existence of a genuine Girls' Rifle Club, and listed himself and five friends as members. The story was read with interest and acceptance, and for several weeks, according to the late Morris Musselman, Hollywood writer and Oak Park classmate, Hemingway filed additional stories about the club's matches and incredible skill. In the spring the Class Book editors, in good faith, asked for a picture of the group. Hemingway was equal to the crisis. He borrowed a shotgun for each of the five marksmen, none of whom had either owned or fired such a weapon, and posed them professionally.

The anecdote restores the proper perspective to any conception of Hemingway as a mere victim of a highly organized school hierarchy. He was as vigorously competitive in Oak Park as he has been in his manhood. This spirited energy has even contributed one element of his artistic creed. "Listen," he told a young writer in 1936, "there is no use writing anything that has been written before unless you can beat it. What a writer in our time has to do is write what hasn't been written before or beat dead men at what they have done."[5]

He is not always as literarily belligerent as that, however, and frequently his artistic pronouncements have been sardonic and relaxed. The Rifle Club burlesque of extracurricular frenzy represented the same healthy self-irony. Hemingway has seldom been able to resist a challenge in any area of his life, but he has rarely solemnized his competitive zeal. The instinct to win has been almost a reflex; his conscious attitude toward the reflex has caused it to become graceful. "I remember," said one classmate, "that often his themes were humorous. And this is something I have talked about since—he was gay in those days, always laughing, carefree. His literary ability was recognized, but one might have predicted that he would be a writer of humor."

It was characteristic of such a temperament that this buoyancy should disguise a more somber aspect of his life and attitudes. Hemingway as an adult has never taken anything easily, nor do many high school students of intelligence and sensitivity have an entirely carefree existence. It is this side of his Oak Park boyhood which has been emphasized by Freudian literary commentators and casual biographers. Hemingway himself has encouraged the legend of a turbulent youth. The occasional tensions of the period have been magnified until the symbol of his boyhood is a runaway vagabondage. Such episodes did occur of course, as they occur for many boys; they are almost a pattern for a certain kind of middle-class American boyhood.

His brief flights from home—sufficiently brief so that he never dropped back in school because of them—were little more than the rebellious independence of a restless boy.

Years later Hemingway declared that the best training for a writer was an unhappy boyhood. This was in part a serious statement, applicable to a degree in his own case; in part, too, it was a sly comment on literature in general and first novels in particular, and an ironic, characteristic belittlement of artistic solemnity. To think of his adolescence in terms of misery or maladjustment is to misunderstand his Oak Park experience and his personality as a whole.

It is true that his adolescence was made difficult by the intensity of his own character and the complexity of his family relationships. Normally his common sense and energy sustained him; occasionally he had bleak moments. The spartan demands of his physician father invariably conflicted with the rich artistic aura which his mother attempted to cast over her family; there was inevitable confusion and bitterness for a boy as responsive and sensitive as their oldest son. The stress of emotional tension, however, contributed to the growing opaqueness of his vision. From his wanderings and escapades he began to acquire a precocious wisdom. Some of the faculty, and an occasional contemporary, sensed in him an unusual awareness. "When I expressed surprise at the sophistication of his books," said a classmate who was the daughter of a teacher, "my father said that he had been more knowing in high school than the rest of us."

Little of this ambivalence was readily apparent. It was never more than a minor factor in an otherwise restless but reasonably well-adjusted period. "I heard stories about Ernest being a 'tough guy,' having run away from home, etc.," said Edward Wagenknecht, "but I never saw anything to confirm any of this." He could hardly have acquired those eight inches devoted to him in the class book had his four years been chaotic or disturbed. The epitaph beneath his extracurricular record summed up the wry, impressed assessment of his contemporaries. "None," they concluded, "are to be found more clever than Ernie."[6]

### III.

The cleverness which his Oak Park classmates discovered in Hemingway went beyond the casual wit and horseplay of high school friendships. It also took the more permanent form of publication. Most of his classmates remembered this role as primarily that of an entertaining reporter and columnist for the school newspaper. He also published a moderate amount of fiction and verse in the literary magazine; his work in the *Tabula* reaffirms those qualities which caused his classmates to greet with eagerness the themes he read in the English courses.

Hemingway never held office on the *Tabula*, and, indeed, the aggressiveness which he brought to the more conventionally masculine activities was conspicuously absent or concealed in his early attitude toward both the magazine and the newspaper. There was a reticence in his attitude toward all artistic or semi-artistic endeavor. Its origins were in his personal background. He lived in a household where creative talent was oppressively honored. For a time he deliberately cultivated the other capacities of his temperament. When his stories did begin to appear in the *Tabula* it was almost by an act of conspiracy on the part of his supporters.

"He never submitted a story or essay to the school magazine while I was on it," said a classmate whose editorial tenure on the *Tabula* covered their junior and senior years. "But Mr. Platt, the magazine's faculty adviser, came with a manuscript, evidently handed to him by Miss Dixon, and I knew that this essay or story about a hunting expedition was considered good enough by the teachers that it was to be printed whether it appealed to me or not."

The story itself, "Judgment of Manitou," published in the issue of February, 1916, is quite naturally without artistic validity, save in the synthetic hindsight of Hemingway's mature work.[7] The dialogue, it is true, was neither forced nor literary, and the narrative was brisk and lucid. To cite the story as a prophecy of ultimate creative force, however, would be bogus. The fiction was noteworthy only in the sense that it is always noteworthy when a high school junior labors long enough to contrive a readable narrative. "Judgment of Manitou" was thoroughly readable. It marked the author as possessing an interest in the mechanics of storytelling. Its rich detail indicated that he enjoyed writing it. More than that, in terms of foreshadowing, it does not permit. Dealing as it did with the scenes Hemingway encountered each summer at the family home in northern Michigan, it could be said to confirm his early absorption in nature and in violence. The vindictive trapper and the young associate whom he murders, their conflict framed in the mysticism of Indian folklore, are reminiscent of a Jack London treatment. It is a savage story, tempered by irony, and those characteristics have been basic in his later work. Had Hemingway become a minor poet, on the other hand, or a slick serialist, "Judgment of Manitou" could be juggled with equal plausibility into becoming a promise of subsequent achievement in verse or in the women's magazines.

The story's utility as an index to this phase of Hemingway's apprenticeship lies in certain negative areas. Its literacy documents the sound education he was receiving. The story is superior to most adolescent fiction by virtue of its control and lucidity. Sixteen-year-old authors normally produce material that is throttled by false starts and frequent climaxes; the ending is frequently without relation to the beginning, and characters tend to appear from nowhere and dissolve with equal ease. "Judgment of Manitou" was clear and precise. The orderly presentation reflected the discipline Hemingway had received in the fundamentals of composition. The absence of stylistic affectations was a tribute to the good taste of his teachers. "Judgment of Manitou" was an unpretentious story, elaborate only in its relatively complicated plot. Its sturdy clarity was far more durable as a base.

By his junior year, indeed, when Hemingway wrote this story, he was in some ways unusually thoughtful about writing, although the bulk of his energy was still absorbed by more conventional outlets. He was responding to his teaching in a brooding, undramatic way. One of the most acute of his classmates, herself very much interested in writing, could remember that at this time she had not read widely enough to grasp all the subtleties of elementary literary technique. "When Ernest one day spoke of an author's style," she said later, "I knew that he had either read more or was more sensitive than I." She recalled that some of Hemingway's classroom exercises were entirely beyond her. "He wrote a story about an Irish detective named O'Hell that was outside my orbit."

Hemingway's next work in the *Tabula* demonstrated this same kind of approach, an instinctive professionalism which was a blend of inclination, reading, and the example of persuasive, unaffected teachers. "A Matter of Colour" was published in the following issue of the *Tabula*, in April, 1916.[8] The story was in some ways an improvement over its predecessor, particularly in its less obvious reliance on coincidence. Hemingway's principal strength, however, continued to be his utilization of material which he had either experienced or observed. He dealt with the prize fight world he was just then encountering through his boxing lessons in a Chicago gym.

He made no attempt to impose a statement on the story. Its basic structure was an ironic anecdote about a crooked fight. The denouement was withheld until the final line; everything hinged upon the information of that last sentence. The treatment reflected the current debt to O. Henry. It was pure gimmick, a build-up for a vaudeville punch line. The story was presented as a monologue by a veteran fight manager. Old Bob Armstrong spoke in language which was an attempt to reproduce an authentic idiom, but, like the narrators in most professional magazine fiction of the period, he was so carefully shaped into a recognizable type that his speech became a single heavy cliché. Occasionally Hemingway permitted the dialogue to flow without the hackneyed phrases. " 'It can't be helped,' says Dan. 'That bag wasn't fastened proper; I'll fight anyway.' " The primary significance of Hemingway's *Tabula* stories is to emphasize the crucial apprenticeship which lay ahead of him in journalism, in war, and in the European associations of the 1920's. His high school fiction demonstrates that he was blessed with an acute interest in all new experience, a ready narrative style, and a sound training in clear self-expression. The rest would come only after a series of increasingly more sophisticated tutors and a vast amount of personal growth and application.

The momentum of English III, out of which had come "Judgment of Manitou" and "A Matter of Colour," was nevertheless an important factor. It sustained Hemingway's instinct toward creative writing even during his senior year, when most of the impulse was being satisfied by his work for the school newspaper. The first issue of the 1916-17 *Tabula*, published in November, featured another story drawn from the northern Michigan material.[9] "Sepi Jingan" was also largely dialogue, a tale of violence and revenge told by an Ojibway Indian. This time Hemingway avoided the artificiality of total monologue. There was a base of fragmentary exposition; the narrator asked occasional questions that kept the Indian's speech fluid.

The most promising characteristic of "Sepi Jingan," however, was Hemingway's introduction of a statement. His conception of the two previous stories had never gone beyond the anecdotes themselves. Now he created another dimension by inserting the paradox of an Ojibway killer who was also a kind, decent man, patient with the questions of the young summer resident, tender with the dog, Sepi Jingan, and more deeply concerned about the merits of various pipe tobaccos than the savage memories of the manhunt he was describing. The statement was clumsily handled at times, nor, understandably, had Hemingway yet learned to make a thesis unobtrusive and implicit. The dialogue, however, was smoother, partially cleansed of the tendency to entertain his classmates with smart hyperbole, and to the clarity of narrative there had been added a calm, worldly discernment.

The edge of the full moon showed above the hill to the east. To our right was a grassy bank. "Let's sit down," Bill said. "Did I ever tell you about Sepi Jingan?"

"Like to hear it," I replied.

"You remember Paul Black Bird?"

"The new fellow who got drunk last fourth of July and went to sleep on the Pere Marquette tracks?"

"Yes. He was a bad Indian. Up on the upper peninsula he couldn't get drunk. He used to drink all day—everything. But he couldn't get drunk. Then he would go crazy; but he wasn't drunk. He was crazy because he couldn't get drunk."

The knowledgeability took various forms, as has the knowledgeability of his mature work. It was not always as adult as the mature estimate of Paul Black Bird's misery. Occasionally Hemingway was content to mine only slapstick from this capacity for understanding. One of Miss

Dixon's annual assignments to her upperclassmen, for example, was the composition of a ballad. Hemingway's precocious handling of this exercise was printed in that same November, 1916 issue of the *Tabula*.[10] It was an ancient device whose entire forty-eight lines consisted of variations on the author's query as to what he should write about and how he should rhyme it. The first stanza stated the approach and content of the other five.

> Oh, I've never writ a ballad
> And I'd rather eat shrimp salad,
> (Tho' the Lord knows how I hate the
> Pink and Scrunchy little beasts),
> But Miss Dixon says I gotto—
> (And I pretty near forgotto)
> But I'm sitting at my table
> And my feet are pointing east.

The whole lively jest, "How Ballad Writing Affects Our Seniors," indicated something more than confident charm and an affection for Kipling. There was a glossy finish that was alien to the solemnity of the *Tabula;* even the HE-SHE jokes in the SMILES department, where the ballad was printed, were heavy by comparison. The technical dexterity, unremarkable in any large sense, was impressive in a high school student. It was a variation of the increasing sophistication which had encouraged him to attempt the paradox of "Sepi Jingan."

Hemingway confirmed this sleek facility with several other poems during his senior year. His range extended from a neat burlesque of James Whitcomb Riley through solemn lines about the moral superiority of a Great Lakes stoker to his effete passengers.[11] He also collaborated with his friend and teammate, Fred Wilcoxen, in some impressionistic, Sandburg-like free verse about a football game.[12]

The heroic aura of "Athletic Verse" must have been largely
the contribution of Wilcoxen, the star athlete of the Class of
1917, a three-letter man who had been on varsity squads
as early as his sophomore year. Football for Hemingway
had been largely an unavoidable chore. "Football," he explained later, talking about the experiences which had been
helpful in learning to write, "I knew too much about and
it did not interest me really and I have never written a line
about it."[13]

Ironically, however, Hemingway's senior year was spent
in the creatively unfruitful competitions—as opposed to
boxing or fishing—of high school sport. He not only played
varsity football all that fall, but even in his writing he was
for a time restricted to sports material for the weekly newspaper. It was in the *Trapeze*, in fact, rather than the *Tabula*,
that Hemingway's apprenticeship really began. Journalism
would be the basic ingredient of his formal training, at least
until 1922, and his vocation from 1920 until 1924. His newspaper career was thrust upon him in Oak Park in the winter
of 1916, when he was sixteen.

*IV.*

Between January, 1916 and May, 1917, Hemingway's
by-line—usually Ernest M. Hemingway, as it remained
throughout his newspaper work—appeared more than thirty
times in the *Trapeze*. The *Trapeze*, a characteristic secondary school paper, was in no way more typical than in the
emphatic prominence it gave to sports coverage. Hemingway's assignment to the varsity contests thus certified him
as an acceptable reporter in the estimation of the editors and
their faculty adviser. The latter, indeed, subsequently declared that by the end of his junior year Hemingway "was
recognized as the best writer on the staff."

It was to Arthur Bobbitt, in fact, that Hemingway owed

his initial push into journalism. In 1916, when the history teacher was first appointed its sponsor, the *Trapeze* was being published irregularly. It was largely the preserve of one or two students. Bobbitt reorganized it as a weekly, with a fixed publication schedule and a conventional student hierarchy of editors, business staff, and reporters. Bobbitt vividly recalled the occasion when he recruited Hemingway; he told the story many times to colleagues and students. His classmates, Bobbitt suggested to Hemingway one day in study hall, had often spoken about his writing ability. Hemingway replied that he didn't want to write for the paper. "I'm not interested in writing," he said.

It was the same synthetic resistance which a few weeks later caused Hemingway's reluctance to publish his fiction, requiring the intercession of Mr. Platt and Miss Dixon before "Judgment of Manitou" was submitted to the *Tabula*. "No, I don't want to," he repeated to Bobbitt, but he got the article in by the deadline, and though Bobbitt had to repeat his arguments for the next issue, Hemingway, the adviser recalled, "soon became an enthusiastic reporter."

The material Hemingway wrote for the *Trapeze* in the winter and spring of 1916 was competent but in no way exceptional. There were several others on the staff who seem by their work to have been as able reporters as he; one of his contemporaries, in fact, maintained later that "it seems strange now, but most of us thought he wrote very indifferently." In reality the quality of Hemingway's early reportage was a compromise between the retrospective enthusiasm of Mr. Bobbitt and the skepticism of the classmate. He wrote seven by-lined articles that first year, and was sufficiently capable, and interested, so that when the staff was chosen for senior year he was named as one of the six editors.

Hemingway was even more productive as an editor than as a reporter. He wrote twenty-four stories between November, 1916 and May, 1917. There was scarcely an issue during that period in which his by-line did not appear at least once; several times he had as many as three articles in a single number. The stories were usually five or six hundred words long. Although Hemingway was functioning as a reporter rather than a columnist, he could not always maintain the objectivity of conventional reportage. "As usual," he noted bitterly in a description of a one-sided loss by the home team, "Oak Park was without the services of their constantly ineligible stars and Standish joined the missing pair due to parental objection to his swimming."[14]

Such editorialization would have been red-penciled by Mr. Bobbitt, who supervised the paper very closely. Bobbitt, however, as of the issue of December 22, 1916, had delegated faculty sponsorship of the *Trapeze* to a young instructor named John Gehlmann. Like his superior, the new adviser had no professional newspaper background, but he was a perceptive, energetic man who encouraged every reasonable form of student initiative. Gehlmann was at times a particular ally of Hemingway, for the latter soon grew restless under the drab bondage of sports writing; on his own Hemingway launched what was by far the significant enterprise, either journalistic or creative, of his high school writing.

*V.*

In 1917 Ring Lardner was probably the contemporary writer most widely read in the Chicago area. His column in the Chicago *Tribune* was one of the municipal glories, revered by subscribers of all ages. Hemingway's contemporaries testify to their own excitement when they encountered Lardner. For many of them he was the first contemporary writer they read. "In the Wake of the News" was an intoxicating diet after the required staples of late

Victorian literature. Hemingway's own response to Lardner
was instantaneous. He documented his homage with a series
of *Trapeze* adaptations.

The most impressive aspect of Hemingway's use of the
*Tribune* columnist as a model was the imaginative way in
which he transferred the latter's techniques into a high
school framework. The boy's work ultimately became more
than an imitation; it was original as well as derivative. During the winter of his senior year Hemingway made four
awkward, repetitive experiments; by the spring he was
using the form with confidence and success. He was no
longer content simply to replace Lardner's situations and
characters with high school facsimiles. He used instead a
Lardnerian treatment of authentic high school material. In
a column of May 4, 1917, addressed to "Dear Marce"—
his sister Marcelline was editor that week—he demonstrated
the authenticity of his adaptation. The paragraph was an
effective parody of adolescent conversation and attitudes.

Say, Marcelline, did you know that there is 5 pairs of
brothers and sisters in school and invariabsolutely it is a
strange coincidence that the sister is good looking and the
brother is not? Schwabs, Shepherds, Condrons, Krafts and
Hemingways, is it not most peculair that except in one
family the sister is awful lot better looking than the brother.
But we are too modest to say which family is the exception.
Huh? Marce?[15]

Hemingway also understood the Lardner device of self-
derision. "The *Trapeze* is short of stuff," he wrote, a paragraph or two later, "and so don't get sore if I string this
out because anyway you should give me lots of space because we are sisters and brothers." The basic structure of
the entire treatment, in fact, indicated a comprehensive
grasp of Lardner's principal effects, confirming Mr. Bob-

bitt's subsequent statement that Hemingway "took articles from the Chicago papers and studied them carefully." The young satirist completed the seven hundred word column —it was called "Ring Lardner Returns"—with a sly gibe at Oak Park conservatism, which he had already mocked in paragraphs about smoking and gambling.

Well, Marce, I had better quit now but if you and Mr. Gehlmann let this go thru you will be glad because think of the joy it may bring to some suffering heart,

"Lovingly?"

"Ernie"

In fairness to Gehlmann, this derision should have been directed not at him but at the superintendent, the late M. R. McDaniel. The latter frequently chided the young faculty sponsor about Hemingway's columns. "I was always having to fight criticism by the superintendent," Gehlmann once said, "that Ernie was writing like Ring Lardner—and consequently a lost soul!" McDaniel remained unimpressed by Hemingway's mature work. Ultimately the *Trapeze* material of Hemingway's adolescence became one of McDaniel's favorite jests; he was fond of reminding Gehlmann that Hemingway got his start under the history instructor's sponsorship. "He held me responsible for the malodorous writings from Ernie's pen," Gehlmann remembered.

Official opposition, even as mild as Superintendent McDaniel's, had a predictable effect on Hemingway. He was back in strength in the next issue. This time, however, he gave his column a new title. "SOME SPACE FILLED BY ERNEST MACNAMARA HEMINGWAY," it read, with an ironic subheading: "Ring Lardner Has Objected to the Use of His Name."[16] The approach of graduation, as well as the superintendent's distaste, seemed to furnish Hemingway a heightened creative momentum, for the bulk of his Lardner material was written in the last weeks of his senior year. He published another of his columns in the issue of May 25.[17] The tone of the article, a series of personal paragraphs, was explicitly in the pattern of his previous satires. Hemingway bowed out of Oak Park in the role of professional iconoclast.

"Mr. Dale Bumstead," he began, "gives a dinner dance tomorrow night at the Country Club. Messers Morris Musselman, Fred Wilcoxen, Ernest Hemingway, Abraham Lincoln and General Joffre will not be among those present, all having perfect alibis." Hemingway also returned to the locally profane topic of gambling. "Several members of the Trap Shooting Club," he declared, "are exhibiting pieces of silver ware of the Ohlsens' home as trophies of the meeting held there Saturday night. The silver ware is always the last stakes that Ray puts up." He violated, with relish, the Oak Park mores on drinking. "A new party enters the race next fall in the person of the anti-prohibition party. Its leaders, led by Tom Cusack, nominated the modest editor of these columns and announced their slogan as 'Hemingway and a full Stein!' "

Hemingway's valediction was thus an amiable roundhouse swing at faculty, community, and classmates, not the less pointed for its amiability. The junior class paid tribute to him in the first editorial of their *Trapeze* tenure, citing "the humor of Airline [Morris Musselman's column] and Ring Lardner" as having given "more pep to the issues."[18] Even an unliterary classmate who deplored Hemingway's subsequent career conceded later that "at the time we were in high school, Ring Lardner was in his prime and Ernie ran a column in the *Trapeze* imitating Lardner and it was quite good."

Hemingway's work for the *Trapeze* had an importance far larger than the recognition it brought from his contemporaries. It provided him with a personal direction. Mr.

Bobbitt felt with justice that the *Trapeze* experience was "the opening wedge for the newspaper experience which Ernest went into immediately upon graduation." Had he attended the University of Illinois, as he indicated to his classmates that he would, Hemingway planned to major in journalism.[19] He had found in the high school newspaper experience, and particularly in the freedoms of a column, at least the beginnings of a tangible objective. He wrote approximately fifteen thousand words, and once a week he sat with the other five editors and read and edited the work of the reporters. He was chosen to write the Class Prophecy, and his treatment of the assignment was characteristic of his *Trapeze* columns; he created an elaborate melodrama, with a martial setting, in which he cast his classmates in roles precisely the reverse of their temperaments.[20]

His careful adaptations of Lardner had been an invaluable opening exercise in some of the technicalities of idiomatic prose, as well as a profitable experiment in various levels of humor, burlesque, and satire. Years afterwards, at Lardner's request, Hemingway autographed a book for him, inscribing it "To Ring Lardner from his early imitator and always admirer, Ernest Hemingway."[21] Hemingway outgrew Lardner, as he has outgrown most of his models and tutors. Like the *Trapeze*, however, Lardner was an important agent in the establishment of direction. "There was plenty to admire," Hemingway said later of Lardner's work.[22]

In June, 1917, following his graduation from high school, the *Trapeze* and Lardner and writing as a whole were put aside for the annually welcome escape to the Hemingway summer home in northern Michigan. Here, in the immense delights of fishing and camping and a masculine world, with a group of friends more important to him than his high school associations, Hemingway extended each summer another element of his apprenticeship. It was an element whose importance does not become wholly apparent until

1920, when he used this Michigan material in his free-lance work for the Toronto *Star Weekly*. The summer of 1917, however, was a difficult one for any eighteen-year-old American as aggressive and restless as Hemingway. For such a boy the events in Europe marched their distracting shadows across even the woods of Michigan.

# *KANSAS CITY*

" . . . in Kansas City he really began
to learn."        MAXWELL PERKINS[1]

---

*I.*

Hemingway's restlessness became more acute with each
week that passed in the summer of 1917. The war, and his
father's unalterable opposition to his enlistment—"the boy's
too young," the doctor had said, and there the discussion
ended—made his situation intolerable. He talked about getting away for good, and about making his way in the world,
and it was finally agreed that in the fall he should go to
Kansas City and get a job. Kansas City had several things
to recommend it.

Carl Edgar, a Horton Bay friend, would be there, working for a fuel oil company, and though Edgar himself was
also very anxious to get into the war, he was at least an
older man, mature and conscientious. Doctor Hemingway
hoped that he would have a steadying influence on his son.
Hemingway himself had crossed over to Edgar's Pine Lake
cottage almost every day during the early summer. He
observed with envy his friend's prosperity and independence. In July, just before Edgar went back to Kansas City
at the end of his vacation, Hemingway told him he would
definitely be there in the fall. Edgar was delighted with the
plan. To someone of his own tastes the boy's ingenuousness
and, Edgar once explained, his enthusiasm for "fishing and

the out of doors in general," were appealing characteristics.

In Kansas City, too, lived Doctor Hemingway's younger brother, Tyler Hemingway, a successful, socially prominent businessman. Tyler Hemingway could not only provide a local regency of family supervision, but he would also be able to find his nephew a newspaper job; he had been a classmate at Oberlin of the late Henry J. Haskell, then chief editorial writer of the Kansas City *Star* and for some years its Washington correspondent.[2] "I wanted to work on the *Star*," Hemingway declared flatly many years later, "because I thought it was the best paper in the U.S." Few of the *Star*'s readers, and not many informed Americans, would have disagreed with him. The Kansas City *Star* was in 1917 one of the half-dozen great American newspapers.

The *Star* had been for almost twenty years the natural target of talented, ambitious Midwesterners. Through its city room during this period there passed a stream of young, obscure reporters who during the next generation would form a kind of self-perpetuating cadre in the editorial rooms of the Hearst empire, in the Curtis publications in Philadelphia, in the executive offices of other, *Star*-derived Midwestern papers, and in the writers' wings of Hollywood studios. Innumerable smooth, professional storytellers served their apprenticeships under the stern discipline of William Rockhill Nelson, his lieutenants, and his professional heirs.

Like the revered New York *World*, with which it was often compared, the *Star* infected its staff with a curiosity about mankind and a craftsmanlike regard for clear, provocative, good—as opposed to "fine"—writing. Unlike the *World*, which preferred to hire reporters of proven quality, the *Star* insisted when possible on training its own men. The late Courtney Ryley Cooper, gossiping about his own *Star* days, recalled that the invention of a mythical background of experience had not helped his application for a job on the paper. "Young man," the assistant editor told him, "when a man becomes a member of the staff of the Kansas City *Star* we give him his experience. We don't want men from big papers, and we don't want boomers who run around the country from one paper to another. We train our men, and we train them well."[3]

The atmosphere of the *Star* was a fresh and exciting one, for which nothing in Hemingway's brief high school journalism could have prepared him. "They worked us very hard," Hemingway remembered thirty-five years later, "especially Saturday nights. I liked to work hard though, and I liked all the special and extra work." His zeal, of course, would have been no surprise to his editors on the *Star*; it was what they expected to get from every young reporter lucky enough to work for the *Star*. They expected too that sixty-dollar-a-month cubs would quickly master the paper's celebrated style sheet.

This was a long, galley-size, single page containing the 110 rules that governed the *Star*'s prose. It had been developed by the man who made the *Star*, the legendary Colonel Nelson, and two of his first editors, T. W. Johnston and Alexander Butts. To it had been added the discoveries about reportorial frailty of successive *Star* editors. It survives today, printed now in the pamphlet form which has become standard practice on good newspapers; although, then as now, it contained the customary local prohibitions and idiosyncrasies of particular editors, it was in its essentials a remarkable document. The *Star* included several rules which went far beyond the conventional instruction in spelling, punctuation, and grammar. These were the rules which made a *Star* training memorable. The style sheet's first paragraph—and it remains the initial paragraph in the current style book—might well stand as the First Commandment in the prose creed which is today synonymous with the surface characteristics of Hemingway's work.

Use short sentences. Use short first paragraphs. Use vigorous English. Be positive, not negative.

Nothing Hemingway might learn in the next decade of apprenticeship would supplant this precept. The inevitable verbosity he had brought from high school theme-writing, despite the efforts of Miss Dixon and Miss Biggs, as well as the prose vices of premature independence in *Trapeze* reporting, could not survive in such an atmosphere. Rule 1 was an edict observed with evangelical devotion by the *Star*'s copyreaders and, more important, by the man who was most directly in contact with young reporters and their work.

C. G. (Pete) Wellington was in 1917 the assistant city editor of the *Star*. He is regarded by the scores of writers whom he has trained as the man who was the keeper of the *Star* style sheet. He was in the direct line of descent from Nelson, having been hired away from the Topeka *Capitol* in 1912 by the colonel's lieutenants. In the early 1940's, when it became necessary to expand the old style sheet, it was Wellington—by then managing editor—to whom the chore was automatically handed.

For him it was no chore. Accuracy and readability were his twin gods. If a particular point was not covered by the style sheet, one could be sure in 1917 that the assistant city editor could supply a principle. In the hands of such a man —patient, severe, devoted to the paper in general and to readable, lucid prose in particular—the style sheet was never a rhetorical prison. It was a kind of bellows with which words were controlled and structured. For most of the *Star*'s reporters the style sheet and its phrases remained in their minds long after they had left Kansas City. Hemingway—who worked there for only seven months—could recall in 1952 that "you were never to say a man was seriously injured. All injuries are serious. He was, as I recall, slightly injured or dangerously injured. There were many other things like this," he added, "that made extremely good sense." Hemingway then translated his memories of the style sheet into another idiom, giving his description the kind of freshness that would have pleased Wellington.

"They gave you this to study when you went to work," Hemingway explained, "and after that you were just as responsible for having learned it as after you've had the articles of war read to you."

Wellington's young reporters invariably reacted positively to this atmosphere of diligent and thoughtful professionalism. If one worked even briefly in this world where short sentences and vigorous English were truly important things, then he would, fundamentally, write that way forever, just as he would always write with the emphasis on freshness and originality. They used to say that on the *Star* you could write a story backwards if you made it interesting enough. This becomes believable when Rule 3 of the style sheet is analyzed.

Never use old slang. Such words as *stunt, cut out, get his goat, come across, sit up and take notice, put one over*, have no place after their use becomes common. Slang to be enjoyable must be fresh.

At a time when the habits of a vocation are formed, Hemingway was being given the training that would make him so apt a pupil during the coming five or six years. Language and words could never from this point on be lightly regarded. The effort would always be toward authenticity, precision, immediacy. There was a legend on the *Star* that the city desk once accepted in a reporter's story the line, "He hit the girl he was engaged to's brother." The myth vividly indicates what was wanted by the *Star* and, above all, by assistant city editor Pete Wellington.

Hemingway's sense of obligation to Wellington has always been profound, and he has recorded it scrupulously on several occasions. "Pete Wellington was a stern disciplinarian, very just and very harsh," Hemingway said once, "and I can never say properly how grateful I am to have worked under him."

Wellington has been described by the playwright Russel Crouse—on the *Star*'s sports desk in 1917 and a friend of Hemingway there—as a fine teacher because "he had the wonderful habit of putting his arm around you and then talking to you as though he was a friend instead of a boss." This was the man who read Hemingway's copy and discussed it with him, whether it was merely the phoned-in facts of a General Hospital stabbing, or a story written by the boy on his return to the city room. It was the kind of teaching, bolstering as it did the creed of the style sheet, and a tradition of great *Star* stories and reporters of the past, which was invaluable. Each of the *Star*'s rules becomes more meaningful to the importance of the period to Hemingway when it is thought of as being explained to the boy by Wellington. The assistant city editor was particularly insistent on the observance of Rule 21:

Avoid the use of adjectives, especially such extravagant ones as *splendid, gorgeous, grand, magnificent*, etc.

Wellington translated this into an understandable prose code for his young reporters, just as, when they violated the *Star*'s edict on short sentences, he would shrug and say, without rancor but severely, "Why the hell do you want to tangle your reader up? Do you like listening to someone who talks like that?"[4] American journalism was just emerging from a period of heavy, turgid prose. Like the *Star* rules, Wellington's careful, frugal use of adjectives, in which the fresh and evocative was always sought, was evidence of the *Star*'s creative attitude toward prose.

"Those were the best rules I ever learned for the business of writing," Hemingway told a young newspaperman in 1940. "I've never forgotten them. No man with any talent, who feels and writes truly about the thing he is trying to say, can fail to write well if he abides by them."[5]

*II.*

Hemingway scrambled eagerly through this professional world. Thinking back to what gave Hemingway his drive on the *Star* in 1917, Dale Wilson, a contemporary there who later became Sunday editor of the Milwaukee *Journal*, decided that his friend "would have been satisfied to be the top assignment man on the *Star* and merit the approval of Pete Wellington." The others who knew him in Kansas City also recalled him clearly on the basis of those seven months of eagerness. They remembered him in terms of his energy, his charm, and, above all, as someone who wouldn't sit still.

"He liked action," said Pete Wellington in 1951. "When he was assigned to the General Hospital he had an irritating habit of riding off with the first ambulance to go to some kind of cutting scrape without letting the city desk know that he was leaving the post uncovered." Wellington felt this could be related to Hemingway's subsequent work. "He always wanted to be on the scene himself, and I think that trait has been evident in his later writings."

Other young *Star* reporters of the period, most of them with literary ambitions of their own, were sometimes less tolerant of Hemingway's bustle. "When Ernest was on the paper here," according to Landon Laird, a *Star* veteran who today conducts its drama column, "he was always bouncing up to the now departed No. 4 police station at 15th and

Walnut to ride squad cars with Officer Bauswell and others. Bauswell was a character, and much more productive of the excitement in which Ernest revelled than a city room possibly could be." John Selby, the novelist and editor, remembered Hemingway as "forever disappearing into the receiving ward of the city hospital or onto the tail of an ambulance."

It took Hemingway a few weeks to maneuver that General Hospital assignment, however. Until he acquired it he was restless and "not too satisfied," said Frances Davis, who shared the Federal Building beat with him before becoming better known as Frances Lockridge of Mr. and Mrs. North fame. "He wanted to ride ambulances." When he got the assignment it meant he had survived the *Star*'s thirty-day trial period; he was no longer on probation. His new beat was not by any means a sinecure. "You had to be pretty fair to get away with it," according to Clifford Knight, who covered the General Hospital himself and then made the familiar *Star* transition into a successful novelist. Hemingway was now a reporter. Russel Crouse, not given to exaggeration, later declared that he was "a good reporter."

"I covered the short-stop run," Hemingway said in 1952, "which included the 15th Street police station, the Union Station and the General Hospital." Hemingway remembered the small details of his daily routine. "At the 15th Street station you covered crime, usually small, but you never knew when you might hit something larger. Union Station was everybody going in and out of town . . . some shady characters I got to know, and interviews with celebrities going through." The third area of his beat was the one where he found most of his action. "The General Hospital was up a long hill from the Union Station and there you got accidents and a double check on crimes of violence." On another occasion, more than twenty years after he left the *Star*, even his senses could respond to a discussion of the paper, and he talked to an interviewer about how "when the fog came in the fall, you could see Hospital hill pushing up, almost smelling its antiseptic concord of odors."[6]

Wellington, who saw Hemingway at least briefly during almost every day of his seven months on the paper, remembered him personally and as an attentive pupil. "He was a big, good-natured boy with a ready smile," Wellington said years later, "and he developed a friendship with all those on the staff with whom he came in contact." Wilson Hicks, a contemporary who became a national magazine editor, remembered their Kansas City cub days as both industrious and buoyant. "Ernest was conscientious about his work," Hicks declared, "but he would also come back from a story laughing about the people involved, and characterizing them in ways he couldn't write in the paper."

It was Carl Edgar, his friend from Horton Bay, who was most thoroughly exposed to Hemingway's enthusiasm. Hemingway had found his uncle's Warwick Boulevard home too reminiscent of Oak Park; after a few days he accepted Edgar's offer to share his small apartment. The older man usually worked late, and since Hemingway had to be at the *Star* each morning by eight o'clock, they saw each other only at night, when they would meet at the rooms on Agnes Street and discuss the day's affairs. "Hemingway felt the charm and romance of newspaper work fully," Edgar conceded later. "He would talk for hours about his work, frequently when it would have been better to go to bed." Edgar also sensed that Hemingway considered the job essentially as a means to an end. "I believe that the writing itself interested him principally," Edgar maintained. This was also Wellington's analysis, and the assistant city editor often heard from Hemingway the dramatic promise, not unique in a city room, that "he would write the great American novel."

The *Star*'s milieu, in fact, was one in which only the most perverse of young men could have ignored the writing of fiction. "Every newspaperman I knew," Russel Crouse recalled, "was secretly working on a novel." On the *Star*, too, there was a factor which did not operate on many papers. This was the famous institution inaugurated by Colonel Nelson and known as either the exchange or the literary department. Nelson had insisted that considerable space be given in the *Star* to reprints of modern and classical literature, and to masterpieces of art. The literary department clipped magazines, quoted from new books and old, and ransacked American and foreign newspapers for material that would both interest and elevate subscribers to the paper.

A young man who worked on the *Star* learned to write declarative sentences, and to avoid hackneyed adjectives, and to tell an interesting narrative; and, because of the literary department, he learned to do these things in a school which was interested in a more complex aspect of writing than the mere coverage of the day's events. "The editorial room of the *Star*," said Clifford Knight, the detective story writer who worked for the *Star* for more than ten years, both before and after Hemingway's tenure there, "was something more than just another newspaper. There was an atmosphere there that was unique." In 1952 it was still vivid in his mind. "There were good men there in the top spots, as good as there were in the business, and after the paper went to press and things slacked off, you could go and talk to almost anybody; you could dream dreams and talk about the novel you were going to write some day."

Literary critics have sometimes patronized Hemingway as the victim of an abbreviated and inadequate education. On the contrary, in addition to the admirable instruction given at Oak Park High, he was the recipient of an extremely literate and concentrated training, general as well as vocational, on the *Star*. It was an education to which, like any young man, he would be more attentive than he would have been to similar instruction at, say, the University of Illinois. "The *Star*," according to Clifford Knight, who grew up in its circulation belt before he joined its staff, "was a cultural bath." It served this function both for those who read it and for those who wrote it.

No matter how single-mindedly he pursued ambulances, a young man could not be unaffected by such an atmosphere. This was not the dipsomaniacal city room that Hollywood invented, nor was it the monotony which is frequently the American newspaper of reality. "It was literate and alert," John Selby testified in 1952. "People did read, not only the current stuff, but generally. The shop bristled with novels being written."

It would be naive to imagine, however, that Hemingway spent all his time in the literary department. He was already doubtful of whatever was not experienced. The exchange department, had he thought consciously about it, would have seemed to a degree a quaint make-believe. Hemingway belonged only occasionally to the group which discussed literature and art in reverent, almost academic terms. Although some of his friends were among those who gathered regularly with John Patrick Gilday and the older men from the literary department, and though he himself was responsively interested in fiction of all kinds, Hemingway, when the paper was put to bed, turned to a spokesman of a different approach to fiction.

*III.*

Lionel Calhoun Moise became a legend in American city rooms by the time he was thirty.[7] During the rest of his life the legend extended in depth of anecdote without changing its essential pattern. Witnesses to Moise's career are invariably in doubt as to whether it was his talent as a writer or his color as a personality which contributed most strongly to their memory of him.

Of his stature as a journalist they were never in doubt. Experienced colleagues, who had read a thousand perishable accounts of the day's events, always remembered one or two by Moise when the rest had blurred away. He had the kind of agile talent which once enabled him to write three hundred entertaining words every day for a month on the phenomenon of Halley's comet. He is preserved in the minds of his contemporaries as a symbol of a vanished species, the boomer, the nomad reporter who acknowledged no master, moving turbulently from job to job, able neither to write a dull story nor be a dull companion. He was notorious as a cop-slugger and barroom brawler, a *Front Page* character who, in Russel Crouse's memory, "was a good tough reporter of the old school who loved to get drunk and throw typewriters out the windows."

The anecdotes about his brawls and his drinking and his women were legion. Defining the relationship between Moise and Hemingway, a contemporary concluded that if Hemingway had written his fiction before 1917, younger newspapermen in Kansas City might have described Moise as "like a character out of Hemingway." Hemingway remembered him in 1952, the year of his death, as "a very picturesque, dynamic, big-hearted, hard-drinking and hard-fighting man," adding that he (Hemingway) had "always regretted that his talent was not disciplined and canalized into good writing."

Moise, as Hemingway inferred by that brief epitaph, was more than just a dissolute, professional he-man. "If Hemingway learned anything on the *Star*," according to Wesley Stout, a famous Kansas City reporter who later became editor of the *Saturday Evening Post*, "it was from Moise, whose footsteps he dogged. Moise had many theories about writing, which he was not unwilling to share." Moise was particularly emphatic on the requirements of good prose. His description of his own work is an excellent indication of what he taught Hemingway. He was fond of pointing out that copyreaders hated to read his stories because he wrote transition sentences to tie each paragraph tightly to its predecessor. "Not," he explained to another of the *Star* cubs who always surrounded him, "these choppy, bastard, journalese paragraphs that can be cut out easily when a story had to be shortened."

He was, for all his romanticism and his saloon gregariousness, a sharply critical man, capable of expressing his beliefs in pungent epigram. "It is a regrettable indication of a great nation's literary taste," he once said, "when it chooses a national anthem beginning with the words, 'Oh, say.'" His advice to the young reporters was always the same; it is the precise advice Hemingway has continued to give novices. Moise urged an ambitious associate to quit his job on the overstaffed *Star* and take one with the Kansas City *Journal*. "With its ridiculously small staff," he explained, "the *Journal* will run you ragged with writing reams of copy—and the only way to improve your writing is to write."

Moise's temperament and creed had an understandable appeal for Hemingway. He and the older man became good friends. Russel Crouse told another *Star* associate, in 1930, that his own most vivid recollection of Hemingway in Kansas City was as "a companion of dat ole davil Moise." From Moise—and from others like him, "storybook newspapermen," Wilson Hicks recalled, "men like Tod Ormiston and Harry Godfrey"—Hemingway received aspects of a set of attitudes toward experience, as well as a pattern of writing habits he could add to the more important ones he was acquiring from the *Star*'s atmosphere in general and from Pete Wellington in particular. Moise was blunt and doctrinaire on the qualities which fiction must possess.

"Pure objective writing," Moise often said, "is the only true form of storytelling." The writers he admired were Saint-Simon, Mark Twain, Conrad, Kipling, and Dreiser. "No stream of consciousness nonsense; no playing dumb observer one paragraph and God Almighty the next." He would lean forward emphatically, an impressive and persuasive lecturer. "In short, no tricks." Moise, unlike others to whom Hemingway was temporarily indebted, neither envied nor belittled the younger man's success. "I have since heard Hemingway quoted," Moise said in 1952, in one of the last letters he wrote, "to the effect that this and other pronouncements influenced him for the good." Moise's ironic wit was still active. "But," he added, "he probably was not himself." Growing more serious, Moise was literate and assured in his analysis of Hemingway's work. "Like all real writers, Hemingway owes his well-deserved eminence not to any 'influence' but to his ability to select from a host of influences—part of that little thing called genius." He had read Hemingway's stories with care and approval. " 'The Killers' is an example of pure objectivity; dialogue, action, and a minimum of description."

Moise's importance to Hemingway, though by no means as lasting and crucial as Pete Wellington's, was sharp and direct. Almost half a century after he broke in Moise as a green cub on the *Star*, Marvin Creager, his first city editor, remembered that even then Moise had "a flair for the intellectual and a thirst for knowledge." Creager, who subsequently became editor of the Milwaukee *Journal* and made it one of the great Midwestern dailies, remembered too that Moise read widely and "understandingly." He could concentrate on "things that most cub reporters would find heavy going." As a combination of tutors Wellington and Moise complemented each other in a way that would have been hard to duplicate. Their mutual concern with Hemingway—the one's official and stern, the other's friendly and convivial—made the *Star* another profitable step in apprenticeship. Wellington was a natural teacher to whom the entire staff looked for guidance and praise; Moise, as a contemporary remembered him, was "the idol of all the cubs." It was a formidable piece of good fortune; Hemingway, above all, was an apt and industrious pupil.

*IV.*

One of Wellington's clearest memories of Hemingway on the *Star* was that he took "great pains" with his work. Wellington recalled specifically that he labored carefully in fashioning "even the one-paragraph news story." Here again the *Star* offered a discipline not characteristic of American papers. Its treatment of news stories lent itself to a prose exercise of which Hemingway, determined as he was to learn to write, was in desperate need.

Every page of the *Star*—including the front page—was jammed with stories. Page one, with its unorthodox seven columns, seldom contained in 1917 and 1918 more than three or four long stories. The rest of the page was filled with as many as twenty-five items of one or two paragraphs. They might be of state, national, or international origin, but as a rule most of them were locally derived and written by any one of the staff reporters. These were the one-paragraph stories over which Wellington recalled Hemingway toiling. They demonstrate the paper's crisp, declarative style as well as its stress on the colloquial. They show Wellington's insistence that narrative be clear and interesting and precise. In 1940, just after the publication of *For Whom the Bell Tolls*, Hemingway told an interviewer that during his seven months on the *Star* he was trying to tell simple things simply. He remembered that he had been "enormously excited under Pete Wellington's guidance to learn that the English language yields to sim-

plicity through brevity."[8] Hemingway was especially indebted, he declared, to Wellington's concept of flexible
narrative rather than the rigidly inverted, conventional news
story, with its artificial dogma of lead, secondary lead, and
key qualification points. In some ways—as indicated in this
front page story of March, 1918, typical of the kind over
which Hemingway labored—the *Star* was training its staff
in narrative as much as in reportage.

A well dressed young woman entered the jewelry division of the welfare loan agency yesterday. She presented
a worn pawn ticket. It was for a wedding ring pawned nine
months before.

"I never intended to come back for that," she said. "I
didn't wear it and it always seemed just an expression of
sentiment and I believed I was an unsentimental woman.
But my husband was drafted and I thought I'd like to have
the ring to remember him by in case he never comes
home."[9]

The most rudimentary extension would alter this kind
of *Star* paragraph into the fragmentary sketches Hemingway was producing five years later in such work as "A
Very Short Story" and "The Revolutionist."[10] The *Star*
stressed reader interest far more than it emphasized the
traditional—and confining—*who, what, where,* and *when*
of conventional journalism. The city desk also encouraged
the use of dialogue, and insisted that the speech have authenticity and crispness. The news section carried at this time,
for example—and presented as a straight news story—an
account of the trial of a Negro woman accused of operating
a confidence game. Having explained briefly that the prisoner specialized in love-crossed matrons, the *Star*'s reporter
focused on the central character.

"I'se Alicka, the Wonder Woman," she told her clients. "Tell your fortune, bring back your lovers, fix everything up, all for a quarter. Cross my palm, lady; cross my palm."[11]

Alicka swindled the woman out of not only her quarter but also a considerable amount of jewelry. Greedy at the spectacle of this easy victim, Alicka returned later and was apprehended by a policeman. The latter accused her bluntly of theft.

"You're right, copper," Alicka answered. "Take me along. You fool men all time butting in and spoiling everything."

She pleaded guilty and was fined fifty dollars; dispatched to the state farm for female offenders, she said to the judge, according to the *Star*'s story: "That ain't so bad. I'll charm them fool niggers at the farm. Watch Alicka."

Frequently the now characteristic, undercut Hemingway climax, full of unstated, ironic implications, was coupled in these *Star* paragraphs with the blunt, declarative idiom on which Wellington insisted.

A warrant charging Joseph C. Wirthman, who owns several drug stores in Kansas City, with selling liquor without a license was issued by the prosecutor today. The complaint was made by George Herne, representative of the Society for Suppression of Commercialized Vice.

Wirthman was arrested and pleaded not guilty. He waived preliminary hearing and trial was set for August 13 before Judge Ralph S. Latshaw. He was released on $500 bond signed by his attorney.

Herne said he bought a 25-cent bottle of whiskey in Wirthman's store at Thirty-first Street and Troost Avenue July 1. Herne complained to Shannon C. Douglas, assistant prosecutor, that several men, whom he recognized as Second Ward politicians, followed him to the Criminal Court Building today and threatened him. Wirthman is a former alderman.[12]

When Hemingway was preparing himself intensely at the end of his apprenticeship for the heavier burden of full-length fiction, he conceived the exercises which were eventually published as a group in the expatriate volume, *in our time*, in 1924. The relationship is explicit between these important creative experiments and the short news paragraphs Hemingway wrote for Pete Wellington in 1917 and 1918. In 1924, in fact, Hemingway went back to his *Star* instruction not only for the method but also on two occasions for the material itself. Save for the minor licenses permitted a fictionalist, they might be the very items— known on some American papers as brighteners—which daily enlivened the *Star*. They contain all the characteristics Pete Wellington valued, sharpened now by the five years of Hemingway's subsequent apprenticeship. Hemingway had retained the entire technique of the *Star*, even to the idiosyncrasies of spelling and the terminology of streets and precinct.

At two o'clock in the morning two Hungarians got into a cigar store at Fifteenth Street and Grand Avenue. Drevitts and Boyle drove up from the Fifteenth Street police station in a Ford. The Hungarians were backing their wagon out an alley. Boyle shot one off the seat of the wagon and one out of the wagon box. Drevitts got frightened when he found they were both dead. Hell Jimmy, he said, you oughtn't to have done it. There's liable to be a hell of a lot of trouble.[13]

In the second 1924 exercise based on *Star* material and methodology, Hemingway described the old Jackson

County jail at Missouri Avenue and Oak Street. William Moorhead, the *Star*'s police reporter for forty years, who took Hemingway with him on a number of assignments in 1918, found Hemingway's picture "an accurate description of the dismal, massive brick building." Hemingway several times mentioned to friends a Kansas City criminal with the same name as the central figure of this hanging scene. "They hanged Sam Cardinella at six o'clock in the morning in the corridor of the county jail," Hemingway began the 1924 sketch.[14] The abrupt exposition was only one of several stylistic reminders of Wellington's teaching.

Even during his brief seven months on the *Star* Hemingway wrote a number of stories which startled his associates by their effectiveness and maturity. As was always the practice, such successes were an occasion for general congratulation; it was the cherished compensation for the low salaries and rare by-lines. Hemingway received the accolade several times, in particular for a story which he himself remembered, many years later, as "very sad, about a whore." It was a simple vignette of a shabby girl who walked back and forth, weeping, outside a soldiers' dance sponsored by a socially prominent local organization. The girl intently watched a particular soldier as he danced with his smartly dressed partners. Hemingway's exposition was wholly implicit; he avoided both sentimentality and cheapness. The treatment was instinctive anticipation of one of the strengths of his later work. The story impressed George Longan, the city editor, as much as it did Wellington. There were enthusiastic prophecies about the eighteen-year-old boy's journalistic future.

Hemingway himself had a more realistic, vocational memory of the story. "It was around then they decided maybe I should be allowed to write occasionally as well as telephone." The incident increased both his stature on the paper and his conviction that he could write well if he worked hard enough at it. He became a close friend of the assignment editor of the *Star*'s morning edition, the *Times,* and when he finished his own assignments he would cover stories for Charlie Hopkins. Hopkins was always short-handed; he made the most of such a windfall. He became very fond of Hemingway, and about this time had a long talk with the boy concerning his future. When Hemingway was back in Oak Park in May, 1918, he told Fannie Biggs a little bit about that conversation with Hopkins. "Don't let anyone ever say that you were taught writing," Hopkins had told him. "It was born in you."

It was a pleasant thing to hear, of course, but Hemingway was already too sophisticated in his trade to really believe it. He had been taught a great deal at the *Star*. Now he was ready to move on to another lesson. The war was still very much on his mind. Although he had been turned down twelve times by the medical examiners of various units, he suddenly got the break he had been hoping for.

### V.

It was another *Star* friendship which led Hemingway into the war. Ted Brumback was the son of a socially prominent Kansas City family. An undergraduate at Cornell from 1913 through 1915, he had left college for a year after a golfing accident that cost him an eye. He returned to Cornell for the academic year 1916-17, but at the close of the spring term, in spite of his vision, he was accepted by the American Field Service as an ambulance driver. He was on active service in France from July until November of 1917. His enlistment up, he returned to Kansas City, a glamorous figure who had served with the Chasseurs Alpins. Brumback, with his local connections and literary ambitions, had no difficulty obtaining a cub reporter's job on the *Star*. Hemingway, a dynamo of furious energy at an office typewriter, attracted Brumback's attention on his first day in the city room.

"Every tenth letter or so," Brumback wrote later, "would print above the type line. He didn't seem to mind. Nor did he mind when the two keys would jam."[15] Hemingway finished abruptly and called for a copy boy. He turned to Brumback. "That's rotten looking copy," Hemingway said. "When I get a little excited this damn type mill goes haywire on me." He got up and held out his hand. "My name's Hemingway," he told Brumback. "Ernest Hemingway. You're a new man, aren't you?"

The two young men became close friends. Years later, in the 1930's, Brumback was traveling in California, wandering casually in a battered Ford, when he encountered another ex-reporter from the *Star*. One of the first things Brumback mentioned was that he had not only known the author of *A Farewell to Arms*, but had shared the same tent with him in Italy, and, he said, "had seen and done everything that Hemingway did over there." In 1936, when he wrote for the *Star* a brief memoir of his friendship with Hemingway, Brumback described him in much the same terms as had his other Kansas City contemporaries. "He was a big, handsome kid," Brumback wrote, "bubbling over with energy. And this energy was really remarkable. He could turn out more copy than any two reporters."[16]

Brumback told Hemingway, of course, about his experiences in France, and so as early as Christmas, 1917, Hemingway was talking to Carl Edgar about joining some sort of ambulance unit. In April the opportunity finally presented itself. Hemingway and Brumback were able to capitalize on it, appropriately, because of their connection with the *Star*. The legend was that when one day a wire service story came to the telegraph desk, dealing with the Red Cross's need for volunteers with the Italian Army, the two young men cabled applications before the paper used the item. Wilson Hicks, who had also been part of their plan, decided at the last moment to stay in Kansas City and wait for the American army. On April 30, 1918, therefore, Hemingway and Brumback drew their last pay from the *Star*. Together with Carl Edgar and Charlie Hopkins, the *Times*'s assignment editor, they went up to northern Michigan for a final fishing trip.

From Kansas City Hemingway took with him not only the lessons he had learned about writing but also a trained reporter's eye which would enable him to profit considerably more from his Italian experiences than if, for example, he had been able to enlist directly from high school the previous June. He took with him too a reservoir of material upon which he could draw when he began his serious writing in 1919. The two harshly moving short stories, "A Pursuit Race" and "God Rest You Merry, Gentlemen," are the memorable harvest of his *Star* assignments.[17] Prior to their publication in 1927 and 1933 he had written what he later called "some good stories about Kansas City" which were lost, without carbons, in the late fall of 1922.[18] Even in 1952, when he was asked about his memories of Kansas City, Hemingway was still planning to go back to the period for material.

"I was always going to write about Kansas City myself," he said. "I know it just as it was then." Those had been seven lucky months in 1917 and 1918; Hemingway had made the most of them. He was better prepared for a part of his apprenticeship which would be in its way equally important to him.

# *ITALY*

"It was a hell of a war as I recall,
But a damned sight better than no war
at all."

*Mademoiselle from Armentières*

## *I.*

Hemingway and Brumback were in New York, waiting
for a ship to Europe, by the second week of May, 1918.
Their orders had been forwarded from Kansas City to
Horton Bay; they left hastily for Manhattan, still wearing
their fishing clothes. The Red Cross issued their uniforms
on May 12 and enlisted them as honorary lieutenants. A
week later the unit was part of a Fifth Avenue parade—
marching downtown from 82nd Street to the Battery—
and was reviewed by President and Mrs. Wilson. Hemingway was jubilant about finally getting into the war; Brumback remembered him as "delirious with excitement."[1]

Back in Kansas City the paper had printed pictures of its
two former reporters and a paragraph or two about their
personal histories, declaring prematurely that the pair would
sail that week "from an Atlantic port for Italy."[2] The
article stressed Brumback's previous service in France and
Hemingway's persistent campaign to deceive medical examiners about his own imperfect eyesight. Although few
of the new drivers had been forced to exercise Hemingway's tenacity of martial purpose, they were nevertheless
an enthusiastic and enterprising group. Hemingway, at

eighteen, was one of the youngest. In 1920, in fact, when he was working on a newspaper in Toronto, a Canadian reporter concluded that the American's exceptional maturity must have come from a wartime association with older men. Brumback, his closest friend in the unit, would normally have graduated from Cornell the previous year. William D. Horne, Jr., a young New York businessman with whom both Brumback and Hemingway quickly became friendly, had been a member of the Class of 1913 at Princeton. Most of the unit had either attended or finished college. Even Zalmon Simmons, Jr., an heir to the mattress fortune, although he was young enough to have been a prep school senior in 1917, had the advantage of an earlier enlistment in France with the American Field Service.

The Red Cross ambulance corps in Italy was modeled on the American Field Service units. All the original personnel in Italy, for whom Hemingway's group had been signed on as replacements, had been recruited in Paris from men who had served with the Field Service ambulances in France. The structure and atmosphere of the American Field Service, with its heroic record of work with the French, dominated this new world into which Hemingway was being initiated. Its history clarifies the Italian milieu.

*II.*

The American Field Service and its successor, the Red Cross ambulance corps in which Hemingway served, testified to the humanitarian impulse which was so strong a factor in American attitudes toward, and participation in, World War I. The impulse has been obscured by the subsequent disillusion of that generation and by the shamefaced skepticism with which many of them later regarded their youthful idealism. The novels and plays of the 1920's told their bitter narratives in such sardonic terms that the memory of World War I has become an embarrassment. War-time slogans were soon endowed with irony as though no good had ever existed in them. In reality, whether they went overseas with such advance units as the Field Service and the Red Cross, or whether they enlisted in more conventional military units, the bulk of Hemingway's generation traveled east in the crusading idealism of their President. This is verified by an examination of such American volunteers as Hemingway and his associates and predecessors.

The volunteer organizations had from the beginning a strongly literary and academic background.[3] One of their first sponsors was Henry James. In November, 1914, Macmillan published in London—and sold for a penny—a twelve-page pamphlet by the novelist called *The American Volunteer Motor-Ambulance Corps in France*. James, addressing himself to "the editor of an American journal," told of the work of Richard Norton of Boston, founder of the corps, and appealed to other Americans for funds and vehicles with which to continue the work. The pamphlet was distinctly in the prose of James's late period. He described the suffering of the wounded. "Carried mostly by rude arts, a mercy much hindered at the best, to the shelter, often hastily improvised, at which first aid becomes possible for them, they are there, as immediately and tenderly as possible, stowed in our waiting or arriving Cars, each of which receives as large a number as may be consistent with the particular suffering state of the stricken individual."

James had touched immediately on one of the basic elements of the entire volunteer episode. It was a spirit of humanitarianism which moved Richard Norton and the several thousand who followed him during the next four years. These Americans were profoundly disturbed by the suffering of the wounded. Norton's ambulances, replacing the slow, springless horse-drawn wagons of the hard-pressed

French Transport Corps, as the Red Cross would later come to the aid of the Italian command, were able to get the wounded from the first-aid stations in a matter of minutes. Late in 1915, though it continued to receive assistance from England's St. John Ambulance, Norton's unit became formally associated with the American Red Cross. They had carried 28,000 wounded, and, as Norton wrote to his brother in New York, "our cars relieved the suffering of over six thousand individuals between September 25 and October 9." When the United States declared war in April, 1917, there were more than one hundred Red Cross ambulances on the western front.

The American Field Service, in which so many of Hemingway's fellow volunteers in Italy had served, developed along the same general pattern as had Norton's unit and the smaller, independent, Morgan-Harjes group. Section One of the Field Service went on duty in Alsace in April, 1915. By 1916, at the time of the Verdun emergencies, the unit was operating one hundred and twenty-five ambulances, donated by American philanthropy and manned by American drivers. The enlistment of almost exclusively undergraduate or recently graduated personnel was already well established. Hemingway's own section in Italy contained a high proportion of college men, from institutions as diverse as Stanford, Princeton, Boston University, Illinois, the University of California, Dartmouth, and Pennsylvania State College.

This was the characteristic which impressed John Masefield, who was sent to France in 1917 by the British Government to inspect the American volunteers. "These drivers are men of high education," he wrote in *Harper's*. "They are the very pick and flower of American life, some of them professional men, but the greater number of them young men on the threshold of life, lads just down from college or in their last student years." Membership in the various ambulance groups was an extension and renewal of high school and college, with a fraternity aspect that included the hazing of new men, the publication of collegiate-like newspapers, and the celebration at the front of Yale's upset victory over Harvard in 1916. The volunteers practiced the martial truth enunciated by one of Evelyn Waugh's characters in 1940. "Most of war seems to consist of hanging about," says the young Commando officer in *Put Out More Flags*. "Let's at least hang about with our own friends."

The camaraderie was intensified by the nature of the work and the organization of the corps. The Red Cross ambulance unit in Italy was divided into five sections. The sections were small enough—less than fifty men, in the case of Hemingway's Section IV[4]—so that real intimacy naturally developed. The friendship which emerged in Section IV between Hemingway and Bill Horne remained an active one for many years. Several of the other drivers made a point of looking up Hemingway in Paris in the very early 1920's, long before he had become a celebrity. A number of the members of Section IV settled in or returned to Chicago after the war; although few of them had any direct business relations, they continued to hold informal Ambulance dinners for the next thirty-five years. Their service in Italy was not only an absorbing adventure; by and large it was one of the most memorable of their experiences.

It was also difficult, responsible, and frequently dangerous. The hours varied according to the particular requirements of the sector. When the work was light, the shift was twenty-four hours on, twenty-four off. "During the busiest periods," according to the Red Cross's *Report of the Department of Military Affairs* in Italy, the work was "divided evenly between the nights and the days." In the case of night attack periods, of course—and

Hemingway's service coincided with the July counter-
offensive along the lower Piave—the cars were driven
without lights. In their letters and diaries the drivers expressed again and again their horror when at the end of
a long drive, under shelling, they discovered they had been
driving not an ambulance but a hearse. "These are nights
that bear no relation to reality," one of them wrote. "Morning comes like the relief from pain."

Later it became fashionable to mock those writers who
had been in the ambulance service, and to treat their overseas service as a comfortable, rather ridiculous sinecure.
"With the Ambulance Boys in France and Italy," commentators sneered in the 1930's, reducing the experience
to the level of juvenile tales of adventure. Some of the
volunteers themselves took this attitude, as if ashamed of
an ill-advised chapter of their youth. Hemingway, characteristically confident of the evidence of his own memories of Italy, resisted belligerently the shifting climate of
opinion in 1935.

I thought . . . about what a great advantage an experience
of war was to a writer. It was one of the major subjects
and certainly one of the hardest to write truly of and those
writers who had not seen it were always very jealous and
tried to make it seem unimportant, or abnormal, or a dis-
ease as a subject, while, really, it was just something quite
irreplaceable that they had missed.[5]

### III.

Hemingway, crossing the Atlantic in late May of 1918
to join this atmosphere of adventure and service, in which
he would take his first lessons in war, made the most of
whatever excitement was available. The *Chicago*, a vener-
able possession of the French Line, was traveling without

destroyer escort. Hemingway was delighted with the rumors of a U-boat operating along the American coast; he and Brumback stood expectantly on the blacked-out deck.[6] Nothing happened. The *Chicago* was in every way a disappointment. There was little to occupy the monotonous trip except poker in the bar, where the game was the twenty-four-hour one of all troopships, or a crap game with allies who might cover you in French, English, Belgian, Italian, or American money. "Hemingway tried it," Brumback wrote later, "but found he was behind, although he'd won." Once there was a flurry of excitement as they suddenly changed course. A barrel on a raft had been sighted; it was said to be the prelude to sinister German trickery. No lurking sub materialized. "Hemingway," Brumback said in 1936, "felt he'd been cheated."

His disappointment was softened by their arrival in Paris in the midst of the first shelling of the city by Big Bertha, the new, long-range German gun. At the Gare du Nord Hemingway gave Brumback his instructions. "Tell the taxi," he commanded his friend, "to drive up where those shells are falling. We'll get a story for the *Star* that'll make their eyes pop out back in Kansas City." A heavy tip to the driver allowed them to begin what Brumback recalled, with restraint, as "one of the strangest taxi drives I shall probably ever experience." They spent over an hour driving through Paris trying to catch up with the bursts. Finally they succeeded. "The shell hit the facade of the Madeleine," Brumback wrote, "chipping off a foot or so of stone." Perhaps by design, or perhaps merely by virtue of his own *Star* training, Brumback described the incident in 1936 in a facsimile of Hemingway's own prose. "No one was hurt. We heard the projectile rush overhead. It sounded as if it were going to land right in the taxi with us. It was quite exciting."

Paris, after they had exhausted the possibilities of Big

Bertha, soon became as monotonous as the *Chicago*. "This is getting to be a bore," Hemingway told Brumback. "I wish they'd hurry and ship us off to the front." A day or two later, fortunately, they did leave for Italy; by the middle of June Hemingway was sending excited postcards to Kansas City. The frustrations of bogus U-boats were forgotten. From Milan they were hurried by truck on an emergency basis to a scene of complete devastation outside the city. "Having a wonderful time!!!" Hemingway wrote back to a friend on the *Star*. "Had my baptism of fire my first day here, when an entire munition plant exploded."[7] His use of the cliché was probably in part ironic; his outward response to the catastrophe was not phrased in the idiom of Henry James and Richard Norton. "We carried them in," he went on, "like at the General Hospital, Kansas City."

This was his public personality, however, the bravado his contemporaries had noticed in him as a reporter, and his antidote, as well, to the solemnity of the Red Cross atmosphere. The scene made a deep impression on him, so vivid that he returned to it fourteen years later in his angry, antiwar story, "A Natural History of the Dead." His 1932 memory of the impressions of the 1918 scene, like his simultaneous gibe at the cold, academic humanism of the period, was harsh and specific. "Regarding the sex of the dead," he wrote, "it is a fact that one becomes so accustomed to the sight of all the dead being men that the sight of a dead woman is quite shocking. I first saw inversion of the usual sex of the dead after the explosion of a munition factory which had been situated in the countryside near Milan, Italy. . . . I remember that after we had searched quite thoroughly for the complete dead we collected fragments. . . . Many fragments we found a considerable distance away in the fields, they being carried farther by their own weight."[8]

In 1918, not yet nineteen years old, Hemingway's primary concern was to find more of the same. "I go to the front tomorrow," he wrote back to Kansas City. "Oh, Boy!!! I'm glad I'm in it."[9] From Milan the entire contingent of twenty-two drivers moved on to Schio, ninety miles to the east, where they joined Section IV and relieved those men whose enlistments had expired. Once again, as with Big Bertha in Paris, their arrival seemed a signal for the unprecedented. Almost immediately, Brumback recalled, the Austrians violated an unwritten pledge by which each side had previously refrained from shelling certain towns. Schio had been such a town. Hemingway was as excited as he had been in Paris. "We set off," Brumback remembered, "running for the [railway] station to get there before the next shell arrived." The bombardment was over by the time they reached the target, but Hemingway consoled himself with the certainty of Italian revenge. "Visiting team's started playing dirty ball," Hemingway told his friend. "We'll hear from the home team on that."

Schio itself, in addition to the charm of its lost immunity, had a special interest for two former reporters. Section IV, not content with the multitude of Red Cross bulletins issued in Rome, was publishing its own newspaper. The paper was printed once a month in nearby Vicenza, under the heartily macabre name, *Ciao*, Italian for "good-bye." *Ciao*'s four pages were in format and treatment a duplication of an American high school paper. "All the hysterics of Section IV," the front page promised.[10] Its "Weather Report" was in the same style: "Clear: with bombing moon, possibility of sky becoming overcast before morning with planes, with resulting hail." The June issue, which contained an editorial urging the new drivers to "uphold the reputation of the Section," also asked for prose contributions from the recruits. "We know that there is talent among them." Hemingway needed no urging. The very issue which included

the address of welcome to his group also included a story
in the Lardnerian manner he had last used in the *Trapeze*
in 1917.

Hemingway's article—"Al Receives Another Letter"—
was the longest single item in the paper.[11] Its confident
expertness was in sharp contrast to *Ciao*'s conventional paragraphs of fraternal banter and heavy, Wilsonian purpose.
There was an illusion of effortless flow and a consistency
of treatment that made the article superior to Hemingway's
Oak Park columns. The story was organized with a coher-
ence that stemmed directly from the severe city room and
discipline of Kansas City. The material was particularly
impressive in its display of Hemingway's precocious mastery
of this new milieu. The paragraph exploited the familiar
malapropisms, grammatical distortions, and personal vani-
ties of Lardner's buffoons. These were transferred by
Hemingway, however, with complete authenticity, from
the world of Lardner's Jack O'Keefe and a stateside army
camp into the new atmosphere of the Red Cross ambulance
service.

Well Al we are here in this old Italy and now that I am
here I am not going to leave it. Not at all if any. And that
is not no New Years revolution Al but the truth. Well Al
I am now an officer and if you would meet me you have to
salute me. What I am is a provisional acting second lieutenant without a commission but the trouble is that all the
other fellows are too. There aint no privates in our army
Al and the Captain is called a chef. But he don't look to me
as tho he could cook a damn bit. And the next highest
officer he is called a sou chef. And the reason that they call
him that is that he is chef of the jitneys and has to cook for
the 4ds. But he has a soft job Al because there are only one
4d. lefts.

Hemingway used some of the identical phrases that were occurring in Lardner's *Saturday Evening Post* satires in 1918 —Jenahvark, for example, and Gerry Baldy—and he employed the same sardonic exposure of the author of the letter. The story was an excellent one, about eight hundred words long, and as technically finished as anything Hemingway had yet written. "Do you remember that fellow Pease Al that I wrote you about what was our captain? Well he is a p.s.l.A.w.a.c. now just like the rest of us and he speaks to me pretty regular now and yesterday he darn near called me by first name. But what are we fighting for anyway except to make the world safe for the Democrats?" The satire established Hemingway firmly in the minds of his companions, several of whom not only recalled the story, many years later, but also remembered the delight with which he had written it.

"Al Receives Another Letter" was the extent of Hemingway's published work during the war, although he persistently thought of himself as a writer, and continued to write a good deal during the late summer of 1918. One of the drivers remembered that Hemingway told him he would have preferred to be a war correspondent, but lacked the necessary experience. Bill Horne, who was interested in Hemingway's writing from the beginning, declared later that Hemingway was "writing short stories" during the period. He remembered that "some of these were good stories, too," adding, quite rightly, that so far as he knew "none of those which I read or heard discussed was ever published." Horne also felt that this material could not have been written during this period with Section IV in late June; Hemingway, he pointed out, "was awfully busy being an ambulance driver." The necessary opportunity and leisure were given Hemingway very shortly. He was seriously wounded on July 8, 1918, and spent the next three months in the American Red Cross Hospital at Milan.

*IV.*

Hemingway was one of the few severe casualties among the American drivers in Italy. The way in which he was wounded was an indication both of his eagerness for action and his genuine desire to serve the Allied cause. Hemingway, according to Frederick Spiegel, another young Chicagoan with whom he shared several ambulance assignments, was "extremely conscious of the war as a 'crusade for democracy,' and burning with the desire to have a share in it." His behavior at Schio documented such testimony.

The area to which they were assigned was enviously designated by the other sections as the Schio Country Club. They were quartered on the second floor of an abandoned woolen mill. In front of the mill was a flat meadow where the drivers played baseball. Beside the mill was the stream from which it had previously drawn its power. The Americans swam and sun-bathed there. Hemingway's reaction to this routine, broken only by relatively uneventful ambulance runs, was a natural one. The front was near enough so that he was highly conscious of it, and yet for the moment it was as inaccessible as if he were once again spending the summer at Horton Bay. The Italian command to which Section IV was attached was apparently dug into the mountains for an indefinite time. There was no indication that the Austrians would ever attempt to dislodge it. Hemingway, according to Brumback, was speedily "disgusted with the war."[12] He told his friend that the only shots being fired were practice shots.

"I'm fed up," he said after a week of baseball and swimming. "There's nothing here but scenery and too damn much of that." He thought of getting out of the ambulance corps altogether, "to see," he told Brumback, "if I can't find out where the war is." If that failed, he hoped that he might at least be able to get transferred to a sector on the

Piave River. "They play ball down there," Hemingway announced bitterly. While he waited for an opportunity to get in the game—which Lardner's *Saturday Evening Post* busher had been calling the real worlds serious—Hemingway had to be content with unwarlike duties in the mountains. Section IV was equipped largely with Fiats, and he was detailed to an Italian ambulance. Brumback drew one of the section's six Fords, with assignments in the flat land below their headquarters. "I'm in the Alps," Hemingway wrote back to Kansas City, making the best of a bad job, "riding in a Fiat."[13]

The driving itself was at first exciting and novel. For a time he was contained by the drama of hairpin turns banked by thousand-foot drops. The road from Schio up Monte Pasubio to the advance line dressing posts was a well-made one, but so narrow that the barbed wire on either side almost touched the fenders. High-jinks on mountain roads, like swimming in the mountain stream across the abyss from Austrian emplacements, was a sorry substitute for guns and action and the great crusade. Frederick Spiegel remembered Hemingway's discontent after ten days of idle play and commonplace duty. "He became increasingly itchy."

His ultimate solution was a blend of the two alternatives he had discussed with Brumback. He left the ambulance corps, though not the Red Cross, and wangled his way further east to the more active Piave front. With several others from Section IV he volunteered for duty with the Red Cross Canteen. He obtained the new assignment at the moment when the Italians were making their counter-offensive all along the Piave, attempting to push the Austrians back across the river. "So," Brumback wrote later to Doctor Hemingway, "he got to see all the action he wanted."[14] The new job was in every way a forward area operation. The canteens were operated at seventeen points along the front, some in the mountains, some—like

Hemingway's—in the plains, but none of them more than a few kilometers back of the trenches.

Each canteen included two units, a small hut which contained both the Red Cross lieutenant's quarters and a supply storeroom, and a larger, adjoining hut with a kitchen and a large rest room for the Italian soldiers. The canteen served hot coffee, chocolate, jam, and soup. The soldiers brought their own bread. There were also rations of candy and tobacco. The room contained writing tables, A.R.C. postcards and letterheads, and reading material. The walls were decorated with flags and patriotic inscriptions. The canteen was thus a kind of soldier's club, the equivalent of the NAAFI's and Red Cross units of World War II, available both to passing troops and to men from the command fighting in the nearby trenches. The officers allowed their troops to leave the trenches three or four times a week to come back to the canteen. Hemingway took charge of such a canteen in late June of 1918.

"The work done by these officers," reported the Department of Military Affairs in Italy, "was of a nature which called upon all the resources of the versatile and adaptable American temperament." The canteens were frequently in the range of shell fire; one American lieutenant was killed only a few weeks before Hemingway himself was wounded. Several of the canteens were destroyed or damaged by Austrian fire. Hemingway, however, was no less restless than he had been in Kansas City on the Federal Building beat. He had not come to Italy to supervise the pouring of hot coffee nor the distribution of patriotic literature. He resumed his single-minded campaign for martial action.

He had made friends immediately with the Italian officers in the trench units, and now he persuaded the local commander to allow him to come up to the trenches themselves. Every day thereafter Hemingway mounted his bicycle at the canteen and rode to the front, "laden down," Brumback

wrote to Doctor Hemingway, "with chocolate, cigars, cig-
arets, and postcards."[15] Brumback, who pieced together the
story after Hemingway was wounded, also told his friend's
father that Ernest "thought he could do more good and be
of more service by going straight up to the trenches."
Hemingway followed this routine for six days. He had
achieved his goal; he was in the war. He became a familiar
and welcome figure; the Italian soldiers were always asking
for the *giovane Americano*. Hemingway threw himself into
the front-line atmosphere with the same intensity, heightened here by conviction and dedication, which he had
shown in high school and in Kansas City. With his gifts
for absorbing a new world he saturated himself in the
sensations of trench life. Out of those six days, and the
abbreviated seventh, supplemented by a few more weeks
with the infantry in October, Hemingway would create
during the next fifteen years not only *A Farewell to Arms*
but also several fine short stories.

Hemingway has always valued enormously his experience
of war. Even at eighteen he sensed instinctively its potential
utility as material and as an area for self-discipline as observer and student. His behavior during this period was
neither ghoulish nor abnormally farsighted in terms of his
future vocation. It was the same instinct which impelled a
writer of another generation, in another war. "All the time
I was overseas," Norman Mailer said shortly after the publication of *The Naked and the Dead* in 1948, "I had conflicting ideas, wanting, the way everybody else did, to get
the softest job, to get by with the least pain, and also
wanting to get into combat and see it."[16] Hemingway regarded the opportunity in an even more intense way, since
his own temperament and the general climate of feeling
made involvement even more natural for him in Italy in
1918 than for Mailer on Luzon in 1944.

Hemingway was consciously shaping himself and his attitudes in 1918. "I learned about people," he said later of this period, "under stress and before and after it." That has been the fundamental theme, after all, of all his creative work. Six days in the heavily engaged lines along the Piave in July, 1918, only a few yards from the Austrian positions, provided an excellent basic training in stress. "Also," Hemingway added drily on that same occasion, "learned considerable about myself." Even the letters he wrote home in 1918 showed his concentration on the reality around him in the trenches. His language seems stilted and familiar today, the phrases dulled by a thousand young men exposed to later twentieth-century wars, but they must have shocked Oak Park by their vivid enunciation of the force of his interest in his situation.

You know they say there isn't anything funny about this war, and there isn't. I wouldn't say that it was hell, because that's been a bit over-worked since General Sherman's time, but there have been about eight times when I would have welcomed hell, just on a chance that it couldn't come up to the phase of war I was experiencing.

For example, in the trenches, during an attack, when a shell makes a direct hit in a group where you're standing. Shells aren't bad except direct hits; you just take chances on the fragments of the bursts. But when there is a direct hit, your pals get spattered all over you; spattered is literal.[17]

His removal from this scene he had struggled so long to achieve was pathetic in its swift finality. He said later that he was already regarded by the Italians as having a charmed life, but at midnight on July 8, near the tiny village of Fossalta, two weeks before his nineteenth birthday and seven days after his first admission to the trenches, he was struck by the exploding fragments of a trench mortar which landed a few feet from him. He was handing out chocolate to the Italian soldiers. According to the legend which developed in Section IV, however, testimony to his comrades' recognition of his temperament, Hemingway was said to have been wounded a moment after he had seized an Italian rifle and began firing toward the Austrian lines. An instant later, it was rumored, he saw an Italian sniper fall in No Man's Land. As Hemingway went out to bring him in, the shell from the mortar exploded.

Hemingway did, in reality, show considerable heroism, but this came after he was wounded rather than before. An Italian standing between him and the explosion was killed instantly; a second, standing a few feet away, had both legs blown off. A third soldier, another of those who had been waiting for chocolate, was badly wounded. Hemingway, having regained consciousness, "picked [him] up on his back" and carried him to a first aid dugout.[18] The scene was forcefully recorded, with only minor variations, in *A Farewell to Arms*. Hemingway told Brumback he did not remember how he got to the dressing station, nor that he had carried in the soldier. An Italian officer described the events to him the next day.

A few years later, when Hemingway's early fiction was causing certain critics to identify him as merely a callous recorder, Hemingway told Maxwell Perkins, his editor at Scribner's, that he had "not been at all hardboiled since July 8, 1918—on the night of which I discovered that that also was vanity."[19] He developed a private ritual for both the exorcism and utilization of his wound. One of the novels about war which he has always admired for its authenticity is Frederic Manning's *The Middle Parts of Fortune*.[20] "So each year in July," Hemingway explained in 1942, "the anniversary of the month when I got the big wound, I read [it] and it all comes back again as though . . . it were this morning before daylight and you were waiting there, drymouthed, for it to start."[21]

The fact of being wounded, and as seriously as he was, had immense psychological implications for Hemingway; these implications quite naturally converge on his artistic position and work. The wound permitted him to assume the role of semi-professional soldierhood at the very least, with the privileges and responsibilities attending that role. His front-line service was brief and unmartial, but the wound qualified him as a combat man and deepened his absorption in war as a temporary arena for the study of men and the practice of his creative energy. Because of the shock of the wound, and the three months of enforced idleness, Hemingway was able to evaluate, even if only in an elementary way, the experiences he had endured and observed. The brevity of his service, he later concluded, was an advantage to him as an artist. "Any experience of war," he said in 1952, "is invaluable to a writer. But it is destructive if he has too much."

Hemingway had enough war, in the early summer of 1918, to give him confidence in his judgments and a sound base for the acquisition of further experience through observation. In the hospital at Milan he talked to men who had also survived the front, and one could learn from that, too. From a young English officer he first heard, and adopted as "a permanent protecting talisman,"[22] the lines from *Henry IV*: "By my troth, I care not; a man can die but once; we owe God a death . . . and let it go which way it will, he that dies this year is quit for the next." Four years later there occurred his second major lesson in war, when he covered the Greco-Turk fighting as a correspondent. The profit he drew from the Near East campaigns was made possible because of his initiation in Italy. He was able to learn quickly and accurately in Thrace and Macedonia because he had been blooded at Fossalta. It is on this basis that World War I must be included in his literary apprenticeship. Hemingway summed it up many years later.

When you go to war as a boy you have a great illusion of immortality. Other people get killed; not you. . . . Then when you are badly wounded the first time you lose that illusion and you know it can happen to you. After being severely wounded . . . I had a bad time until I figured it out that nothing could happen to me that had not happened to all men before me. Whatever I had to do men had always done.[23]

He paid a heavy price, as he has all his life in every area of experience, for his knowledge and insight. He received two hundred and twenty-seven separate wounds from the mortar and was hit simultaneously in the leg by a machine gun round. "My feet," he wrote his family from Milan, "felt like I had rubber boots full of water on (hot water), and my knee cap was acting queer. The machine gun bullet just felt like a sharp smack on the leg with an icy snow ball."[24] After he regained consciousness the second time he was carried three kilometers by stretcher. The road was being shelled, and the bearers—as, again, in *A Farewell to Arms*—dropped him frequently. The dressing station had been evacuated during the attack; he lay for two hours in a stable waiting for an ambulance. An Italian ambulance ultimately moved him to another dressing station. "I had a lot of pals among the medical officers," he told his family. Twenty-eight shell fragments were then removed from his legs. He drew pictures, in his letter home, to indicate to his family the size of the fragments.

Hemingway spent five days in a field hospital before he was fit to be moved to the base hospital in Milan. He had another operation there, and another, and then another; he had a dozen operations in all. His right leg was in a plaster splint for some weeks. "I wouldn't really be comfortable now," he wrote after six weeks in the hospital, "unless I had some pain."[25] His closing sentences were boyishly ironic. "As Ma Pettingill says, 'Leave us keep the home fires burning.'" Brumback visited him several times, and reported to Doctor Hemingway that his son had stated with conviction that he now intended to stick to ambulance work. These were merely the thoughtful words of a good son. A few weeks after his convalescent leave ended in the early fall, Hemingway managed to get himself assigned to the Italian infantry. He served with them during October and until the Armistice in November. Thus, when the war ended, he was a bona fide fighting man. He was recommended for and received the silver medal of valor for his conduct at Fossalta, and because he earned the medal the hard way he has always had a combat soldier's sensitivity to both the significance and limitations of ribbons.

Hemingway was discharged by the Red Cross on January 4, 1919. A few days later he sailed for New York on the steamship *Giuseppe Verdi*. He had acquired, in addition to the immeasurable extension of his education, a personality and a role. He had been a foot soldier, the elite of fighting men. "That's one good thing about being an infantryman," he wrote in 1950 in *Across the River and Into the Trees*. "You never have any dreams except bad dreams." He would forever hold a blunt contempt for what he once called "the military politicians of the rear." His judgments about men at war, because of the nature of this first Italian chapter, would always be deeply felt and very accurate. The lugubrious phrase of the period, "the baptism of fire," could be applied to him quite literally and with dignity. He had yet to discover, with veterans of every war, that one did not shed it when he picked up his discharge papers.

## V.

Hemingway landed in New York on January 21, 1919. He immediately received at the age of nineteen the first of many attentions from the press. The New York *Sun* carried a five hundred word story on page eight about his war record and wounds. He was described as the first wounded American to arrive home from the Italian front, "with probably more scars than any other man, in or out of uniform, who defied the shrapnel of the Central Powers." Manhattan had not yet become bored with its returning heroes; Hemingway's personality, as well as the fact that he had been "before the war a reporter for the Kansas City *Star*," made the *Sun*'s reporter doubly responsive. Hemingway was also an excellent subject; the vividness of the story's phrases about his wounds clearly came from him. As for his future plans, Hemingway was thinking exclusively in terms of writing. He thought he was "qualified to take a job on any New York newspaper that wants a man that is not afraid of work and wounds." The interview was an indication of the sort of thing one of his friends referred to when he said later that Hemingway "tasted blood early" as far as notoriety was concerned, and that, leaving aside his gifts and natural capacity for success, he could scarcely have been expected to settle down to a conventional, Oak Park life.

Hemingway, however, did go home to Oak Park briefly. His effect on the community, and on his own generation in particular, was spectacular. "I remember him distinctly," a contemporary recalled in 1940, "walking up the street in his blue uniform, and limping, with a cane."[26] He was invited to speak at the high school. In the assembly hall he discussed his experiences and, one of his audience later reported, "held up a pair of shrapnel-riddled trousers for the students to see." He told them that it was the first speech he had ever made, and that he intended it to be his last, but he discussed the war in lucid terms; one of the listeners maintained years later that "the repercussions in Oak Park to that speech are still remembered." The garments worn on the night of July 8th, however, were his principal props. Frank Platt, the head of the English Department and faculty sponsor of the Burke Club, as he had been during Hemingway's student days, brought his former pupil to a meeting of the club. Hemingway displayed his khaki jacket, pants, and shoes to the boys, enumerating his wounds, according to Platt, and allowing them to examine the holes for proof. "Hemingway limped a little," Platt recalled, "but he had escaped death."

There were several things, on the other hand, which modified the pleasant triumph. There was another operation on his leg, and there was the familiar disenchantment with suburbia. There was no G.I. Bill through which one could solve or delay the situation by going to college, even had he wanted, and he had not been able to save any money from the scanty Red Cross allowance. The anticlimax was obviously substantial. He did a good deal of restless walking around the village, and he developed a cynical manner toward the girls whom he occasionally took out. He told an older friend one day that he was deeply in love. "A great temporary happiness," Hemingway explained, "has overcome me." There were stories about his presence in the Italian saloons of Chicago, and vague gossip about a party he went to with some ensigns from the Great Lakes Naval Station. Krebs, the central figure of the short story Hemingway wrote in 1924 about a veteran's homecoming, "tried . . . to keep his life from being complicated" by family pressures and obligations. Finally Krebs decided to go away altogether. "Still," he reflects, assessing his gains and losses, "none of it had touched him. He had felt sorry for his mother and she had made him lie. He would go to Kansas City and get a job and she would feel all right about it."[27]

Hemingway himself made a different, less abrupt adjustment to his rehabilitation, and one that was thoroughly appropriate to his personal interests and his intense desire to learn to write. He went up to northern Michigan and stayed there a long time, fishing, writing, reading. He came back to Chicago several times, and in the summer of 1919 he located Ted Brumback, who was working there on the old *Journal*. "He looked the same," said Brumback, who had last seen him in the Milan hospital a year before, "but he limped."[28] Hemingway persuaded Brumback to come up to Michigan. At night, as they sat around the campfire after a trout dinner, Hemingway outlined his plans. He intended to get a job on a newspaper and write in his spare time. As soon as he could make a living from his fiction, he would devote all his time to it. He was buoyant and confident with Brumback, telling his friend that he expected to be able to support himself as a fiction writer after "a short time."

Carl Edgar had also gotten home in 1919, and he visited Hemingway for a few days in Oak Park. Later, during the summer, Edgar saw a good deal of him at Horton Bay. Edgar was much impressed by the impact the war had so evidently made on Hemingway. "He came back," Edgar once said, "figuratively as well as literally shot to pieces." Edgar concluded that the intensity of Hemingway's desire to write was directly connected with the war. "He seemed to have a tremendous need to express the things that he had felt and seen."

Hemingway worked hard in Michigan and stayed on after his own family and the rest of the summer colony had gone home. "I put in a fall and half [a] winter writing up in Petoskey, Michigan," Hemingway said many years later, describing the extent of the preparation which preceded his first expatriate publication in 1923. It was a period of discouraging rejection. "I worked and wrote," he said on another occasion, "and couldn't sell anything." The chronology of rejection—which, except for his journalism, would continue until 1922—had begun, actually, during the war. From Milan Hemingway had mailed to a friend in Chicago

a number of stories which she tried unsuccessfully to sell
for him in the United States.

In retrospect, however, the period he spent in northern
Michigan in 1919 was of great profit. The area as a whole,
as well as its associations and implications, gave Hemingway the material for a large part of his earliest published
fiction. One of his first stories, "Up in Michigan," was
drawn from it.[29] Of the fifteen stories in *In Our Time*, the
collection which in 1925 brought him his first important
critical recognition, seven stemmed directly from the peninsula country he had fished and hunted since boyhood. The
solitary weeks he spent there in 1919, coming as they did
as an aftermath to his Italian experiences, allowed him a
rich perspective. A number of his wartime friends came up
to Michigan with him for short vacations that year, including Bill Horne and several others from the ambulance corps.
"Hemingway, to my own certain knowledge," Horne said
many years later, "never threw off his experiences in the
war." The force of those experiences, and the fact that he
had this northern Michigan interval in which to assess them,
made possible the kind of strong, dimensional treatment he
gave to Horton Bay in the early 1920's.

# TORONTO

"The Toronto *Star* laid great emphasis
on human interest."  J. H. CRANSTON[1]

---

*I.*

Horton Bay, to which Hemingway owed so much in the formation of his interests and attitudes, also provided him with the next opportunity in his literary apprenticeship. It was through a summer friendship in the northern Michigan colony that he received his introduction to the Toronto *Star.*

The late Ralph Connable, for many years head of the F. W. Woolworth chain in Canada, with headquarters in Toronto, had a summer home in Petoskey, Michigan. He had come originally from Chicago, and was an old friend of the Hemingway family. He was particularly fond of Doctor Hemingway's oldest boy, who called him Uncle Ralph. When the young veteran was at loose ends after the war, spending a restless summer in Michigan in 1919, Connable suggested that he come up to Canada. He could live at the Connable home in Toronto, acting as a kind of tutor to their young son. This would give him plenty of time for his writing, or, if he preferred, Connable was sure he could be of help in terms of a local newspaper job.

Such generosity was characteristic of Connable, a cheerful, gregarious man who had overcome the Canadian antagonism toward Americans. Connable was a particular favorite because of his legendary sense of humor; an obituary referred to him as "one of the city's best known practical jokers." The Toronto *Daily Star* devoted most of its full-column notice of his death in 1939 to a chronicle of his most celebrated jests. He was a man of frank, open kindness, shrewd and friendly, and with the sort of tolerant understanding that was required by a restless, rather bitter young man. The whole sequence of events, both in its personal as well as its vocational aspects, was as fortunate as that which had led Hemingway to Kansas City in 1917.

His informal duties in the Connable household in the late fall of 1919 occupied only a part of his time and energy. Connable turned him over to one of his own friends, Arthur Donaldson, head of the Toronto *Star*'s local display advertising. Donaldson, in turn, took Hemingway down the hall to the office of Gregory Clark, at that time feature editor of the *Star Weekly*.[2] Another chapter in Hemingway's apprenticeship had begun. He would be associated with the *Star Weekly*—as well as its parent paper, the *Daily Star*—for virtually the whole of the next four years. The Toronto Star Limited, the organization within which the two papers operated, was as appropriately suitable to Hemingway's training requirements at this stage as the Kansas City *Star* had been ideal as a preliminary school. The American and Canadian papers, indeed, were of such diverse natures that had his relationship with them been reversed—had he gone to Toronto in 1917 and to Kansas City in 1920—the entire pattern of his apprenticeship would have been seriously altered and damaged.

*II.*

In Kansas City Hemingway had worked under conscientious editors who took with the greatest seriousness their responsibilities to the profession in general and to young reporters in particular. Through Pete Wellington, and through the entire company and atmosphere of the Kansas City *Star*, Hemingway had been indoctrinated in the necessities of accuracy, in the obligations of vigorous prose, and in the requirements of forceful narrative. It had been a school with high, harsh standards, rigidly enforced. Few such standards existed on either of the Toronto papers owned by the late Joseph E. Atkinson.

Atkinson's weekend publication, the *Star Weekly*, was in particular dedicated largely to the indiscriminate entertainment of its subscribers. It was published on Saturday, because of legal prohibitions against printing and selling a paper on the Sabbath. It included a news section that was necessarily sketchy, and a conventional front page coverage of local, national, and international events, but its primary function was as a weekly magazine which Atkinson hoped ultimately to distribute throughout Canada.

The *Star Weekly* was the first Canadian paper to use American color comics. It exploited in full the reader values of an excellent illustrated section. It had several cartoonists, notably the late Jimmy Frise, who were as good as their metropolitan New York colleagues. More important, from Hemingway's point of view, the *Star Weekly* emphasized feature material on a virtually limitless range of topics— Atkinson placed certain flexible boundaries on sex and blasphemy—and bought most of its material, in 1920, from free-lance writers. The magazine also possessed an editor who, though he contributed nothing directly to Hemingway's training, was sympathetic and generous to young men of the American's talent and temperament.

The late J. Herbert Cranston, editor of the *Star Weekly* in 1920—its editor, in fact, from 1911 until 1932—was a man of considerably more literary interests and judgment than his employer. Cranston's personality and values, plus his pressing need for inexpensive writers, made the *Star*

*Weekly* a natural progression in Hemingway's apprentice-ship. All Hemingway's gifts for narrative and for ironic impressionism were encouraged in such surroundings and under such an editor. Cranston, like the harassed editors of all such publications, guided his staff as best he could be-tween the requirements of a semi-literate audience and the decencies of responsible writing. No one understood better than he the nature of the medium.

"The *Star*," Cranston said many years later, just before his death in 1952, and long after he had been forced out of the editorship to make room for Hearst-like techniques he could not stomach, "laid great emphasis on human interest. It knew that the masses derived much more entertainment from reading of the doings and foibles of ordinary indi-viduals like themselves than of those in the seats of the mighty."

Cranston was a mild, pious man. Reserved and serious, he was deeply committed to the personal conviction that through the *Star Weekly* he could do more than merely conspire in the creation of an enormous circulation. He hoped that in the magazine he could establish a worthy vehicle for young Canadian writers. There has been a very real hostility toward both the *Star Weekly* and the *Daily Star*, coming from some of those who have worked for the papers and from thoughtful Canadians who mistrust the papers' ethics. Cranston himself, both as an individual and as an editor, never inspired anything but good will and respect. "He was a lovable editor and loyal friend," accord-ing to one of his former contributors, "who was never equipped to oppose the utter ruthlessness of the men who successfully developed the *Star*'s circulation."

Cranston had none of the ascetic leadership of Pete Wellington. He prided himself on the temperate quality of his editorship. "I could not drive," he said later, analyzing the differences between his own editorial techniques and those of the men who were closer to the owner. He was content to function as editor in an old world, modest sense of the role, preferring even to buy his material through correspondence rather than personal contact. Cranston had, nevertheless, a realistic sense of the tone and treatment which were required for large circulation material. For a young writer like Hemingway, who had already learned the fundamentals of his trade, but needed the opportunity to exercise them, he could be of value simply by his recognition of work that would interest a broad audience.

"The *Star*," Cranston declared in 1951, "aimed to give the people largely what they wanted to read rather than what they ought to read if they would become intelligent citizens." As a contributor to the *Star Weekly*, Hemingway was encouraged to nourish and enlarge his instinct for interesting material. His editor emphasized an ancient principle in the pursuit of their audience. "We always sought to get an article started with a striking anecdote," Cranston once explained, "which would whet the appetite of the reader for more. The bait offered in the first few paragraphs must be such as would securely hook the fish." Such principles were always conditioned by Cranston's deeply cherished hope that he could establish the *Star Weekly* as a magazine of genuine literary stature.

It was not an easy objective, either in the light of his audience or of his employer's goal of dominating Canadian journalism. Cranston quite naturally fought a losing battle. His twenty-one-year tenure, however, was not a steady chronicle of defeat. If his editorship were graphed in points of partial success and total failure, in his attempt to realize this private ambition, the chart would show that Hemingway began to write for the *Star Weekly* at about the moment of maximum fruition in Cranston's ideal. Between 1920 and 1927 Cranston enjoyed his greatest freedom from owner and executive supervision, and with it the greatest success in the development of talented young writers.

Immediately after the war, in Cranston's own memory of the period, he "gradually built up a fine array of staff writers, and added one or two outstanding staff artists." Shortly after Hemingway arrived in Toronto, Cranston—probably under pressure from above—also began to alter the editorial point of view. "We now sought," he recalled, "to give a larger number of entertainment features, and possibly fewer information articles. By that I mean humorous articles, Leacock, Lardner, and many others, some of them American syndicate, and encouraging humor wherever we could find it in Canada." The division between the *Daily Star* and the *Star Weekly*, above all, was well defined at this time. "The two papers," Cranston remembered nostalgically, "were almost two completely separate entities in the early days."

Hemingway thus became a contributor at the instant when the increasing circulation made Cranston's appetite for young writers a sharp one, and when the new emphasis on humor and entertainment was still balanced in part by the earlier requirement of more serious treatment. There was a small literary renaissance in Toronto in the 1920's, and although the *Star Weekly* played no formal part in the movement—it would be ludicrous to imagine it as an agent of revolt or innovation—many of its writers participated actively in the attempt to vitalize Canadian literature. Their more serious work was often made possible by Cranston's ready purchase of their journalism. This was Cranston's greatest contribution to Canadian letters, and the closest he came to the realization of his private ambitions for the *Star Weekly*.

One of the men Cranston helped remembered him in terms which clarify the nature of the editor's role in Hemingway's apprenticeship. "Looking back," said Merrill Denison, today a writer in the field of industrial history, "I now realize that he must have picked men for both their writing skills and mental outlooks, and having accepted them, let the men themselves proceed pretty much on their own." Cranston, according to another writer who worked with him, was "shy and retiring, wrote little himself, but spent his energies discovering and encouraging talent wherever he found it." Hemingway reached Toronto in the first weeks of 1920 in need of both encouragement and discovery. Cranston remained his friend and supporter during the whole of the young American's turbulent association with the *Star*. He never made any attempt to identify himself with Hemingway's subsequent successes, beyond a brief note in his *Canadian Who's Who* biography in which he listed Hemingway among a half dozen others to whom he "gave first publication." The legend developed within a younger generation of Canadian writers that Cranston was the man who discovered Hemingway. Cranston himself was always frank to admit that he never looked upon the American "as likely to develop into anything out of the ordinary."

Cranston's bequest was his immediate recognition of such gifts as Hemingway had at the time, and his bestowal of the opportunity to exercise and extend them. Newspaper men of the period invariably testify to Cranston's consistent good taste as an editor. He was, according to Tim Reid, a prominent Canadian publicist and former city editor of the *Daily Star*, "an excellent judge of a story." Cranston encouraged Hemingway from the beginning by his willingness to buy whatever the latter submitted. At their first meeting they "chatted about the kind of thing the paper wanted," Cranston recalled; after that "the ice was broken and for a number of weeks Hemingway's name appeared regularly in the paper." Cranston characterized the young man's work as written in conventional newspaper style, with considerable wit. This was the quality, in fact, which most pleased the editor. "Hemingway," Cranston declared in 1952, "could write in good, plain Anglo-Saxon, and had a certain much prized gift of humor."

It was as a humorist, therefore, that Hemingway presented himself in much of his *Star Weekly* material in 1920. Humor continued to be at least an important ingredient in all of his work for the magazine and, to a lesser degree, the *Daily Star*, during the next four years. His style and attitudes matured as he ranged experimentally through the various levels of burlesque, mimicry, satire, and irony. All of these qualities have been important in his fiction; his debt to Cranston and the Toronto papers was thus a large one in those terms alone.

### III.

Hemingway's first story for the Toronto *Star Weekly*, published on February 14, 1920, without a by-line, established immediately this satiric impulse.[3] It was one of his few unsigned articles for either the *Daily* or the *Weekly* until late in 1923, when, though an experienced and well-paid reporter, he was being disciplined by the assistant managing editor. In February, 1920, however, the *Star Weekly* quite naturally printed without a by-line a story which was only a little over five hundred words long.

Hemingway made the most of the situation's potential. His ironic account of the snobberies of a Toronto scheme for renting works of art must have pleased Cranston, always searching as he was for wit that was neither too subtle nor too broad. Hemingway's treatment, in which he isolated and emphasized nuances of speech and affectation, was calculated to mock the world he was describing—a world not unlike Oak Park—and entertain the less genteel subscribers for whom he was writing. It was deft and promising, evidence of high spirits and precocious gifts of mimicry as much as of any genuine talent. Certainly, however, it was verification that he could establish himself as a free lance with this weekly magazine whose needs were so neatly tailored to his current assets and requirements. No one but a clairvoyant could have foretold from the article that he would ever write any notable fiction; nor, on the other hand, was there anything in it so clumsy or dull that such a prophecy could be outlawed. It was an encouraging start; it gave him a toehold in journalism and all the benefits of regular deadlines.

Three weeks later Cranston bought and printed another Hemingway story, this one equally shaped from and for the humorous prerequisites.[4] Cranston also gave him his first Toronto by-line. The lead paragraphs displayed the readiness, basic to the later success of his fiction, with which Hemingway has always been able to grasp and quickly identify himself with whatever world he happens at the moment to be inhabiting. Canada in 1920 was experiencing a mild nationalism, expressed in a struggle with England for political release, in the literary renaissance to which Cranston contributed the *Star Weekly*'s money, and in a spasm of anti-Americanism. A Toronto audience, in Cranston's principle, would inevitably rise to the bait of Hemingway's opening lines.

The land of the free and the home of the brave is the modest phrase used by certain citizens of the republic to the south of us to designate the country they live in. They may be brave—but there is nothing free. Free lunch passed some time ago and on attempting to join the Free Masons you are informed that it will cost you seventy-five dollars.

His second paragraph linked this crisp but seemingly unproductive lead with his general topic. "The true home of the free and the brave," Hemingway wrote, "is the barber college. Everything is free there. And you have to be brave." His prose had the exaggerated hyperbole basic to this type of humor. "For a visit to the barber college requires the cold, naked valor of the man who walks clear-eyed to death." The scene established, Hemingway picked up the narrative, shifting to dialogue that was easy and colloquial. He milked the situation with the expertness of a vaudeville routine. The story was semi-professional; its tricks and effects indicated his growing facility and confidence. He was maintaining in his writing an intensely personal flavor. It was clear that if he did not remain a hack too long he had enough individuality to escape the formula prisons of feature writing.

This was made abundantly evident by his third story, which was published the next week and preserved the ironic direction of his work.[5] His article on "How To Be Popular in Peace Though a Slacker in War" was savage and personal. Its satire was observant, keyed again to an audience whose casualties in World War I had been appalling; Toronto's pride in its war record was belligerent and anti-American. Hemingway's lead exploited a characteristic blend of mock rhetoric and abrupt colloquialism.

During the late friction with Germany a certain number of Torontonians of military age showed their desire to assist in the conduct of the war by emigrating to the States to give their all . . . in munition plants. Having amassed large quantities of sheckles through their patriotic labor they now desire to return to Canada and gain fifteen per cent. on their United States money.

Employing derisively the stock phrases ordinarily used to justify draft-dodging, Hemingway declared that "through a desire to aid these morally courageous souls who supplied the sinews of war," he would offer a few hints for "the returning munitioneer" who wanted to be popular. He suggested that it would be wise to come back to a different town, and he also had advice on how to handle the problem of a discharge button. He gave explicit instruction, still in the parody of a technical or academic manual, on the matter of dress. "Go to one of the stores handling second-hand army goods and purchase yourself a trench coat. If you cannot get a trench coat buy a pair of army shoes."

The war, quite clearly, was a genuinely compulsive factor in all Hemingway's attitudes in 1920. His instinct toward satire had been sharpened by his experiences in Italy and by the disillusioning contradictions he observed in Chicago and Toronto. Had his reaction to the war been less positive he would have used it a great deal more in his work for the *Star Weekly*. Gregory Clark, the *Weekly*'s feature editor and principal staff writer, who became a close friend of Hemingway during this period, observed this aspect of the young American with great interest. He felt that Hemingway was enduring a chaotic interlude of adjustment. "He was lost," Clark said many years later, "in the lovely confusion of trying to understand his past. He was trying to orient himself to the experiences he had been having."

Clark was equally struck by Hemingway's gifts as a writer. "His use of words," Clark said in 1952, "was precise, aware. His diction—his choice of words, I mean—was extraordinary." He remembered as a disturbing mannerism the way in which Hemingway was continually shadow-boxing, either during a conversation or while others were talking; Clark felt it indicated a basic lack of confidence. Hemingway, however, soon adjusted to his new friends. Before long, according to Cranston, he had "tall tales to tell of his war experiences." The fourth of Hemingway's 1920 pieces of satire, in fact, was another version of wartime slackers, less bitter than the one about Canadian munitioneers, but no less denunciatory in its mockery, this time, of service men who had not been in combat.[6] It was particularly significant as an indication of Hemingway's instinct for the general pattern of fiction. Save for the first paragraph, the article was composed almost entirely of dialogue between two Canadian veterans. Even that single paragraph of exposition was itself a conventional opening for pulp fiction. "Two returned men," Hemingway began, "stood gazing up in infinite disgust at a gang of workmen tearing down a building on King Street."

In the remaining twelve paragraphs of dialogue Hemingway established the two men as legitimate combat veterans, supplying a refrain of wit in the resistance each old soldier showed toward hearing the other's reminiscence. The speech as a whole, to be sure, had the synthetic, stock realism of readable magazine fiction of the period, but the authenticity of some of the idiom and language rhythms was unmistakable. It was the speech of Canadians of the working class, still retaining some of the old country inflections. It could never have been confused with the words of a veteran of the A.E.F., nor was it altogether like the talk of an English Tommy. It was an elementary distinction, perhaps, but a conscious distinction nonetheless, and one not always made by newspapermen older and more experienced than Hemingway.

Hemingway's affinity for dialogue, and his concern with its accurate use, was plainly evident in his work during the spring of 1920. He tended particularly to rely on it in these satiric articles. On March 13 the *Star Weekly* printed Hemingway's acid portrait of the mayor of Toronto.[7] The seven-hundred-word character sketch was an extended display of the gift for caricature which Hemingway had demonstrated in the story on renting works of art. The article had an uncompromising frankness that was fresh and startling. Its lucidity verifies Hemingway's memory of the solitary work he had done in Michigan between his return from Italy in 1919 and his arrival in Toronto in early 1920. When Gregory Clark summed up his specific memories of Hemingway's Toronto journalism, this particular sketch was the only one which still remained clear in his mind. "It was good," Clark recalled in 1950. "Maybe we didn't know how good."

Mayor Tommy Church was presented by Hemingway as he appeared during an evening at the fights in Massey Hall. T. L. Church advertised himself widely, and was generally accepted as, a zealous devotee of all sports. The synthetic pretense by a vote-conscious politician enraged Hemingway. He built the portrait around this aspect of the Mayor's personality.

Mayor Church is a keen lover of all sporting contests. He is an enthusiast over boxing, hockey and all the manly sports. Any sporting event that attracts voters as spectators numbers his Worship as one of its patrons. If marbles, leap frog, and tit-tat-toe were viewed by citizens of voting age, the Mayor would be enthusiastically present. Due to the youth of the competitors the Mayor reluctantly refrains from attending all of the above sports.

Hemingway maintained that after the last bout that night Mayor Church said, "Meeting's dismissed," thinking he was at the City Council. The final paragraph reaffirmed the lead. "The Mayor," Hemingway wrote, "is just as interested in hockey as he is in boxing. If cootie fighting or Swedish pinochle, or Australian boomerang hurling are ever taken up by the voters, count on the Mayor to be there in a ringside seat. For the Mayor loves all sport." It was one of the stories which Cranston, like Clark, could remember years later. He recalled it as "a lively description of Mayor

Tommy Church," written "in characteristic Hemingway style with plenty of punch in it."

Hemingway's punch was not restricted in his 1920 journalism to the thoroughly humorous or satiric. There was another block of material substantial enough to illustrate, like the satires, other characteristics of this stage of his apprenticeship. Hemingway wrote for the *Star Weekly* five stories about fishing and camping. They were long and detailed. In wordage they exceeded the satiric group; they were also less impressive as prose. Perhaps Hemingway was too familiar with the material to erect with care the neat structures and developments of several of his satires. The treatment was loose and patronizing. Stylistically, with occasional exceptions, the stories tended to look back toward the high school *Trapeze* rather than forward to the early fiction. They were virtually essays, clear and interesting, but without the sense of form which characterized his portraits and denunciations. His manner was stern and didactic.

"Sporting magazines," he began a story printed on April 24, "have fostered a popular fiction to the effect that no gentleman would catch a trout in any manner but on a fly on a nine foot tapered leader attached to a double tapered fly line cast from a forty-five dollar four and a half ounce rod."[8] The instructional impulse, basic to all successful journalism, was a strong one in Hemingway. He explained the motivation behind this deceit. "Out door magazines," he pointed out, "are supported by their advertising." He maintained that the advertisers were manufacturing expensive products "suitable to the understocked, over-fished streams of the Eastern United States." Myth and fraud clarified, Hemingway concentrated on the various kinds of live bait. The remainder of the article—almost a thousand words—was an elaboration of his belief that "worms, grubs, beetles, crickets, and grasshoppers are some of the best trout baits."⁹

The articles about fishing and camping indicated Hemingway's concern with expository writing. Cranston bought three more for June and August issues. They preserved the subjective intimacy of most of Hemingway's journalism. He was already following wherever possible the fundamental edict of his creative writing; a man should write only about what he has known. The first two stories were timely lectures on how to spend a vacation in the woods.¹⁰ The third, its emphasis on the more profitable drama of rainbow trout, was much the best of the trio, less coy and labored.¹¹ Hemingway found a Canadian angle for this account of fishing experiences that had been primarily in Michigan. "The rainbow," he wrote, "has recently been introduced into Canadian waters. At present the best rainbow trout fishing in the world is in the rapids of the Canadian Soo." The inflated rhetoric of high school prose still clung to his writing. "It is a wild and nerve-frazzling sport," he went on, "and the odds are in favor of the big trout who tear off thirty or forty yards of line at a rush and then will sulk at the base of a big rock and refuse to be stirred into action by the pumping of a stout fly aided by a fluent monologue of Ojibwayan profanity." His precise sense of landscape, as he catalogued the physical characteristics of the trout river, was sharper and more mature.

A high pine covered bluff that rises steep up out of the shadows. A short sand slope down to the river and a quick elbow turn with a little flood wood jammed in the bend and then a pool.

A pool where the moselle colored water sweeps into a dark swirl and expanse that is blue-brown with depth and fifty feet across.

There was the recurrent suggestion of his instinct for fiction as he pointed out that "the action is supplied by two figures that slog into the picture up along the trail along the river bank with loads on their back that would tire a pack horse." He remained in the present tense, dramatizing the fishermen and their excitement. His narrative of the catch itself was energetic and declarative, cleansed for the moment of garrulous journalese. "He tore down the pool and the line went out until the core of the reel showed. He jumped and each time he shot into the air we lowered the tip and prayed. Finally he jumped, and the line went slack and Jacques reeled in. We thought he was gone and then he jumped right under our faces."

Hemingway provided a kind of final installment to this fishing and camping series with an account of lake trout he had encountered in Michigan in September of that year.[12] The story was not written, however, until after he returned from Horton Bay—it was published in the *Star Weekly* on November 20—and he justified its out-of-season quality with an entertaining lead in which he described the "opening of the great indoor fishing season." His paragraphs were slanted expertly with local allusions. "More fish are caught in clubs at this time of year," Hemingway wrote, "than ever were taken from the Nipigon. Bigger trout are taken around the tables in King Street cafeterias than in the prizes offered by the sporting magazines. And more fish get away within the confines of Toronto than are lost in all the trout streams of Christendom."

In this way, with winter anecdotes about the great catches of spring and summer, Hemingway completed his essays on northern Michigan. They had as much body as most of the journalism Cranston was able to buy for the *Star Weekly;* they had more durability than some of it. They contained occasional paragraphs of vigor and imagination. They were competent and effective in terms of the medium for which they were designed; it would be unrealistic to belittle the expository and narrative gifts they represented in a twenty-year-old high school graduate. It would be equally unrealistic to aggrandize them. The articles emphasize again the crucial importance of experiences and associations which would occur during the next three years. In 1920 Hemingway was neither more nor less promising than any talented undergraduate of wit and energy. On the other hand, he was exposed to dangers that do not normally exist for a young writer in undergraduate circles. An extreme vocational adaptability was already apparent in his free-lance work. It was evident in the casualness with which he had warmed over some of the camping material for a second *Star Weekly* serving.

*IV.*

On April 10, in the same issue in which was printed the satiric exercise in dialogue about the two Canadian veterans, there appeared a second story by Hemingway.[13] It was longer than its companion, and so different as to seem the work of another writer. It represented a kind of journalism Hemingway produced for the *Star Weekly* with increasing frequency; it was almost a scenario of his work during the fall of 1923. At this stage in his career, however, its glib facility was alarming. The 1920 treatment displayed a journeyman capacity for manufacturing a salable story from wholly stale material. Hemingway wrote about teeth, the causes and manner of their infection, and the merits and disadvantages in having them extracted.

The story was as shrewdly presented as a patent medicine, slick with heavy wit, and admirably lucid. No amount of clarity, however, could disguise its pedestrian quality. Hemingway quoted at length, like the weariest of hacks, from "a leading Toronto dentist." His nine final paragraphs

—about six hundred words—were an unacknowledged popularization of the charts and texts which hang in a dentist's office. Hemingway had an immense capacity for hard work, and an impressive willingness to learn; his talent nevertheless required severe tutoring if it weren't to degenerate into mere fluency.

That the article was more than a momentary cynicism was verified by a story published two weeks later.[14] Hemingway here produced what was little more than an anecdote. Less than five hundred words, its only resemblance to his conscientious satires was that once again he exposed a popular illusion. His theme was that "big department stores cannot obtain insurance against changes of style." He explained that a corollary of this was the technique by which unsold clothes were being sent by the Toronto stores to small cities "in the mining district, bush or country," where they were re-offered for sale as the latest Toronto models. The article was spun from the rhetorical question, "What becomes of the old style, and the unsuccessful styles?" Hemingway enlarged on the commercial hoax, and ended with a single sentence paragraph whose crisp paradox may have been the material's original attraction. "These little stores on the edge of things are the real graveyard of dead styles."

The story was at best an abortive execution of a commonplace conceit. Like the rest of his work in 1920, however, it convinced Cranston that in Hemingway he had located a writer of uncommon inventiveness. Verbally as well as in prose, Hemingway evidently overwhelmed the editor. "He had been a vagabond," Cranston once explained, on the basis of what Hemingway told him in Toronto, "from the day he decided he had had enough of school." Cranston enlarged on this on another occasion, describing Hemingway's boyhood as having been spent "riding the rods and sleeping in tramp jungles." Hemingway was taking over as his own all the hobo lore he had heard from Lionel Moise in Kansas City.[15] Canadians, until very recently at least, have been willing to believe almost anything of Americans. Hemingway found Cranston an excellent audience.

"There was nothing Hemingway would not do just for the sheer excitement of it," Cranston maintained, "and he had eaten—or said he had—all kinds of things, slugs, earthworms, lizards, all the delicacies that the savage tribes of the world fancy, just to get their taste." The editor recalled that whenever he "ran out of subjects on which Hemingway might write he was always able to pull a good one out of his adventurous past." The fourth story Hemingway sold Cranston was an illustration, for the Canadian, of this limitless reservoir. Hemingway had known and observed petty criminals in Kansas City, and he had cultivated the friendship of cops and detectives. He now wrote for the *Star Weekly* a plausible analysis of department store larceny.[16] The triviality of the material did not prevent it from being excellent practice—up to a point—for a young writer who wanted to be able to explain and clarify and vivify. The treatment was standard Sunday supplement presentation, of the sort that was being supplied regularly to similar mass circulation weeklies and syndicates in the United States. Such articles consolidated his association with the *Star Weekly*. "I would hesitate to suggest that I taught Hemingway anything," Cranston said later. "He was a born storyteller."

In 1920 the importance of newspaper work to Hemingway derived primarily from the opportunity to write constantly, for publication, in a medium which required narrative that was interesting and forceful. By 1923, when Hemingway completed four concentrated years of feature writing and reporting, his compulsion toward fiction was breaking through the restrictions of the *Star Weekly* formula. Certain final articles, in the late fall of 1923, were transition pieces between the feature and the short story. Even in 1920 Hemingway's instinct toward exposition through dialogue and action was a powerful one. For the issue of June 5 Hemingway wrote a full-column survey of the role which Canadians and Canadian liquor were playing in the violation of American prohibition.[17] Cranston featured it on the first page of the magazine section. It balanced, in terms of page make-up, an article by the late Fred Griffin; as a rule Griffin shared the *Weekly*'s top assignments and columns with Gregory Clark. Hemingway's story was notable for its compact, imaginative style. On this occasion his talent dominated the material. He illustrated his denunciation of ambiguous Canadian laws with an effective vignette.

I saw a slack lipped, white faced kid being supported on either side by two scared looking boys of his own age in an alley outside a theatre in Detroit. His face was pasty and his eyes stared unseeingly. He was deathly sick, his arms hanging loosely.

"Where'd he get it?" I asked one of the scared kids.

"Blew in his week's pay for a quart of Canuck bootlegged." The two boys hauled him up the alley. "Come on, we got to get him out of here before the cops see him."

Crime and violence had a special fascination for Hemingway, and, of course, particularly if it were of American origin, for his employers. He ended his 1920 association with the *Star Weekly*, in the issue of December 11, with an even more specific exploration of racketeers.[18] The story was date-lined from Chicago on December 8. Hemingway gave it authenticity by placing most of his emphasis on the ex-killer from whom he had gotten most of his information. "Perhaps it were better not to describe him too closely," he wrote, "because he might run on to a Toronto paper. But he is about as handsome as a ferret, has fine hands, and

looks like a jockey a little overweight." The phrases have
the outline at least of the brief exposition in "The Killers,"
where the two gunmen's hands, as well as their slight
statures, are emphasized. The *Star Weekly* article even included, as would "The Killers," a juxtaposition of crime
and the ring. Hemingway's final paragraph had a poised,
confident tone, closer now to the idiom of his early fiction
than had been the sometimes forced, precocious material he
had sold Cranston at the beginning of 1920. It is a reminder that he had matured as a writer during these
months. "That's the type of mercenary that is doing the
Irishmen's killings for them. He isn't a heroic or even a
dramatic figure. He just sits hunched over his whiskey glass,
worries about how to invest his money, lets his weasel mind
run on and wishes the boys luck."

It was his fifteenth article for the *Star Weekly*.[19] The
stories had averaged approximately fifteen hundred words.
The fact that they had been largely written in the four
months between March and June pointed to a fairly consistent production of about five thousand words of pub-
lishable material each month. He had been aided in the
formation of regular working habits. He hadn't made
much money—Cranston said later[20] that "his biggest
check was $10"—but he had earned enough and written
enough to legitimately think of himself as a writer and
to feel that, given time, he could ultimately make a living through his work. This was a crucial step. At the age
of twenty-one he could regard himself as a professional. He
would thereby sift all his subsequent experiences in terms of
their possible use in his work. He had worked with men as
able as Fred Griffin and Gregory Clark. He had won their
professional respect and the confidence of his editor. Hemingway's arrivals in and departures from Toronto were
frequent between 1920 and 1924, and in later years his
Canadian friends were sometimes confused as to the precise intervals when specific events occurred. Cranston,

however, stated categorically that as early as 1920, while "he wrote articles for the *Star Weekly* to keep himself in clothes and fodder," Hemingway was also "ambitious to become a writer" and "labored" at his writing "in his spare hours."

## V.

Hemingway returned to Chicago in the autumn of 1920, after spending the summer in Horton Bay. He was reluctant to settle in his family's Oak Park home; in Chicago he lived on the outskirts of the world of people like the retired gunman and the practicing bootleggers. The *Star Weekly* feature work he resumed in 1921 would reflect this world. In the meantime he spent a great deal of time in the Chicago gyms, and in the Italian restaurants. For a while, very broke, he shared a furnished room with Bill Horne, his ambulance corps friend. Eventually he got a job through a want ad in the Chicago *Tribune*. He became an associate editor of *Co-operative Commonwealth*, a monthly house organ by which Harrison Parker, a Chicago advertising man, was publicizing his venture of the moment. Hemingway did not know much about this enterprise when he accepted the position. His brief association with the magazine did not increase his sense of harmony with postwar America. He turned out a good deal of copy for the magazine, however, and in his spare time—and on the magazine's time as well—he continued with his own work. As an episode in his apprenticeship it was by no means comparable to the seven months in Kansas City, nor to the period he had just spent in Toronto. It nonetheless made certain contributions to his literary situation. His transformation from a feature writer in Canada to a house organ editor for a Chicago promoter, brief as it was, is another well-defined gradation in his training.

CHAPTER

V

# *CHICAGO*

"The Cooperative Society of America
. . . . is a colossal shell-game."
*Nation*[1]

*I.*

Had Harrison Parker exercised occasional restraint, and
had he not been seized by political ambitions, he might have
overshadowed Samuel Insull as Chicago's success story of
the 1920's. Parker has nevertheless had a profitable career
as a devotee of the complex holding company as well as the
simpler beauties of prize contests.[2] He has made good use
of the United States Post Office, which has over the years
received many complaints about a variety of promises he
has expressed through the mails.

The Co-operative Society of America—its name deceptively similar to that of the legitimate and highly respected
Cooperative League of the United States of America—was
incorporated by Parker in Chicago on February 20, 1919.
It was created out of the ruins of the recently defunct National Society of Fruitvalers. The new society's assets were
heavily mortgaged properties, of doubtful value, in Muske-
gan, Michigan. Its structure was that of a trust, filed by
Parker's wife. Mrs. Parker subsequently earned $1,522,609
through the sale of certificates in the society, while being
paid a salary of five hundred dollars a week as secretary of
one of the subsidiary companies. The trust named Parker
and two male associates as trustees. A trust was more at-

tractive to Parker than either a corporation or a partnership, since virtually unlimited powers could be assigned to trustees.

Parker and his two lieutenants were now legally entitled to everything that might be contributed in the future to the society by potential subscribers. They were permitted to sell or mortgage such contributions without the consent of the members. They were cited in the trust agreement as "not liable to the members for the results of their incompetence, or for their acts or failures to act." It was stipulated that the trustees were "not to be bonded to indemnify the members for losses arising out of dishonesty." They were authorized to fix their own compensations. The members, on the other hand, as the magazine *Co-operation*—the foremost journal of the authentic co-operative movement—pointed out bitterly in 1921, enjoyed "less opportunity for democratic control than even the usual profit-making corporation."[3] They could neither compel the trustees to pay dividends out of the earnings of the society, nor were they entitled to an accounting. The bait, of course, was easy money.

Parker urged his prospective subscribers to "provide for your old age by investing in the great Co-operative Movement." He also promised an opportunity "to cut the cost of living through the elimination of profiteering on the necessities of life." Before an angry minority of his stockholders managed to bring him into court, convinced that his campaign for governor of Illinois had been financed with their money, Harrison Parker had acquired 81,000 contributors. From them, and through the manipulation of the funds in a set of allied trusts, he received investments of $11,500,000. When the society was finally adjudged bankrupt on October 6, 1922, in the United States District Court in Chicago, it had acquired liabilities of $15,000,000 and retained assets of $50,000.

The remaining assets, which may have formed the seed of what Parker later called the "considerable competence" that permitted him to retire in 1931, had been transferred to a new organization, The Cooperators of America. Parker was its principal trustee. In 1921, when Judge Kenesaw Mountain Landis—whose name Parker had been impudently using in his promotional literature—ordered Parker to sell no more society securities in the state of Illinois, he expressed his horror at what had been revealed about the organization. "It is so unclean, the whole thing," Landis said, almost in disbelief, "no matter where you touch it." The *Nation* published an indignant account of Hemingway's employer in the issue of October 19, 1922. The article described the entire operation as "a colossal venture in frenzied finance."[4] Some of the energy for the venture was provided by idealistic young students from Northwestern University and the University of Chicago; they helped in the local distribution of circulars and conceived of themselves as partners in an evangelical crusade. The sale of securities was also prompted by the flood of pamphlets which Parker circulated throughout the Middle West. The principal vehicle of persuasion, however, was a monthly publication, *Co-operative Commonwealth*. It was as an editor of Parker's magazine that Hemingway supported himself in the winter of 1920.

*II.*

Evangelical idealism was not the impulse which brought Hemingway to the staff of *Co-operative Commonwealth*, although he later admitted he assumed "a co-operative thing was straight because they had tried to start one for marketing apples when I worked on the farm in Michigan." In 1920 he was moved primarily by the fifty dollars a week which the job paid. He accepted on faith the organization's statement that it was patterned after the old Rochdale Co-operatives in England. The Chicago *Tribune* want ad made no mention of the Co-operative Society of America, simply advertising for someone to fill an editing job, with a box number. "He was pretty completely out of a job and money," his friend Bill Horne recalled later, "until this house organ editorship came along." Horne and Hemingway continued to live in the former's attic bedroom at 1230 North State Street for a brief time; then the generosity of Y. K. Smith, the oldest of the Smith family from Horton Bay, enabled them to move into completely different quarters on Chicago's near north side.[5]

Smith, a successful advertising man, was living with his wife in a large, old-fashioned apartment at 100 East Chicago Street. The flat had been sublet from Mrs. Dorothy Aldis, a wealthy, local patroness of the arts then traveling in Europe. "Big-hearted Y.K.," according to Roy Dickey, Smith's former copy chief at the Critchfield agency, "had promptly moved all his indigent friends in to share the apartment." In addition to Mr. and Mrs. Smith, the apartment now sheltered the former's younger sister, Kate, who later married John Dos Passos; a friend of hers named Edith Foley, a free-lance writer; Hemingway and Horne; and Donald M. Wright, another advertising man. Horne and Hemingway shared a bedroom, as did the two young women. Wright, who was not working at the time, slept late in the mornings and had a room to himself.

It was a very pleasant arrangement. Three of the group were old friends of Hemingway. He had known the Smiths since he was twelve, and Horne, of course, was an ambulance corps buddy. All of them, with the exception of Mrs. Smith, were interested in writing and were earning their livings as writers of one sort or another. Smith was a man of culture, widely read and perceptive, and very articulate. Horne and Wright were both advertising men; the latter, a friend and great admirer of Sherwood Anderson, with whom he had done agency work, had literary ambitions. Kate Smith and Edith Foley were collaborating on magazine articles. Smith had a wide acquaintanceship in Chicago, and a variety of interesting people continually visited the apartment in the evenings.

It was not a bohemian atmosphere. Smith had no intention of sponsoring a miniature Latin Quarter. He was himself fastidious and well bred, and he was sufficiently older than the rest so that his point of view established the general tone of their lives, at least so far as the apartment was concerned. Horne, almost thirty, was hard-working and ambitious. Neither Wright nor Hemingway were dissipated men. Their evenings were usually spent in the apartment, both by inclination and because none of the younger tenants had much money. Smith recalled that in their conversations, as well as in the fraternity-type horseplay, Hemingway was invariably the leader. "He was by far the most colorful of us," Smith said later, "and very witty."

Hemingway himself was very fond of Smith. Wright conceived of their relationship as almost that of foster parent and son, and maintained afterwards that Hemingway once told him that he had "learned all I know about many things from Y.K." Smith also was more sympathetic to Hemingway's talent than the others; until Sherwood Anderson joined the group he was probably the only one who sensed the extent of the young man's gifts. The rest had various attitudes toward his work. Horne, of course, was devoted to him, admired every aspect of his character, and, in his own phrase, remained his "hero-worshiper" during the subsequent years. Horne, however, was the least literary of the group. Wright, the most self-consciously literary, thought of Hemingway as a competent journalist, but all their tastes were different; Wright was appalled by Hemingway's turbulent realism and his positive statements about what was good and what was bad in writing. Smith, the most mature and acute, felt that during the winter and spring of 1921 Hemingway had no clear conception of what he wanted to do, but a very real notion of what he didn't want.

"He hated the idea of a nine to five job," Smith said many years later. "He wanted his freedom. He had no illusions about journalism, but he'd concluded that it was at least better than anything else he'd seen."

Despite the absence of a well-conceived philosophy or plan of attack—whose existence would have been startling in one so young and so recently returned from the traumatic experience of war—Hemingway was working far harder than the rest. He was writing a great deal, both for *Co-operative Commonwealth* and on his own. In the evenings, when the others were idling in the living room, Hemingway was apt to be in his room, typing. He stood out from the others in his diligence and his intensity. In 1937 Wright published a brief sketch of the Smith group. He remembered that Hemingway "was trying any and every kind of writing at the time—he even fired out satirical rewrites of world news to *Vanity Fair*, to no avail."[6]

It was during these months, in this mood of almost buckshot literary endeavor, that Hemingway wrote two fragments which were published in New Orleans by the *Double-Dealer*, a little magazine, in the spring of 1922. "A Divine Gesture," the first of these, was a brief, ironic prose sketch, in the manner of Anatole France or such an imitator as Ben Hecht.[7] Elaborately arch, this satire on the triviality of mankind is so alien to Hemingway's literary attitudes, as displayed extensively in the journalism and fiction he wrote in Europe in 1922 and 1923, that it verifies Wright's statement that he was attempting a variety of mediums in Chicago. "Ultimately," the quatrain which the *Double-Dealer* printed in the June issue, was somewhat more characteristic;[8] it was not unlike the poetry of his expatriate pamphlet of 1923, *Three Stories & Ten Poems*. On the whole, however, the *Double-Dealer* material was more truly juvenilia than almost anything he had written since he left high school, abortive concessions to the milieu in which he was temporarily living.

Hemingway was nevertheless completely serious about mastering his trade. "Will it sell?" he would ask his friends at the apartment, after reading one of the stories aloud. "Do you think it will sell?" There was a real irony in his concentration upon salability. While the others discussed art and the artistic verities, and urged Hemingway to concern himself more with the permanent values of literature, he was actually subjecting himself to a rigid professional discipline. He was dismayed and angered, however—as he has continued to be—by too much talking in large, vague terms about writing. "Artist, art, artistic!" he would shout. "Can't we ever hear the last of that stuff!" While they talked about art, with the rather easy intensity of dilettantes, Hemingway talked about story markets, and about the fighters he was watching in Kid Howard's gym; and above all, his friends remembered, he talked about soldiering.

He was inevitably profiting from this literate atmosphere, on the other hand, much as he might despise its garrulous, uncreative aspects. He was himself interested in music and painting and in the specific work of the artists who came to the apartment. He told his friends that music, like writing, had above all to be clear; his conception of painting showed the same earnest fidelity to realism, authenticity, and immediacy. The traditional picture of literary Chicago during the early 1920's is as a sort of cornbelt Florence. The Smith apartment was a miniature of that aspect of the city. Hemingway could not help but be affected by the passionate concern with art and craft. He had simple, absolute convictions as to the functions of writing and the responsibilities of the writer.

"You've got to see it, feel it, smell it, hear it," he once declared to the group. This commandment, basic to all his subsequent work, is confirmed by Hemingway's own memory of what he was attempting in those months.

"I was always working by myself," he said in 1952, in an effort to define his literary debts, "years before I met Ezra [Pound] or Gertrude [Stein]. This is how I would do [it]. For instance I knew I always received many strong sensations when I went into the gym to train or work out with boxers." As he sat in the gym, wrapping his hands and waiting to get in the ring, he would try to identify the various smells. This was the first step of the process. The second step isolated him even more dramatically, in a literary sense, from the rest of the Smith group. This was the step he practiced in the evenings, while the others talked in the living room of art and craft and the creative process. "When I would get back from the gym," Hemingway remembered, "I would write [the sensations] down." Clearly Hemingway was not merely indulging in comforting talk when he told Don Wright that a writer must see it, feel it, smell it, hear it.

Wright, of course, could agree that this was perhaps one kind of writing, although he did not accept it as a total prescription, any more than it would have been accepted by Sherwood Anderson, the contemporary writer for whom Wright reserved his greatest admiration. Hemingway's attitude toward Anderson, who was soon introduced into the group by Wright and Smith, both of them former associates of his in local advertising work, was a revealing one. The other members of the group were constantly razzing Anderson, kidding him affectionately about his flamboyant dress, his extravagant stories, his imaginative flights. Hemingway, however, was always very polite to Anderson,

quiet and attentive. His attitude might have been interpreted as simply that of a young apprentice sitting respect-
fully at the feet of an older and more experienced—and
relatively successful—writer. Smith, who was always intrigued by Hemingway's complex personality and attitudes,
had a different interpretation. "It probably means a storm's
brewing," he said, explaining that in his experience Hemingway handled certain personal relationships like a good
boxer, encouraging his opponent to overextend himself,
growing more tense and silent as a situation developed.

Anderson, on the other hand, was from the beginning
delighted with the young newspaperman. Anderson was
then living on Division Street, not far from the Smith apartment, and he visited them often that winter. He was emphatic in his response to and predictions about Hemingway.
"Thanks," Anderson said to his hosts the first night, "for
introducing me to that young fellow. I think he's going to
go some place." Anderson was already an important figure
in Chicago's literary life. His visits to the Smiths were
notable events. Bill Horne felt that the opportunity to talk
to the various people who came to the apartment was "important to Hemingway's development as a writer," and he
was certain that "the high point of those evenings was when
Sherwood Anderson would come over and spend the evening with us." Hemingway continued to be polite and
respectful, but occasionally he revealed a little of what he
was already thinking. He was thoroughly hostile, inevitably, to Anderson's concept of unconscious art. Once or
twice he was vocally critical of Anderson's style.

"You couldn't let a sentence like that go," Hemingway
once said after Anderson had left, taking with him the
story he had just read aloud. This was the beginning of
Anderson's period of great success, however, and he was
totally unaware of the doubts which existed in the critical
mind of his young friend. Anderson never claimed to have

influenced Hemingway's work as a whole. The most he ever said was that it was "through my efforts" that Hemingway "first got published." Anderson was very explicit about this. "Anyway it is sure," he wrote twenty years later in his *Memoirs*, "that if others said I had shown Hemingway the way, I myself had never said so. I thought . . . that he had his own gift, which had nothing particularly to do with me."[9]

Anderson then added a charitable sentence which confirms the testimony of the other members of the Smith clique. "Absorption in his ideas," Anderson speculated, trying to analyze the impulse which caused Hemingway to satirize him in 1926 in *The Torrents of Spring*, "may have affected his capacity for friendship." Certainly there was no doubt about the intensity or conviction with which Hemingway regarded writing. One was either with him or against him. There could be no compromise or variation. As an attitude this did not encourage permanent relationships with other writers. His mistrust of Anderson was vocational rather than personal. His actual debt to Anderson was a large one.

The praise and sponsorship of a respected, productive writer were of very real value both psychologically and professionally. They contributed to the strength and confidence which would sustain him during the forthcoming period of rejection. Hemingway was bolstered in his artistic intentions by the knowledge that Anderson was achieving recognition with something of the same kind of material as his own. Gregory Clark remembered that Hemingway read Anderson's work constantly in Toronto. Anderson was a spur, a symbol, as well as a tangible material prop, a promise that a man could write what he felt and still find a market. As individuals, however, they were so fundamentally in competition that they could not remain close for any length of time.

"They were very much alike in their vanity," according to Don Wright, "and in the delight they each took in the effect they had on others. Both of them were always saying, 'Look, I put something over, didn't I!'"

The primary value of the winter in Chicago was in the compulsion to produce work constantly. "I think that probably the only thing about this particular deal which contributed to Hemmy's writing future," maintained Horne, who continued to see Hemingway until the 1930's, "was the fact that it kept him writing." There were between fifty and sixty pages to be filled each month in *Co-operative Commonwealth*. Although Harrison Parker took freely from the material of legitimate co-operative magazines, Hemingway was responsible for delivering a good deal of original copy. The magazine stressed human interest stories; Hemingway thus continued in effect the same type of features he had been writing in Toronto. He was also responsible for what he referred to as "thinking and planning of editorials." His hours were elastic. The understanding was that he would do a good deal of his work at home.

Hemingway's job—which he once referred to as "managing editor"—owed its existence to the recent transformation of *Co-operative Commonwealth* into a monthly. The magazine was being slicked up during the autumn of 1920, under the new editorship of Richard Loper, as part of Parker's renewed campaign for members. Hemingway's brief tenure occurred, therefore, during a time when professional standards had replaced the amateurish informality and irregular publication of earlier months. The magazine was now well edited, with excellent layouts, good captioning, clear text, and a lavish use of photographs. There was a skillful reliance on devices that would interest the unsophisticated audience at which the house organ was directed. The magazine emphasized that it regarded "the members as of utmost importance to the co-operative movement," promising "to print all we can about the membership."[10] It included briskly written personal notes, news of engagements and weddings, and descriptions of members' vacations. Hemingway was again being conditioned, as on the Kansas City *Star* and the Toronto *Star Weekly*, to write entertaining and provocative material. Biblical phrases and similes occurred frequently in the articles and editorials; the evangelical quality Parker sought to cast across the movement was always present in neat, controlled rations. The editorials emphasized pious instruction on such topics as, "What Is Idealism?" The magazine's cover and format, even to the size, type, and design, were studiously modeled on those of the legitimate co-operative publications.

Hemingway could not have been placed in an atmosphere better calculated to increase his distaste for certain American values and his determination to avoid permanent bondage to any such employment. The Co-operative Society of America differed from American business as a whole only in the fact that Parker's intentions were fraudulent. His approach to his product, the techniques used in merchandising it, and the audience instincts to which he appealed, were characteristic of the surface appearance of American commercial life. It was incongruous employment for a skeptical young veteran with a fixed set of personal ethics; on the other hand, of course, it sharpened Hemingway's acute sense of the ironic and paradoxical, and increased his personal ambitions as a writer.

Nor was the environment of the Smith apartment one that would increase his satisfaction with the importance or validity of conventional values. The young advertising men and artists who spent their evenings at East Chicago Street —both the tenants and their friends—had in varying degrees the same attitude toward commerce as those which Sherwood Anderson was expressing in his conversation and his work. A few of them were serious students of possible solutions to the ambiguities of materialistic values. Most of them, however, expressed an attitude which was also Hemingway's. They mocked the entire situation both as it involved them personally and in the larger terms of the system as a whole.

"We had much fun after hours," Wright remembered, "telling yarns about the scheming of the low grade morons who were our bosses in agencies and magazines." Smith summed up the general attitude when he said of the presidential campaign of 1920 that "Harding is elected and the Revolution is assured." During the 1930's Wright sold to the trade journal *Advertising & Selling* a series of articles called "A Mid-Western Ad Man Remembers." In one of these he described the Smith group as an example of the "many literary-advertising 'gangs'" then current in Chicago, and included a paragraph or two about "the burlesque advertising plans" with which Hemingway entertained them in the evenings. One of the plans, according to Wright, had to do with bottling blood at the stockyards and selling it "in gooey kidd-ee copy as 'Bull Gore for Bigger Babies.'"[11] Hemingway's skepticism about advertising quickly extended to the Co-operative Society of America. Before long he was regaling his friends with stories about the scheme. Smith remembered the cynical delight with which Hemingway repeated a declaration by one of Parker's front men that "the members've got a voice but not a vote."

"I worked until I was convinced it was crooked," Hemingway said many years later, "stayed on a little while thinking I could write and expose it, and then decided to just rack it up as experience and the hell with it."

Horne remembered distinctly that toward the end of Hemingway's employment with *Co-operative Commonwealth* he "became very much wrought up about it."

Horne also remembered the denunciation Hemingway assembled and optimistically offered to several Chicago newspapers. "I know that none of them would touch it," Horne said, adding, quite rightly, that "Mr. Parker was riding pretty high at that time and the papers probably thought he was too hot to handle." Hemingway continued at the magazine into the spring of 1921. He had met Hadley Richardson, whom he would marry in September—she had come to Chicago from St. Louis to visit Kate Smith, a classmate and close friend—and he was neither personally unhappy nor ethically desperate about his job. He worked hard, both at the office and in the evenings. He was writing constantly, stories and articles that were rejected monotonously by American magazines, avant garde experiments such as those accepted by the *Double-Dealer*, and features and editorials for his employers. "I tried to write, on their time, all the time," Hemingway once explained. He sent a few articles up to Toronto, consolidating his single promising alliance in journalism. Cranston welcomed his contributions. He bought them promptly for the *Star Weekly*. For a time he even elevated Hemingway to the dignity of a personal column.

Three of Hemingway's seven *Star Weekly* articles in 1921 were printed as three-column, rectangular boxes with his centrally-placed by-line in bold-face type only slightly smaller than the twelve-point, single line titles, drawn from the particular material, with which the columns were headed.[12] Cranston presented a fourth article in essentially the same format, retaining the large, single line caption and the three-column box, this time with Hemingway's name in small, conventional *Star Weekly* by-line type at the head of the left-hand column.[13] Another of his stories was given the identical box presentation with a four-line caption.[14] Cranston further stressed the columnist role by using several of these five articles on the same page of their respective issues; there was even an ironic consistency in the regularity with which the *Star Weekly* misspelled his by-line as "Hemmingway."[15]

Hemingway was as pleased as Cranston with the arrangement. When it became clear early in 1921 that the *Co-operative Commonwealth* was a dead end, Y. K. Smith had taken him around to Critchfield's, the Chicago advertising agency where both he and Sherwood Anderson, as well as Don Wright, had all worked at one time or another. Roy Dickey, the copy chief, had no jobs available, and he noticed that Hemingway at least pretended a lack of concern. He told Dickey he already had a job, "supplying a column," Dickey remembered, to the Toronto *Star*. This was in part bravado, since the financial return on these occasional columns was minute, but he could take legitimate satisfaction in the prominence Cranston gave to whatever he received. It was an encouraging antidote to the otherwise consistent rejection. The freedom Cranston allowed his free-lance staff was particularly refreshing after the slanted fraud of *Co-operative Commonwealth*, and, at the other extreme, the doctrinaire principles of Art enunciated in the nightly sessions at the apartment. A columnist's license was a fine safety valve for Hemingway in 1921.

### III.

Hemingway's seven articles for the *Star Weekly* in 1921 —they averaged about a thousand words apiece—reflect, inevitably in so subjective a newspaperman, the influence of the months he spent in the United States after leaving Toronto in the spring of 1920. Two of his stories dealt specifically with the Chicago underworld. All of them made at least indirect use of such American themes as big league baseball, the Muscle Shoals debate, national vacation habits, and various aspects of the American character which would increase Canadian convictions about the vulgarities of their neighbors. Hemingway had showed from the beginning, in his high school parodies as well as his first work for Cranston in 1920, an instinctive sense of audience tastes. His work for *Co-operative Commonwealth* had increased this natural capacity. He was careful to locate a Toronto angle for each of his 1921 articles.

There was an element in this journalistic facility, however, which went beyond the casual expertness of vocational instinct and experience. Hemingway's commitment to satire, previously no more than a recurrent feature of his journalism, was now definite and apparent. His impulse toward irony, evident in his immediate affinity for Ring Lardner, had probably been checked, though never inhibited, in Kansas City. The atmosphere of both the *Star* and the prosperous Midwestern city as a whole, after all, was primarily one of literate optimism. Neither William Rockhill Nelson nor his heirs and editors saw life in a sardonic way. The letters and postcards Hemingway sent home from Italy in 1918 showed that his excitement at first overcame any tendency toward skepticism about the war. Later, after he had been wounded, his attitude began to change. His satiric talent required more maturity and experience than he could have possessed in 1918. It also required a sustained encounter with provocatively deceitful situations. This encounter occurred in a variety of ways in northern Michigan and in Chicago, and in Toronto itself, from 1919 through 1921.

There was a new sophistication in Hemingway's humor. It even permitted him to inject burlesque into his out-of-doors material, relieving what had often been the solemnity of the enthusiast. In May he sent Cranston a column about American resorts.[16] His theme was that the best guarantee of a long, healthy life was to violate the traditional American insistence on annual vacations. He described several

typical summer colonies. "Beautiful Lake Flyblow," he
wrote, "nestles like a plague spot in the heart of the great
north woods. All around it rise the majestic hills. Above it
towers the majestic sky. On every side of it is the majestic
shore. The shore is lined with majestic dead fish—dead of
loneliness."

Most of his wit was more specifically critical than his
sketches of Smiling Lake Wah Wah and Picturesque Bum
View. His first column, published on February 19, 1921,
was organized on the hypothesis that what he called "public
entertainers"—statesmen, politicians, newspapers, artists,
and athletes—could be advantageously traded between nations as players are traded in professional baseball.[17] He
visualized "the biggest literary deal of the decade . . . trans-
ferring Anatole France, Jean-Jacques Rousseau and Voltaire from France to the United States in exchange for
Harold Bell Wright, Owen Johnson, Robert W. Chambers
and $800,000 in gold." He satirized the complacent ignor-
ance of newspapermen. "Rousseau and Voltaire, whose first
name could not be learned at a late hour, are dead."

In another long column about the farce of American
prohibition, printed under the caption, "Chicago Never
Wetter Than It Is Today," Hemingway described a characteristic "members only" speakeasy, at which, he said,
"there has never been any record of anyone being black
balled," and went on to mock the entire experiment.[18]
"There are eight federal prohibition enforcement officers
in Chicago. Four of them are doing office work, the other
four are guarding a warehouse." His whole tone, in fact,
indicated a hostility to contemporary America that went
beyond the necessities of flattering Toronto readers with
tales of American inferiority. He talked often to his friends
in the Smith group about his eagerness and determination
to get back to Europe. His restlessness covered almost every
aspect of the United States. Even what he had seen of

American soldiers overseas contributed to his jaundice. One night in Chicago he tried to explain to Y. K. Smith the difference between the American and Italian temperaments. Characteristically, his metaphor was war, and he discussed the humiliation of the Caporetto defeat for Italian individual and national pride. Then he imagined American soldiers after such a catastrophe. "At this point," he told Smith, "four of them would present themselves as a quartet, billed as The Caporetto Kids."

Hemingway clarified this distaste for American insensitivity and provincial arrogance in one of the paragraphs of his fantasy about trading international figures. He described the ceremonies in Stratford that would follow the purchase of Shakespeare's citizenship by the United States. "The little English town on the Avon," he wrote, "was decked with American flags and all the buildings were placarded. We Wanted Bill, and We Got Him, and Yea Bill! You Brought Home the Bacon were the legends on some of the placards. Floats were borne in a parade depicting Shakespeare wearing the clothes of a widely advertised American tailor and bearing this sign: Big Bill Shakespeare—One Hundred Per Cent. American."[19]

His satire often contained cheap and easy elements, since it was sometimes written in haste and with the vocational cynicism inevitable after his *Co-operative Commonwealth* chores. Occasionally, too, as in a long, dull analysis of the Muscle Shoals controversy, his paragraphs were the bored, automatic contrivances and lazy clichés of a hack journalist.[20] His writing as well as his attitudes could be affected by his study of American fiction markets and techniques. A May story about a Chicago killing confirms in essence at least a vague recollection by his friends at the Smith apartment that he was trying to sell short stories in 1920 and 1921 to the pulp magazine *Argosy*. Unlike most of Hemingway's journalism, the dispatch would be unrecognizable as his were it not for the by-line.

Anthony D'Andrea, pale and spectacled, defeated candidate for alderman of the 19th ward, Chicago, stepped out of the closed car in front of his residence and holding an automatic pistol in his hand, backed gingerly up the steps.

Reaching back with his left hand to press the door bell, he was blinded by two red jets of flame from the window of the next apartment, heard a terrific roar and felt himself clouted sickeningly in the body with the shock of the slugs from the sawed-off shot gun.[21]

The article indicated his capacity for stock language and stale melodrama. The Muscle Shoals story showed another alternative of newspaper work, a degeneration of his imaginative vitality into mechanical competence. These were the two extremes, tempting and secure, in which most gifted young writers foundered when they chose journalism as an apprenticeship. This was bread and butter writing, commendable in a newly married man but a symptomatic warning for an ambitious writer.

He and Hadley Richardson had been married, in fact, for only a little over two months when the Muscle Shoals article appeared. They were married in September in Horton Bay. The wedding party included most of Hemingway's oldest friends—Carl Edgar, Bill Smith, Brumback, and Kate Smith. Since his bride, a gifted pianist who sympathized with his restlessness, was as anxious as he to go to Europe, Hemingway renewed his efforts to arrange some solution that would get them abroad. His determination to escape America must have been strengthened by another ceremony he attended that autumn, this one in Chicago on November 20, 1921. General Armando Diaz presented Hemingway with Italy's Medaglia d'Argento al Valore

Militaire and with the Croce ad Merito di Guerra. Gregory Clark, the *Star Weekly*'s feature editor, who had always been skeptical of Hemingway's Italian war experiences, automatically turned the medals on edge, to check the inscriptions, when Hemingway showed them to him in Toronto the next month. "As long as I live," Clark wrote in 1950, "I shall never forget the cold chill that leaped out, radiating, from my back and over my shoulders and into my cheeks. For on the edge was inscribed: '*Tenente* Ernesto Hemingway.'"

Hemingway and his wife spent the late fall of 1921 in Toronto. His final *Star Weekly* article that year, published on December 17, was a return to the deft humor of personal journalism rather than the pulp techniques of the D'Andrea killing.[22] Cranston again set up the material as a column, with the caption—On Weddynge Gyftes—in large, Old English type. There was a sketch of a troubled bride and groom staring at a group of wedding presents that consisted solely of traveling clocks. Beneath the drawing Hemingway began his wry lament with some verse written in what his lead paragraph called "the best of the late 1921 rhythms."

> Three traveling clocks
> Tick
> On the mantelpiece
> Comma
> But the young man is starving.

This "unpersonal protest against wedding gifts as an institution" was an illustration of the kind of lively talent that now made possible an arrangement by which he and his wife went abroad for the next twenty months. A week before the wedding gifts story was published, Hemingway was "off to Europe to become roving correspondent for the

*Star*, with headquarters in Paris."[23] He went under the sponsorship of John Bone, managing editor of the *Daily Star*, although for a time his overseas correspondence appeared exclusively in the *Star Weekly*. Bone had noticed the quality of Hemingway's feature work for Cranston in 1920 and 1921; the young American had also done a little routine reporting for the city desk in 1921. The assignment gave Hemingway almost complete freedom of movement and a virtually unlimited choice of material. The *Star* agreed to pay regular space rates for all the stories they printed, as well as their correspondent's expenses in getting the stories.

It was from the Hemingways' point of view an ideal solution. Backed by a little money of their own to tide them over between the periodic settlement of the *Star*'s account, they would certainly be able to get by financially. Considering that he was not yet twenty-three, it was an encouraging testimonial to the reputation he had achieved in Toronto and to the confidence which Bone, an unsentimental, exacting editor, placed in him.[24] Like the earlier steps in his apprenticeship, it was an appropriate extension of his development. He required the liberty of such an assignment, away from the Chicago and Toronto atmospheres of markets and slanted journalese and feverish dilettantism. Years later he told his friend Harvey Breit of the New York *Times* that he had never been able to work well when he was bored.[25] He was in 1921 thoroughly bored with North America. One reason his *Star Weekly* output had been as low as it was that year, according to Cranston, was an additional indication of his need for the creative atmosphere of Paris; he "spent much of his time," Cranston said, "working on his fiction."

Sherwood Anderson, of course, was the one man who could most appreciate Hemingway's sensations about the forthcoming escape to Europe. The older writer had himself just returned from his first trip abroad. His conversation was full of the opportunity for literary and cultural enrichment which existed in Paris. Anderson later said that his most vivid memory of Hemingway was a scene which occurred just before the latter left. Hemingway packed all the canned food from his and Hadley's apartment into a knapsack and brought it around to Anderson the night before they went. "That was a nice idea," Anderson wrote in his *Memoirs*, "bringing thus to a fellow scribbler the food he had to abandon. . . . I remember his coming up the stairs, a magnificent broad-shouldered man, shouting as he came."[26] Hemingway's compulsion to go to Europe was a genuine one. The mass expatriation of young American artists had not yet begun. There was nothing imitative in his impulse toward Paris. It was at that moment a necessity in his personal and artistic life. "Greg," he said impatiently to his friend Gregory Clark about this time in Toronto, "you're going to peter out your life on a warm hearthstone." Hemingway had to be moving on, physically and professionally.

CHAPTER

VI

# *EUROPE*

"A friend of mine and a very delightful
man, Ernest Hemingway, and his wife
are leaving for Paris. . . . "
SHERWOOD ANDERSON[1]

*I.*

The Hemingways sailed for Europe on December 8,
armed with letters of introduction from Anderson. They
were also preceded by a note he had sent at the end of
November to Lewis Galantière, a young Chicagoan interested in the arts and then working for the American Section of the International Chamber of Commerce. Anderson
was very generous, speaking of Hemingway as "a young
fellow of extraordinary talent." He did not hesitate to
launch his friend with the same extravagance he would
have employed a few months earlier on a new account for
the Critchfield agency; "he has been a quite wonderful
newspaper man," Anderson told Galantière. He also added
the certification that was apparently already required in the
presentation of young Americans bound for alcoholic Paris.
"He is not like [Harold] Stearns."

As if to confirm this assurance of sobriety, the Hemingways traveled not by way of Cherbourg and a boat train to
the capital, but by the roundabout route to Spain and then
slowly north by rail to France. They were enormously excited by the whole trip. "You ought to see the Spanish
coast," Hemingway wrote back to the Andersons.[2] "Big

brown mountains looking like tired dinosaurs slumped
down into the sea." He described the scene carefully, using
his correspondence, as has frequently been his custom, for
a kind of trial run of prose effects. It was a thoughtful, carefully composed letter; as such it constituted a very graceful
compliment to Anderson.

They settled temporarily at the Hotel Jacob, where
Galantière lived. During the next few days they were too
busy even to mail Anderson's letters of introduction. Hemingway was very happy to be back in Paris. "What a
town," he exclaimed to Anderson. They went to the Dôme
and to the Rotonde, and, like all cheerful tourists, they
thought things must be even cheaper than when the Andersons had been there in 1920. Soon, Hemingway told the
Andersons, he would send out the letters of introduction,
"like launching a flock of ships." In the meantime he had
already begun his first dispatch. "I've been earning our
daily bread on this write machine," he said. The material
he now began to send back to Toronto had the same intimate, impressionistic quality he had sought in the letter to
Sherwood and Tennessee Anderson.

This was in no way a breach of journalistic responsibility.
It was precisely the kind of treatment the *Star* wanted from
a foreign correspondent. That he should have gone abroad
under the sponsorship of the Toronto paper was one further piece of occupational good fortune for Hemingway.
The European bureau of a Chicago or New York paper
would have required a routine of precise, factual reporting.
There would have been a virtual prohibition against the
kind of material—and the kind of handling of that material
—which would form a profitable education for fiction and
its techniques. The *Star*, on the other hand, wanted lively,
entertaining dispatches, intimate and subjective.

Like all Canadian papers of the period, the *Star* relied
primarily on the English and American wire services for

its daily coverage of foreign events. These were supplemented, in the case of the *Star*, by its purchase of the excellent overseas coverage of the Chicago *Daily News*. A paper as nationalistic as Joseph E. Atkinson's, priding itself too on its metropolitan stature, was never satisfied with this compromise. The situation became so intolerable to Canadian publishers as a whole that in 1927 the Canadian Press—comparable in a limited way to the Associated Press—sent a Canadian newsman to London as its staff correspondent.

In 1922, however, the problem could be solved only by sending one's own employees abroad. Two or three papers in addition to the *Star* were at that time represented by correspondents working, like Hemingway, on a part-time basis. The Canadian resident press, such as it was, was not appointed with the intention of providing a better spot coverage than was available through the Associated Press and Reuters. Its job was either to supplement that coverage with the interpretive reporting generally disavowed by the agencies, or to provide colorful material about Europe, its people, and its customs. Anderson, in fact—perhaps unintentionally—had used an excellent phrase in his letter of introduction to Galantière; he told his friend that Hemingway had been hired "to do European letters."

Hemingway's manner as the *Star*'s correspondent was followed precisely by Matthew Halton, who was the paper's very successful London representative from 1932 until 1940. Like Hemingway, Halton's style was lively and informal; like Hemingway, too, he occasionally cabled spot news and background material of immediate Canadian interest. The bulk of both their dispatches, however, was mailed. David Rogers, another *Star* reporter, younger than Hemingway, who went to Europe in 1929 on the same part-time basis, described his own failure in the job as stemming from his misconception of his duties. "My mistake," Rogers said many years later, when he had become a prominent Canadian editor, "was based on the idea that a serious job could be done." The most extensive assessment of Canadian news coverage, a sober volume sponsored by the Institute of International Affairs, severely indicts Canadian foreign correspondents on the same grounds.

"Those staff men who are sent abroad on special or roving assignments," according to Carlton McNaught, author of *Canada Gets the News*, "seldom add appreciably to a newspaper reader's knowledge of significant developments in the countries they visit."[3] Although McNaught, writing in 1940, did not deal with Hemingway's work, he might well have been describing the young American's stories. Hemingway's approach was essentially the type McNaught was condemning. "Their material," he concluded, "is most frequently of the colourful . . . variety which makes entertaining reading." McNaught quoted in confirmation a Halifax editor's conclusion that the Canadian correspondents of this period were "absorbed completely by the feature, human interest and freak stories and give no evidence of thinking about things that should be fundamental." David Rogers, the young reporter who went abroad for the *Star* in 1929, reached the same rueful conclusion. "They only wanted froth," he said in 1952.

Froth, however, was precisely what Hemingway was interested in, froth, that is, in the sense of subjective, expository narrative evoked from responses and emotions and personal interpretations. One of his first stories, mailed to Toronto—probably from Paris, but datelined Vigo, Spain —and published in the *Star Weekly* on February 18, 1922, was a description of this Spanish harbor where he and his wife landed in December.[4] The story contained no illumination of Spain's political or economic situation, but it was vivid and readable; its composition was also of far more value to him as an apprentice writer than would have been the presentation, for example, of an account of tariff nego-

tiations between the American ambassador and the Spanish
foreign minister. His lead paragraph was precise and meta-
phoric. He used a phrase he had already tested in his letter
to Anderson.

Vigo is a pasteboard looking village, cobble streeted,
white and orange plastered, set up on one side of a big,
almost landlocked harbor that is large enough to hold the
entire British navy. Sun-baked brown mountains slump
down to the sea like tired old dinosaurs, and the color of
the water is as blue as a chromo of the bay at Naples.

Hemingway listed the wealth of potential catches in "the
bright, blue chromo of a bay." His description of the pursuit of tuna was clear and forceful; by the standards of his
later work, however, it was still overwritten. In a few
months, after working with Pound, he would be wary of
such easy effects as "a silver splatter in the sea" and "a
bushel full of buckshot."

Two stories datelined Les Avants, Switzerland, fruit of
a Swiss trip in January, 1922, illustrated this same concern
with atmosphere and people, as well as the glib, knowing
vernacular of the experienced traveler-newspaperman. To
the *Star Weekly*, read by subscribers who were both curious about and ignorant of contemporary Europe, he first
mailed a dispatch that analyzed the cost of a holiday in
Switzerland.[5] His story was an elaboration of the monetary
crisis as a result of which "parts of the country that were
jammed with a tourist population before the war now look
like the deserted boom towns of Nevada."

The second Swiss article, which the *Star Weekly* did not
use until a month later, when he was already back in Paris,
was much better, full of sly innuendo and sharp portraiture,
and containing several deliberate touches for a Canadian
audience.[6] He described the terrain, "wild as the Canadian

Rockies," and explained that at each bend in the road were "four monstrous hotels, looking like mammoth children's playhouses of the iron dog on the front lawn period of Canadian architecture." An instinctive storyteller, as Cranston had recognized from the beginning, and himself absorbed in the variety of people he was meeting, he took his readers inside the hotels, which "in winter are filled with utterly charming young men, with rolling white sweaters and smoothly brushed hair, who make a good living playing bridge." He characterized the other guests in a vivid sketch that was not characteristic of standard *Star Weekly* portraiture.

Then there are the French aristocracy. These are not the splendid aristocracy of toothless old women and white mustached old men. . . . The French aristocracy that comes to Switzerland consists of very young men who wear very old names and very tight in the knees riding breeches with equal grace. . . . When the young men with the old names come into a room full of profiteers, sitting with their pre-money wives and post-money daughters, it is like seeing a slim wolf walk into a pen of fat sheep. It seems to puncture the value of the profiteers' titles. No matter what their nationality, they have a heavy, ill-at-ease look.

The paragraph was an indication of the closeness with which Hemingway was observing his new milieu. He returned from Switzerland to Paris to observe some of his countrymen; a few weeks later the *Star Weekly* used a long story which it headlined, "American Bohemians In Paris A Weird Lot."[7]

The dispatch was a revealing one. It contained an intensity of statement and attitude not often found in journalism at the *Star Weekly* level. His point of view was happily chosen. In adopting the thesis that most bohemians are bogus freaks he was both gratifying the prejudices of his readers and permitting himself a deeply felt declaration of artistic principle. Hemingway lashed out at what he saw as the posturings of synthetic artists. At the age of twenty-two he was repelled by the "strange-acting and strange-looking breed that crowd the tables of the Cafe Rotonde."

They are nearly all loafers expending the energy that an artist puts into his creative work in talking about what they are going to do and condemning the work of all artists who have gained any degree of recognition. By talking about art they obtain the same satisfaction that the real artist does in his work. That is very pleasant, of course, but they insist upon posing as artists.

In his anger Hemingway momentarily lost his balance as a working feature writer; his final paragraph revolved around a name which must have mystified his Toronto readers. He told them that "since the good old days when Charles Baudelaire led a purple lobster on a leash through the same old Latin Quarter, there has not been much good poetry written in cafes." He translated poetic activity into a rather cheap idiom his audience might grasp. "Even then I suspect that Baudelaire parked the lobster with the concierge down on the first floor, put the chloroform bottle corked on the washstand and sweated and carved at the Fleurs du Mal alone with his ideas and his paper as all artists have worked before and since."

He was in reality writing an editorial of denunciation, encouraged by his paper's requirements, his freedom as a by-lined writer, and his own convictions. Like any good editorial writer he had provided a brutal illustration of the Rotonde's habitués. He described "a big, light-haired woman sitting at a table with three young men."

The big woman is wearing a picture hat of the "Merry Widow" period and is making jokes and laughing hysterically. The three young men laugh whenever she does. The waiter brings the bill, the big woman pays it, settles her hat on her head with slightly unsteady hands, and she and the three young men go out together. . . . Three years ago she came to Paris with her husband from a little town in Connecticut, where they had lived and he had painted with increasing success for ten years. Last year he went back to America alone.

It was effective journalese; it was also a persuasive statement of his creed. When he summed it up—"you can find anything you are looking for at the Rotonde, except serious artists"—he had written his most successful dispatch as a foreign correspondent. Its lack of compassion was in part justified by its absolute, vigorous conviction. The *Star Weekly* gave it a full column and four banks of ten headlines. As a declaration it was composed of equal parts of his incongruous debt to the mores of Oak Park, the provincialism of his newspaper, and his own passionate belief in the seriousness of art. It also had a finished maturity of prose, and the intense interest in human situations—plus the unscrupulous use of their biographies—which makes more understandable his apparent transformation, during the next four years, from an obscure string correspondent into a finished technician. When *The Sun Also Rises* was published, in 1926, one of his Paris associates, Robert McAlmon, was surprised at its "sleekness."[8] McAlmon would have been less surprised had he known—as few people apparently did—the extent and nature of Hemingway's journalism between 1920 and 1924. It would be some time, however, before he wrote another article as eloquent or as vivid. The stories he sent to Toronto between its publication and the earlier Swiss dispatches were much more typical of his foreign correspondence. They were also more revealing as to his precocious determination to practice his serious writing and his growing impatience with newspaper work.

## II.

By the second week in March, 1922, Hemingway was already writing Anderson that "this goddamn newspaper stuff is gradually ruining me."[9] He described his plans to "cut it all loose pretty soon and work for about three months." It was to his credit that he stuck with the *Star Weekly* chore. His frame of mind makes all the more notable his ability to manufacture, as he did, journalistic drama out of the Wednesday luncheon gossip of the Anglo-American Press Association in Paris. He wrote about Paris hats "with a girdle of stuffed English sparrows," and he wrote from a colleague's reminiscences a breezy description of the recent papal elections and coronation in Rome.[10] The tone was completely appropriate for Anglican Toronto, with its mistrust of Quebec and French Canada. "They crowned the Pope on a plain pine board throne put together just for that. It reminded me of a fraternity initiation when I saw the throne and watched them getting the scenery out the day before."

Although two months of feature writing had already exasperated Hemingway, and although he was thoroughly frustrated by the encroachments it made upon his serious work, he was still intrigued by the sensation of being on the inside. This was the tonic which enabled him to vitalize his foreign correspondence. Years later, trying to define the attitude he had held toward journalism, he explained that he quit reporting because "I found I would put my own stuff into it and then, once written, it would be gone." His determination to have three months for his own work in the spring of 1922 was painfully reflected in the stubborn

industry with which he produced *Star Weekly* material in
February and March, trying to get together enough money
to exchange hack work for a sustained period of creative
writing. He mailed nine articles back to Toronto during
those few days. He had two dispatches in each of the first
three March issues—on the 4th, the 11th, and 18th—and
three in the March 25 number. He returned to French dress
for one brief sketch which contained most of the elements
of his heavy March publication.[11]

His lead was labored and unconvincing, a pretext for a
passage of dialogue between two Frenchmen who had not
seen each other since the demobilization. Hemingway presented them as they met by chance on a bus and discussed
their domestic grievances.

"Your hair, Henri!" said one.

"My wife, old one, she cuts it. But your hair also? It is
not too chic!"

"My wife too. She cuts it also. She says barbers are dirty
pigs, but at the finish I must give her the same tip as I would
give the barber."

"Ah, the hair is a small matter. Regard these shoes."

"My poor old friend! Such shoes. It is incredible."

"It is my wife's system. She goes into the shoe shop and
says, 'I want a pair of shoes for mon mari. Not expensive.
Mon mari's feet are this much longer than mine, I believe,
and about this much wider. That will do nicely. Wrap them
up.' Old one it is terrible!"

The article as a whole was more reminiscent of the Kansas
City *Star* than of conventional foreign correspondence. It
had the inverted narrative and anecdotal quality; it was
vivified by fresh and authentic speech. The dialogue was at
one level merely slick and amusing, but it also had the pictorial quality of a more experienced fictionalist. The lines

with which Henri portrayed his wife were skillful characterization. Hemingway was also experimenting with the problem of translating rhythm and idiom from one language to another—he would be widely praised for this eighteen years later in *For Whom the Bell Tolls*—and there was a neat, unlabored irony in the final complacence of the two husbands. The total effect, however, was artificial. Hemingway was manufacturing the material to a formula, exploiting the exhaustless reader interest in anything strange and alien—particularly if it also increased their smug contempt for the strange and alien—and he was enlivening the treatment with well-written dialogue and a lead that was sharp and startling despite its contrived quality.

The second dispatch which was used that same week, on the following page, reproduced the technique.[12] The headline—"How'd You Like To Tip/Postman Every Time?"—showed that the Toronto copy desk continued to grasp the essential appeal of his method. "Tipping the postman," Hemingway had written as a lead, "is the only way to insure the arrival of your letters in certain parts of Spain." The next step in the formula, once again, was to dramatize the lead.

The postman comes in sight down the street waving a letter. "A letter for the Senor," he shouts. He hands it to you.

"A splendid letter, is it not, Senor? I, the postman, brought it to you. Surely the good postman will be well rewarded for the delivery of such a splendid letter?"

You tip the postman. It is a little more than he had expected. He is quite overcome.

"Senor," says the postman, "I am an honest man. Your generosity has touched my heart. Here is another letter. I had intended to save it for tomorrow to ensure another reward from the always generous Senor. But here it is. Let us hope that it will be as splendid a letter as the first!"

The formula persisted as he returned to the material of his visit to Switzerland during January. The earlier Swiss stories, published a month apart, on February and March 4, had both been datelined Les Avants; this one was mailed from—or at least datelined—Chamby sur Montreux, not far from Lausanne.[13] His subject was the Swiss luge, "pronounced looge," which he described in his lead as not only "the Swiss flivver," but "also the Swiss canoe, the Swiss horse and buggy, the Swiss pram., and the Swiss combination riding horse and taxi." His exposition was provocative and completely individual. The article included several concessions to the Canadian point of view he was apt to ignore in his European journalism for the *Star*. In his lead he explained that the luge was "a short, stout sled of hickory built on the pattern of little girls' sleds in Canada." Hemingway was characteristically lucid as he presented this new sport and its technique.

You go down a long, steep stretch of road flanked by a six hundred foot drop-off on the left and bordered by a line of trees on the right. The sled goes fast from the start and soon it is rushing faster than anything you have ever felt. You are sitting, absolutely unsupported, only ten inches above the ice and the road is feeding past you like a movie film. The sled you are sitting on . . . is rushing at motor car speed towards a sharp curve. If you lean your body away from the curve and drop the right foot the luge will swing around the curve in a slither of ice and drop shooting down the next slope. . . .

The dispatch, dealing with a variation of their own beloved winter sports, had an obvious appeal for Torontonians. Hemingway outlined the hazards of big, slow-moving hay and wood sleds along the run. "It is considered a very bad omen to hit a wood sled," he wrote. The understated humor provided a transition to his final four paragraphs about the lugeing skill of the British colony at Bellaria, on Lake Geneva. A long, single sentence paragraph was calculated to stir imperial pride in the most nationalistic Canadians. "One wonderful sight is to see the ex-military governor of Khartoum seated on a sled that looks about the size of a postage stamp, his feet stuck straight out at the sides, his hands in back of him, charging a smother of ice dust down the steep, high-walled road, with his muffler straight out behind him in the wind and a cherubic smile on his face while all the street urchins of Montreux spread against the walls and cheer him wildly as he passes."

The story had the energetic felicity Hemingway could give to his journalism when he was absorbed by the material or the sensation it aroused in him. His next article, one of the three which appeared in the March 25th issue, had the same vitality and freshness, here even better defined as he turned again to Paris for the intimate, skeptical treatment he always enjoyed writing.[14] His subject was the cosmopolitan's thesis that the real Paris is thoroughly hidden from casual tourists. There was neither obscurity nor padding in his lead; it was the kind of effective feature writing that had won him the European assignment.

After the cork has popped on the third bottle and the jazz band has brayed the American suit and cloak buyer into such a state of exaltation that he begins to sway slightly with the glory of it all, he is liable to remark thickly and profoundly: "So this is Paris!"

Hemingway pointed out the reality. "It is an artificial and feverish Paris," he wrote, "operated at great profit for the entertainment of the buyer and his like who are willing to pay any prices for anything after a few drinks." His sentences were thick with hostility. "The Buyer demands that Paris be a super-Sodom and a grander-Gomorrah and once alcohol loosens his strong racial grasp on his pocketbook he is willing to pay for his ideal." Hemingway's contempt —which contained a good deal of puritanism—was always for the tourist rather than for those who cheated him. For those who truly knew Paris, he maintained, there was a completely different and authentic night life.

On gala nights there is a drummer at the Bal Musette, but the accordion player wears a string of bells around his ankle, and these, with the stamping of his boots as he sits swaying on the dais above the dancing floor, give the accent to the rhythm. The people that go to the Bal Musette do not need the artificial stimulant of the jazz band to force them to dance. They dance for the fun of it and they occasionally hold someone up for the fun of it, and because it is easy and exciting and pays well. Because they are young and tough and enjoy life, without respecting it, they sometimes hit too hard, or shoot too quick, and then life becomes a very grim matter with an upright machine that casts a thin shadow and is called a guillotine at the end of it.

The syntax of the prose and the romanticism of the attitude point to his debt to Kipling; the scene itself is an outline of one of the first episodes in *The Sun Also Rises*. Hemingway finished the article with another of the vignettes of action and dialogue. His eye and his imagination were becoming increasingly engrossed with fictional presentation. It was still overwritten in spots, and some of the phrases were merely the clichés of his material, but he made the scene and the characters a vivid piece of melodrama.

Occasionally the tourist does come in contact with the real night life. Walking down the quiet hill along some lonely street in a champagne haze about two o'clock in the morning he sees a pair of hard faced kids come out of an alley. They are nothing like the sleek people he has just left. . . . Their closing in and a sudden, dreadful jar are all that he remembers.

It is a chop back of the ear with a piece of lead pipe wrapped in the *Matin* that does the trick and the tourist has at last made contact with the real night life he has spent so much money in seeking.

"Two hundred francs? The pig!" Jean says in the darkness of the basement lit by the match which Georges struck to look at the contents of the wallet.

"The Red Mill holds him up worse than we did, not so, my old?"

"But yes. And he would have a headache to-morrow morning anyway," says Jean. "Come on back to the Bal."

The second of his three stories in the issue of March 25 continued in a wholly different area his use of life in Paris.[15] In the only European dispatch he wrote dealing directly with literature—and one of the very few during his entire apprenticeship in journalism—he discussed *Batouala*, the novel by René Maran which had just won the Goncourt Prize. Although Hemingway made two interesting references to the book's literary quality, he was approaching the story as a feature writer rather than a critic or fellow artist. He emphasized the newsworthy fact that Maran was a Negro serving in Africa and at that moment ignorant of the storm his book had caused in France. Then Hemingway declared himself on the non-journalistic aspects of the novel. It was "great art," he maintained, "except for the preface, which is the only bit of propaganda in the book." His attitude was a demonstration of his statement to Don Wright the year before, in Chicago, that a writer had to see and feel and taste his material.

Launched into the novel itself, the reader gets a picture of African life in a native village seen by the big-whited eyes, felt by the pink palms, and the broad, flat, naked feet of the African native himself. You smell the smells of the village, you eat its food, you see the white man as the black man sees him, and after you have lived in the village you die there. That is all there is to the story, but when you have read it, you have been Batouala, and that means that it is a great novel.

Hemingway's by-line had become a familiar one in the *Star Weekly* during March. He deserved a momentary release from hack work. He was balked abruptly by a cable from Toronto that sent him on his first specific assignment. Anxious to get a coverage of the Genoa Economic Conference that would supplement the news agencies' stories, the managing editor ordered him to Italy. On March 27th Hemingway arrived in Genoa. He would at least have an opportunity to take part in the backstage drama he had previously been able to recount only at second-hand from Paris press luncheons. He wrote and mailed one more article before he left Paris, a loose, padded, editorial-like exposé of the myth of French politeness.[16] The *Star Weekly* used it on April 15th, recognizing its editorial quality with a bold-face, single line caption: FRENCH POLITENESS. Again the synthetic paragraphs of contrived exposition were eventually balanced by a neat snatch of dialogue between himself and a guard at the Paris zoological gardens. The park, Hemingway explained, was advertised as open to the public from eleven until three.

"Is the reptile house closed?" I asked.
"Ferme!" the guard said.

"Why is it closed at this hour?" I asked.

"Ferme!" shouted the guard.

"Can you tell me when it will open?" I queried, still polite.

The guard gave me a snarl and said nothing.

"Can you tell me when it will be open?" I asked again.

"What business is that of yours?" said the guard, and slammed the door.

On this note Hemingway left Paris and went south to Genoa. He was bound for a scene where he would find inflationary prices, and where foreigners were ringed by an aggrieved and militant nationalism. The ambiguities of diplomacy, and the brutality of fascism, however, were at any rate more rewarding material than the problems of insolent French officials at the Jardin des Plantes and aggressive Parisians on crowded buses.

### III.

The Genoa Economic Conference was in many ways the most newsworthy of that rash of meetings by which statesmen contributed to the optimism of the 1920's. Its particular drama, as almost every commentator immediately pointed out, lay in the fact that Europe was going to sit down at a conference table together again. Germany was to be received as an equal for the first time since the war. Russia—Red Russia herself—would be admitted, on a very limited basis, to be sure, but her mere presence was dramatic and controversial. Canadian readers would find a material interest in the efforts to reopen commercial relations between western Europe and the U.S.S.R. The blunt American refusal to attend the conference added a further note of newsworthy tension. The meeting's obvious importance to the political fortunes of Lloyd George supplied additional

Dominion concern. It was spot news. Hemingway's dispatches were used by the *Daily Star* rather than the *Star Weekly*.

Five by-lined stories, four of them long and detailed, were published between April 10 and April 24, 1922. For the first time Hemingway cabled some of his material; on April 10 and April 18 the *Star* gave his copyrighted articles a secondary by-line, "Special Cable to The Star by a Staff Correspondent." The other three stories he mailed to Toronto in the customary way; underneath his by-line, as on his *Star Weekly* features, appeared the label, "Special Correspondence of The Star." It took at least two weeks for the mail to reach Canada. The first story he wrote, on March 27—several days before most of the press arrived —was not used until April 13.[17] The *Star* headed it with an italicized introduction. The paragraph did more than remind subscribers of the paper's overseas services to its readers; it was also a timid editorial corrective to the outspoken anti-fascist tone of Hemingway's knowledgeable dispatch.

Ernest M. Hemingway, a staff correspondent of The Star, who has been traveling through Europe writing his observations, is in Genoa to watch the progress of the conference through Canadian eyes. In the following despatch he describes the real danger of disorder resulting from the presence of the Russian Soviet delegation.

In reality, however, Hemingway had been careful to point out that the essential threat to civic peace was from the Fascists. The well-documented point of view was more authentic than the material being filed in this area by most of his opposite numbers on the New York papers and the wire services. The American press sent home the declaration of Red menace their editors wanted. Hemingway, who spoke Italian and knew the country and its people well, gave a different picture. He did not take sides in a clumsily partisan sense. His story was a realistic definition of the actualities of Italian domestic politics. He hinted at the reality ignored by most of the newspaper men; he explained, straight-faced, that street clashes and riots normally involve two opposing groups. He shifted with abrupt effectiveness to an intimate, impressionistic treatment.

There is no doubt but that the Reds of Genoa—and they are about one-third of the population—when they see the Russian Reds, will be moved to tears, cheers, gesticulations, offers of wine, liqueurs, bad cigars, parades, vivas, proclamations to one another and the wide world and other kindred Italian symptoms of enthusiasm. There will also be kissings on both cheeks, gatherings in cafes, toasts to Lenine . . . and general shouts of, "Death to the Fascisti!"

That is the way that all Italian Red outbreaks start. Closing the cafes usually stops them . . . the "Vivas" grow softer and less enthusiastic, the paraders put it off till another day, and the Reds who reached the highest pitch of patriotism too soon, roll under the tables of the cafes and sleep until the bar-tender opens up in the morning.

Hemingway tellingly defined the fascist psychology. "The fascisti make no distinction between socialists, communists, republicans or members of co-operative societies. They are all Reds and dangerous." His description of a fascist counterattack was mocking and alert, and melancholy in its prophecy of worse to come. He sketched the general nature of the group. "The fascisti are young, tough, ardent, intensely patriotic, generally good-looking with the youthful beauty of the southern races, and firmly convinced that they are in the right. They have an abundance of the valor and the intolerance of youth."

As a dispatch reaching Toronto in a batch of conventional wire service material, the story must have startled his Toronto editors with the lucid, informed novelty of its point of view. Good newspapermen, they couldn't deny its professional virtues. It was more than well written. As a piece of reporting it was one of the first realistic statements about contemporary Italy. The fact that its author was twenty-two made it more remarkable. It was one of Hemingway's earliest anti-fascist enunciations, evidence of an impressive personal growth since the 1918 days when he was reacting to World War I in boyish, exclamatory delight; there was an equivalent artistic maturing in the prose and narrative. The story, on the other hand, certainly couldn't be cited as a dispatch seen "through Canadian eyes," as his paper was billing his Genoa coverage. Early in the assignment, in fact, Hemingway received from his home office what one of his Genoa colleagues later recalled as severe criticism "for not covering some important Canadian angle of the conference." He stayed in Genoa only for the opening of the conclave, leaving town long before the rest of the overseas press. His other articles were only infrequently as skillful—though a trifle more sensitive to the Canadian point of view—as his first one. On April 9 he went out to Rapallo with a "flood of reporters" to inspect and interrogate the Russian delegation. The *Daily Star* used his story the next day on page one.[18]

The dispatch was an uneven one, effective only when he turned to paragraphs of description and personal response. A mass interview, in an atmosphere as guarded as Rapallo's, did not encourage impressionism. The bulk of his relatively short cable dealt with the questions that were put to Tchitcherin, one of the principal Soviet delegates. Hemingway's boredom was evident in the careless dialogue. He also missed the drama of the first interview of a Soviet spokesman by the western press. Nor did he mention the ambiguity noted in the New York *Times*, where the late Edwin James recalled that Tchitcherin was a holdover from the Czarist diplomatic corps. He omitted the irony—at that time a new one—of a luxury hotel inhabited by Bolsheviks. On the whole the story documents the verdict of Wilbur Forrest, one of the New York *Tribune*'s three correspondents at the conference, who felt that Hemingway's basic attitude toward his newspaper work was transparently clear. "He didn't give a damn about it," according to Forrest, "except that it provided some much needed funds and gave him an association with other writers."

Much more interesting to Hemingway than the presence of Lloyd George or Tchitcherin, in fact, was the arrival in Genoa of Max Eastman. Eastman was covering the conference for the *Liberator*. Hemingway wasted no time in showing the influential editor all the fiction he had with him. He was already so serious about his creative writing that he had brought with him from Paris, on a newspaper assignment which promised to be laborious and important, what Eastman later recalled as "a sheaf" of his own work. This was the fiction he had been conscientiously writing in Paris whenever he could get ahead of his *Star Weekly* chore. Hemingway and Eastman, the latter once said, "batted around Genoa together quite a lot." When Eastman and George Slocombe of the London *Daily Herald* drove out to Rapallo to visit Max Beerbohm, the young correspondent went with them. Eastman felt their joint conversation was worth making some notes on during the ride back to Genoa. Hemingway, however, smiled and made a revealing gesture and remark. He tapped his forehead and said, "I have every word of it in here." Eastman concluded, on the basis of "the extraordinary realism" of Hemingway's subsequent work, that the statement was literally true.

In the meantime they had attended the opening session

of the conference on April 10. Hemingway filed two stories which were mailed to Toronto and used on pages one and two of the April 24 issue. His response to the initial excitement was enough to make the first one a lively, detailed account of the scene in the Palazzo di San Giorgio.[19] His tone, as he resigned himself to his Canadian obligations, was mocking and cynical. He explained that the hall was "about half the size of Massey Hall," in Toronto; a few paragraphs later he described the chandelier globes as being "as big as association footballs." His skeptical eye did not miss a plaque which honored Machiavelli. Although his colleagues from New York were soon writing of the conference as "a distinct success" and of "the temper of all the delegates" as "excellent and favorable to hard work," Hemingway preferred to linger over the appropriateness of this earlier Italian politician to the contemporary scene. "Machiavelli," he pointed out, "in his day, wrote a book that could be used as a textbook by all conferences, and, from all results, is diligently studied." He found a marble statue of Columbus "rather pompous," and he was even less impressed by the diplomats themselves.

Delegates begin to come into the hall in groups. They cannot find their places at the table, and stand talking. The rows of camp chairs that are to hold the invited guests begin to be filled with top-hatted, white mustached senators and women in Paris hats and wonderful, wealth-reeking fur coats. The fur coats are the most beautiful things in the hall.

The *Star* certainly could not complain that his material duplicated its wire service or Chicago *Daily News* dispatches. He mentioned his friend Eastman, who sat behind him "like a big, jolly, middle-western college professor." He described the head of the Canadian delegation, Sir

Charles Blair Gordon, as "a little ill at ease," and cited the British delegation, derisively, as "the best dressed." His paragraphs began to have the exuberant excess of his high school journalism; he wrote that Joseph Wirth, Chancellor of Germany and head of its Genoa delegation, "looks like the tuba player in a German band." He caught the dramatic moment when all the chairs were suddenly filled save those of the Russian representatives. "[They] are the four emptiest looking chairs I have ever seen."

Hemingway also stomached the opening day speeches. His second dispatch of April 10 concerned a late, defiant statement on disarmament by Tchitcherin.[20] Hemingway, one of the few newspapermen still in the hall—believing, he wrote, "in seeing a game through until the last man is out in the ninth inning"—gave a graphic account of the explosion. He handled the narrative skillfully, introducing suspense in the first paragraph, prolonging it through careful, successive passages, and then, midway through the long story, he reached his well-organized climax.

Tchitcherin rose and his hands shaking spoke in French, in his queer, hissing accents, the result of an accident that knocked out half his teeth. The interpreter with the ringing voice translated. There was not a sound in the pauses except the clink of the mass of decorations on an Italian general's chest as he shifted from one foot to another. It is an actual fact. You could hear the faint metallic clink of the hanging decorations.

Hemingway remained in Genoa another week. He sent out only one more story, a one-paragraph cable on April 18, his contribution to the diplomatic alarm which followed the signing of a treaty, out at Rapallo, between Russia and Germany.[21] He departed on this final note of disillusion, his career as a Canadian foreign correspondent temporarily suspended. He had profited materially from the Genoa assignment, in terms of story payment and expense money, and he had met Eastman and Beerbohm. His journalistic dossier, if not his reputation within the guild, was more professional; he had covered a major diplomatic conference for a metropolitan paper. His equipment as a writer had not been enriched, although the experience had obvious connections with his general mood of political disenchantment. As a reluctant newspaperman his most effective metier—and, in retrospect, the most artistically valuable form—was still the subjective feature story in any area chosen by himself because of his own response to it.

*IV.*

During the late spring and early summer of 1922, as additional financing for a summer of travel and creative work, Hemingway mailed four articles to Toronto on the casual basis of his original free lance understanding with the *Star*. In May, after a day's trout fishing along the Rhone Canal, near Aigle in Switzerland, he wrote an impressionistic, full-column story whose over-all effect was as powerful as anything he had yet done.[22] The eight paragraphs— a little less than a thousand words—were in the diction and tone of similar passages in the short story he wrote in 1925, "Big Two-Hearted River," and in the novel he began that same year, *The Sun Also Rises*. Lacking, naturally, the taut, frequently rewritten sheen of his fiction, the article was nevertheless visual and evocative. "In the afternoon," he began, "a breeze blows up the Rhone valley from Lake Geneva. Then you fish up-stream with the breeze at your back, the sun on the back of your neck, the tall white mountains on both sides of the green valley and the fly dropping very fine and far off on the surface and under

the edge of the banks of the little stream . . . that is barely
a yard wide, and flows swift and still."

Hemingway and his wife hiked over the St. Bernard
Pass and down into Milan from Aosta. On June 24 a pair
of his articles were published in Toronto, one in the *Daily
Star* and the other in the *Star Weekly*—the twenty-fourth
was a Saturday—which completed the examination of fascism he had begun in the Genoa dispatch of March 27.[23]
Some of the material was a rehash of the earlier article,
newly dramatized, however, by the first of two interviews
Hemingway had with Mussolini in 1922.[24] "Mussolini,"
Hemingway wrote, "is a big, brown-faced man with a high
forehead, a slow-smiling mouth, and large, expressive hands.
. . . His face is intellectual, it is the typical 'Bersagliere' face,
with its large, brown, oval shape, dark eyes and big, slow-
speaking mouth." The interview was competent and informed. It particularly impressed John Bone, the *Star*'s
managing editor; when Hemingway returned to Toronto
the next year, in 1923, Bone planned to assign him primarily
to interviewing celebrities.[25]

The portrait of Mussolini, however, was only a partial
one at most. The interview also had some of the easy glib-
ness which thoroughly dominated a Paris dispatch he
wrote in late July.[26] The first phase of Hemingway's European feature work for the *Star Weekly*, begun in February,
1922, intensified in March, interrupted by the Genoa assignment in April, and resumed briefly in May and June,
now sputtered to a momentary halt. Hemingway's frivolous
story about the great aperitif scandal re-emphasized what
his six months' production had already indicated. He had
virtually completed his apprenticeship. Journalism had completed the process of becoming a writer. Leisure, and solitary, rejected experimentation would now make him a
fictionalist. Had he continued to write feature stories for
the remaining six months of 1922—or, indeed, for the rest

of his life—they would have been written, like this August 12 article, tongue in cheek, to pay the rent and finance new travel. "The great aperitif scandal that is agitating Paris," he wrote in his lead, "has struck at the roots of one of the best loved institutions of France." He explained Gallic drinking habits, spinning out the commonplace exposition with a wordy anecdote about the celebration of Bastile Day. He turned with relief to his own work.

The months as a free-lance contributor and part-time foreign correspondent had permitted him and his wife to live in Europe. They had provided modest financing for a few months of serious writing, and, above all, they had provided an invaluable reservoir of observed and experienced material. The qualities that give stature and immediacy to Hemingway's early short stories of 1924 and 1925 —selectivity, precision, uncompromising economy, deep emotional clarification—were never dominant in his journalism of this period. Each one of those characteristics was separately present in every article; sometimes there were paragraphs or entire sections which contained them all. The shaping of them into a single instrument that would dominate each piece of writing came only when he could concentrate without interruption on work he regarded as dignified and worthy. His position would remain a paradoxical and exasperating one as long as he continued in a role for which he had the capacity but not the temperament, and which he therefore regarded with increasing cynicism.

Other newspapermen liked him personally and respected a talent they sometimes recognized even then as exceptional. "He was an erratic and obviously brilliant young man," according to Basil Woon, a Hearst correspondent in Paris in 1922 who saw a good deal of Hemingway both socially and, later that year, professionally. Many of them sensed that he was an alien in their world; that was part of what

Woon meant by erratic. Trying to define the impression Hemingway made in 1922, Wilbur Forrest said many years later that he would have prophesied a career as "an artist painter instead of a famous novelist." Forrest remembered with impersonal distaste that Hemingway "lived in the Paris Latin Quarter and was among artists, a hanger-on at the Dôme and Rotonde sidewalk cafés." Forrest thought of him as "some sort of genius in a garret." Hemingway himself, of course—as his *Star Weekly* indictment of Paris bohemians demonstrated—had nothing but contempt for the kind of life Forrest automatically assigned him. Momentarily liberated from hack work, Hemingway began in the summer of 1922 to build in the little magazines and in the literary associations of Paris the foundations of his future.

# PARIS

"Gertrude was always right."
ERNEST HEMINGWAY[1]

*1.*

In terms of its actual contribution to the final body of his creative work, 1922 was not a productive year for Hemingway. Although he told Anderson in May that he had "been working like hell at writing,"[2] very little of the material of these months survived. Some of the verse he wrote was published the next year in *Poetry* and the *Little Review*, and he continued work on a novel which was never published. A large part of his time, however, was necessarily given to newspaper work, despite his anxiety to be free of it, and he spent many weeks traveling, in Spain, in Switzerland, in Italy, and in Germany.

It was in these terms that the year was of primary profit to him. He was able to write effectively about northern Michigan because in 1919 and 1920 he had both renewed old associations with it and simultaneously seen it from fresh perspectives. His mastery of the European material came from the same kind of saturation in the atmosphere at several stages in his personal and artistic development. Of the fifteen stories in *In Our Time*, five dealt specifically with expatriation; they were the fruit of his European encounters and observation in 1922, 1923, and 1924.[3] This same intimacy with Europe would give authenticity of atmosphere to *The Sun Also Rises* and *A Farewell to Arms*.

From his expatriation there also emerged all the less tangible assets that come to a responsive young man exposed to the contrasts of a culture that is not his own but which illuminates the one he has temporarily abandoned. There was instruction to be absorbed not only from the newspaper work and from the countries and their people, but also from the literary associations that had been non-existent or abortive in Toronto and Chicago. Anderson's letters of introduction provided the immediate entrée. Hemingway's charm and intensity extended the introductions into friendships.

"Gertrude Stein and me," Hemingway wrote to Anderson in March, 1922, three months after reaching Europe, "are just like brothers, and we see a lot of her."[4] Miss Stein was equally pleased with Hemingway; she told Anderson that she and Alice Toklas were having "a good time" with the Hemingways and hoped "to see more of them."[5] Hemingway had also met James Joyce and read part of *Ulysses*. Ezra Pound had become both literary sponsor among the little magazines and sparring partner at the gym. He sent six of Hemingway's poems to Scofield Thayer at the *Dial*, and "took" a story for the *Little Review*. Hemingway's greatest admiration, however, was for Anderson's good friend in the apartment at 27, rue de Fleurus. "We love Gertrude Stein," Hemingway scrawled in pencil at the end of the letter to Anderson.

Gertrude Stein herself recalled the appearance of Hemingway as "the first thing that happened" when she and Alice Toklas returned to Paris in 1922 from Saint-Rémy.[6] She remembered him as "an extraordinarily good-looking young man." His eyes, she felt, writing ten years later, when their friendship had become sour and bitter, were passionately interested rather than interesting, and he "sat in front of Gertrude Stein and listened and looked." Soon he began to talk, and they talked a great deal together, and

Hemingway invited her and Miss Toklas to the apartment he and his wife had taken near the place du Tertre. That night Miss Stein read everything he had written up to that point. She did more than read it; she "went over" it. She rather liked the poems, but found the unfinished novel wanting. "There is a great deal of description in this," she told Hemingway, "and not particularly good description. Begin over again and concentrate."

It was as good advice as he would ever get. His talent was substantial, as his newspaper work showed; like most young writers he was largely content to exercise and extend the talent. That writing could be a laborious and exacting process had not previously occurred to Hemingway. He had worked hard, it was true, precociously hard, during those compulsive months in Michigan in 1919 and in Chicago and Toronto during the following two years. He had withstood frustration and rejection, but the conception of writing as concentration, as heavy, aching effort, was essentially a new one. Certainly he had never heard such doctrine from Anderson, the only writer of any stature with whom he had been in close contact. Hemingway, indeed, had mistrusted Anderson's apparent indifference to technical concerns.

The fact that this was a misconception on Hemingway's part, which subsequent critics shared with him, did not alter the illusion's effect on his susceptibility to new and seemingly different influences. In his conversation, as, later, in his memoirs and reminiscences, Anderson enjoyed posing as a virtually automatic writer, one to whom his art was merely natural storytelling. Actually, of course, as the manuscripts of *Winesburg, Ohio* show, Anderson's stories frequently went through a series of complicated revisions.[7] He successfully presented himself, however, as the romantic artist of instinctive creativity. To this he added what were for Hemingway the distasteful affectations of bohemianism. It becomes wholly natural, therefore, that Hemingway should have graduated so readily to Gertrude Stein—who herself, on the other hand, had the greatest admiration for Anderson's work—and should ultimately disavow Anderson with *The Torrents of Spring*.

In 1922, however, Anderson was as much of a literary model and influence as had yet existed actively in Hemingway's experience. He had absorbed from the older man more than most commentators were subsequently willing to allow. Hemingway not only listened carefully to Anderson's ideas in Chicago in the winter of 1920 and the spring of 1921, but also eagerly read what Anderson had published. As late as the fall of 1923 Hemingway discussed Anderson's work extensively with Morley Callaghan, the Canadian newspaperman and writer, with sympathy and understanding. Hemingway shared with Anderson an insistence on sex as a basic human drive. Like Anderson, Hemingway was drawn to the examination of youth and its distresses. They also shared a sense of the importance of emotion and feeling. "Turning her face to the wall," Anderson had written of one of his early characters, "[she] began trying to force herself to face bravely the fact that many people must live and die alone, even in Winesburg." This is a recurrent theme in Hemingway, altered and made peculiarly his own by his insistence that the process is always aggravated and controlled by the requirements of a fixed decorum. Even after their separation in December, 1921, when Hemingway left Chicago for Europe, Anderson remained an important factor in Hemingway's position. It was to Anderson that he wrote from abroad in the late winter and early spring of 1922, discussing his work and his ambitions; during these first months in Europe he also talked constantly about Anderson.

Hemingway lunched frequently in Paris that year with Frank Mason, the local correspondent for Hearst's International News Service.[8] Mason was himself mildly interested in serious writing. Their luncheons, however, invariably included a third writer. The late Guy Hickok was for many years the Brooklyn *Eagle*'s European correspondent.[9] He was a reporter of considerable experience, an excellent journalist, and a thoughtful, imaginative man. The conversations at these luncheons invariably concentrated on writing. Mason's most positive memory of Hemingway's interests during those first months of 1922 was that he spoke repeatedly of Sherwood Anderson, and, more specifically, that he expressed many times his intention to model his own literary career on Anderson's. Three years later Hemingway told Scott Fitzgerald that his first pattern had been Anderson's *Winesburg, Ohio*. The evidence of two short stories Hemingway wrote before he could have fully grasped Miss Stein's teaching confirms this. Both "Up in Michigan" and "My Old Man" were written earlier than the rest of the stories published in 1925 in *In Our Time*. They can be fairly described as Andersonian. There were those who even accused Hemingway of having virtually plagiarized "My Old Man" from Anderson.

This was an absurd charge, but certainly such derivation of treatment as the stories indicate is from Anderson as much as from Stein. The treatment of sex in "Up in Michigan," violent, painful, and equated with naturalness and virtue, is wholly Andersonian. The language and narrative device of "My Old Man," as well as the material and point of view, are similarly reminiscent. Neither of the stories was dependent on Anderson's work in any compulsive or unhealthy way. Hemingway himself, when he learned of the accusations against "My Old Man," attempted certain distinctions between his own work and the older man's. He told Edmund Wilson that he didn't think "My Old Man" stemmed from Anderson at all, because, he said, "It is about a boy and his father and race-horses. Sherwood," Hemingway explained, "has written about boys and horses. But very differently. It derives from boys and horses. Anderson derives from boys and horses. I don't think they're [the stories] anything alike."[10] Hemingway was positive about one thing. "I know I wasn't inspired by him." Even the idiom of Hemingway's letter to Wilson, written in November, 1923, is now that of Stein rather than of Anderson, particularly in the last lines.

I know him [Anderson] pretty well but have not seen him for several years. His work seems to have gone to hell, perhaps from people in New York telling him too much how good he was. Functions of criticism. I am very fond of him. He has written good stories.

Hemingway's debt to Anderson continued to be both personal and artistic. Frank Mason recalled Hemingway's admiration for Anderson as being centered on the life Anderson led as much as on the work he produced, and on his attitudes as a writer as much as on his treatment of material. The Hearst correspondent, who never cared particularly for Hemingway, also had the impression that the younger writer had been struck by Anderson's gift for publicity and the exploitation of his personality. Hemingway's relationship to Gertrude Stein was very different than this.

*II.*

The association between Hemingway and Miss Stein was foreshadowed, in a sense, even before they had either met or heard of one another. Hemingway's newspaper work had already indicated a characteristic which has remained basic to his temperament. He was always intensely interested in how to do a thing. He was absorbed by method.

Thus he had written in Toronto in 1920 a detailed discussion of how to catch trout bait, how to fix the bait on the hook, how to then locate the trout themselves; he wrote articles in 1921 about how bootlegging operated and how American gunmen worked, and, in 1922, how to handle a Swiss luge. This was one of his primary attitudes toward experience. It was fundamental to his interest in war, politics, and sport. He would put some of this into his description of young Krebs, who in "Soldier's Home" sits on the porch reading a book about the war. "It was a history," Hemingway wrote, "and he was reading about all the engagements he had been in. It was the most interesting reading he had ever done. He wished there were more maps. . . . Now he was really learning about the war."

The same zealous concern with method is explicit in Hemingway's reaction to bullfighting, big game hunting, and the subtleties of guerrilla war. Once he even wrote in *Esquire* a precise explication of how to drive an automobile in a heavy snow storm. This concern with method gave to his journalism, as it would to his fiction, a vast air of knowledgeability. The concern was thoroughly genuine. Originally encouraged by the cool lucidity of his father, it was extended by his own instinctive curiosity and enriched by the exacting skepticism of such tutors as Pete Wellington, Lionel Moise, and, later in 1922, William Bolitho, the South African journalist. In terms of his serious writing, the aspect of his life, after all, with which he was most deeply concerned, it was only natural that he should be looking for some orderly method.

He had found the beginnings of such a method in the style book in Kansas City, and in the counsel of the *Star*'s editors. He was discovering other fluencies and effects through his feature stories for the *Star Weekly*. Sherwood Anderson, of course, offered no precise methodology. What one got from him were thematic attitudes and an integrity of vision. Gertrude Stein, however, was immensely concerned with method, both in her own work and in what she was writing and saying about prose. Hemingway acknowledged his debt to her technique very specifically in 1923. "Her method," he told Edmund Wilson, "is invaluable for analyzing anything or making notes on a person or a place."[11] The method itself, or at least that part of it to which Hemingway responded between 1922 and 1924, the period of Miss Stein's greatest personal importance to him, revolved principally around the arrangement and exploitation of specific kinds of words to represent and emphasize a desired effect.

"The question of repetition," Gertrude Stein said later, "is very important."[12] This was definite and tangible. How she herself had done it Hemingway could discover in her *Three Lives;* he could also find it, at a more involved level, in the volume she had just finished. "This *Making of Americans* book of Gertrude Stein's," he wrote Anderson in May, 1922, "is a wonderful one."[13] His own work began to reflect the method. It was particularly apparent in "Up in Michigan," which can be regarded as a transition piece; the story is a blend, in a very loose way, of his joint obligation to Anderson and Stein. The third paragraph of "Up in Michigan"—"I had this conception of the whole paragraph," Miss Stein once said[14]—is wholly a use of repetition for emphasis and clarification.

Liz liked Jim very much. She liked it the way he walked over from the shop and often went to the kitchen door to watch for him to start down the road. She liked it about his mustache. She liked it about how white his teeth were when he smiled. She liked it very much that he didn't look like a blacksmith. She liked it how much D. J. Smith and Mrs. Smith liked Jim. One day she found that she liked it the way the hair was black on his arms and how white they were above the tanned line when he washed up in the washbasin outside the house. Liking that made her feel funny.

The paragraph illustrates what Miss Stein had in mind when she later described Hemingway as "such a good pupil."[15] Hemingway, as part of his apprenticeship, performed an invaluable exercise through which he studied her method in the most intense way. He copied the manuscript of *The Making of Americans* for her, getting it ready for the publisher whom he swore he would find for it, and then he corrected the proofs. Correcting proofs, Gertrude Stein felt, was like dusting. "You learn the values of the thing," she said, "as no reading suffices to teach it to you."[16] The way Hemingway used the word "liked" in the paragraph from "Up in Michigan" indicated what he had learned.

Hemingway's first use of the lesson was entirely conventional. "Liz liked Jim very much." Here, in the lead sentence, it says no more than one says casually about a dozen people each day. Then, by repetition, Hemingway strengthened and qualified it. He showed the variety and sensation of her liking. He displayed its immediacy. This was the quality Gertrude Stein had attempted to imbed in *The Making of Americans*. Hemingway also indicated his grasp of her declaration that the twentieth century was not interested in events. Midway through the paragraph, as his tutor herself did constantly, he gave the repetition a new element by using "like" as a different part of speech. Finally, as the paragraph ended, Hemingway conceived another variation, again an echo of Miss Stein's own susceptibility to it. This was "liking," the gerund. "Liking that," Hemingway wrote, "made her feel funny." The paragraph, above all, had been sprung from a previous use of the verb in the story's opening lines. "He liked her face,"

Hemingway had said of Jim Gilmore, "because it was so jolly but he never thought about her." The way in which Liz liked him, however, was shown to the reader to be very different.

Later, of course, Miss Stein became waspish about this sort of thing. "It is so flattering," she wrote of Hemingway in 1933, "to have a pupil who does it without understanding it."[17] She was indulging in her own variety of sour grapes. The paragraph from "Up in Michigan" refutes her belittlement. Sometimes, to be sure, Hemingway mishandled the method. It was a slippery technique, deceptively simple. His use of the verb "found" in the seventh sentence, although it had a value of precision, was clumsy and overstudious, Steinian in an awkward sense. There were also more serious aberrations of the method. "Mr. and Mrs. Elliot," Hemingway began the story of that name in 1924, "tried very hard to have a baby. They tried as often as Mrs. Elliot could stand it. They tried in Boston after they were married and they tried coming over on the boat. They did not try very often on the boat because Mrs. Elliot was quite sick."[18] Like an ugly caricature of the method, the line runs through the entire story. The repetition, smart and glib, did not qualify and enlarge the word and its representation. It was being used for effect in its most limited sense. The method had to be more than a trick; it was not designed for the aggrandizement of café wit.

His debt to Miss Stein, clearly, went beyond such elementary conceptions as this. She helped him discover not only what he was seeing, and how to communicate the sight, but what to look for. It was she who explained that he must look at his material, and at each new experience, as certain painters—Cézanne, in particular—looked at their own compositions. His own subsequent dictums on writing are often variations and extensions of what she had either told him or helped him to learn. He went beyond her as a writer in the same proportion that he was able to enrich her method by giving it a practical, muscular program of training; the program supplemented the fact that unlike Miss Stein, as critics subsequently observed, Hemingway had something to write about. He told a young writer who came to him for advice in 1935, and to whom he gave not only counsel but also a job as night watchman on his boat, that he should watch what happened when they went fishing. "Remember what the noises were," Hemingway told him, "and what was said. Find what gave you the emotion; what the action was that gave you the excitement. Then write it down," he instructed his pupil, as Miss Stein, less specifically, had instructed him, "making it clear so the reader will see it too and have the same feeling that you had."[19]

Hemingway then described the whole process of an apprenticeship with a phrase from the arduous months he had put into musical training as a boy in Oak Park. "That's a five finger exercise," he told the young writer. He also told him to do precisely what Gertrude Stein had attempted in *The Making of Americans*, in which, she said, she wanted "to make a description of every kind of human being until I could know by these variations how everybody was to be known."[20] In 1935 Hemingway rearranged the precept, as he did most of what he heard from Miss Stein, to give it a more available form. "Then," he continued to the young writer, "get in somebody else's head for a change. If I bawl you out try to figure what I'm thinking about as well as how you feel about it." Hemingway stated a principle which has permitted him to survive all the fluctuations of literary fashions. "As a man," he explained, "things are as they should or shouldn't be. As a man you know who is right and who is wrong. You have to make decisions and enforce them. As a writer you should not judge. You should understand."

Hemingway was a good teacher because he had learned these things for himself, taking a method and a handful of rather arbitrary enunciations and shaping them to his needs, material, and objectives. Whatever he said about writing he knew to be true, for him, because he knew it worked. He knew how it was done. Hemingway had built in the interval between 1922 and 1935 an elaborate codification upon the blueprint Miss Stein had given him. He had taken it beyond anything she could do with it, and for this, of course, she could not forgive him. He himself always acknowledged his obligation with frankness. The greatest tribute he paid her was made in 1924, in a letter to her discussing the work he was doing. "[Writing]," he said, "used to be easy before I met you."[21] He had always been willing—anxious, indeed—to work hard at his writing, but she had helped show him how to make it profitably hard. This became one of his fundamental beliefs. This was his attitude in 1935, toward his own apprentice, whose work, Hemingway found, was at first abominable. "Still, I thought, many other people write badly at the start and this boy is so extremely serious that he must have something; real seriousness in regard to writing being one of the two absolute necessities."[22]

Hemingway's relationship with Gertrude Stein has been interpreted in several ways. On the whole the definitions have fallen into one of two extremes. The early critical commentary saw him as a complete disciple. In this it followed the line Miss Stein laid down in 1933, when she said, speaking of the influence of herself and Anderson on Hemingway, that he "had been formed by the two of them."[23] Later it became fashionable to disparage his debt to her. This occurred in part because few critics have been willing to study what she was doing in her own work. It has been easier to study Hemingway. He himself, as has been so frequently the case during his career, gave a more realistic—and verifiable—account of the debt and its variety of distortion. Speaking of his obligation to both Stein and Pound, he said in 1951 that "they were both very kind to me and I always said so." He related this to the literary commentators who are both too eager for and too wary of literary influences. "This," he went on, "is regarded in critical circles like pleading guilty at a court martial." He remembered that she had told him that he "might be a good writer of some new kind." She also reminded him that "no classic resembled any previous classic."

This sort of instruction was available from various Paris sources for any young man as serious about writing as Hemingway. The burden of later identification, however, falls most heavily upon Miss Stein as the source. She was a better instructor than most writers, both by temperament and situation. She was not—at least during the beginning— oppressively the teacher. She could stimulate as well as lecture. She enjoyed instruction without overprizing it. Her salon had the effect of a classroom, but it lacked the trappings. Hemingway was still of an age in which he could respond to her as he had responded a few years earlier to Margaret Dixon and Fannie Biggs. He was anxious, above all, to be a pupil.

Miss Stein's instruction, though it was generally given verbally, survives for our scrutiny in her own work. It is itself a clarification of the lessons Hemingway was receiving and the exercises he was performing. The direction of his writing, and his evolution from journalist to writer, is illuminated by the steps she had already taken and the statements she would subsequently make. She talked constantly about landscape in writing, and tried to communicate it through her prose. In August, 1924, Hemingway wrote her about a story he had just finished, "the long one I worked on before I went to Spain where I'm trying to do the country like Cézanne. . . ."[24] Each phrase of the letter's sentences contained implicit citation of the tutorials he had attended. "It's about 100 pages long," he continued, "and nothing happens and the country is swell, I made it all up, so I see it all. . . ." Miss Stein had been emphatic in her insistence that a writer must create rather than merely report. Hemingway was following the advice, in the composition of "Big Two-Hearted River," and sharing with her the results of the instruction.

During the first three years of their friendship, from 1922 through 1924, Hemingway relied heavily, in a general way, on her judgment. Their relationship was never in any sense a collaboration, but he showed her his work and trusted her evaluation. When Robert McAlmon asked him in 1924 for a contribution to the forthcoming *Contact Collection of Contemporary Writers,* Hemingway rather diffidently sent him "Soldier's Home," adding that Miss Stein had read it and liked it. Earlier, when he and McAlmon were readying Hemingway's *Three Stories & Ten Poems* in 1923, Hemingway took the proofs and cover to Miss Stein before sending them back to McAlmon. During the first months of their association, in 1922, Hemingway apparently even typed out samples of his early journalism for her; among her papers is a typescript of an article which had been printed in the *Star Weekly* early in 1921, a year before he met her.

Miss Stein, however, was not optimistic about the indefinite extent of journalism's contribution to an apprenticeship. She felt that in addition to encouraging a writer to report rather than make, newspaper work also weakened him through its reliance on artificial supports. "Newspapers," she said later, as she had often explained in earlier conversations, "want to do something, they want to tell what is happening as if it were just then happening."[25] She easily persuaded Hemingway that such journalistic immediacy was not a genuine immediacy. It was a primer lesson which Hemingway knew more intimately than she; her conclusions were painfully clear to him. She was very specific in her declaration that Hemingway should stop being a newspaperman. After reading the stories he had written before he reached Paris, Hemingway remembered thirty years later, she advised him "to get out of journalism and write as she said that the one would use up the juice I needed for the other. She was quite right," Hemingway said in 1951, "and that was the best advice she gave me."

### III.

Despite Miss Stein's injunction, and his own anxiety, to abandon journalism, Hemingway was still economically bound to newspaper work in 1922. In terms of his education, of course, thinking still of Europe as the school in which he matured, there still remained some profit to be drawn from journalism, both as it provided a vehicle for constant writing and as it enlarged the range of his experience. In the late summer of 1922, therefore, Hemingway resumed both his travels and his journalism. The one could not exist without the other. Back in Paris in August, after a long walking tour in Italy with his wife and an English friend, the Hemingways set out again. This time they were accompanied on part of the trip by another American newspaperman, Bill Bird, and his wife.[26]

The final form in which Hemingway's journalistic treatment of this German trip emerged was in some respects different from the earlier pattern of his European correspondence in 1922. It was the first genuine series of articles he delivered. The series also had a new publication history. He mailed seven articles to Toronto from Germany between August 17 and the first few days of September; with the exception of one of the last stories, they were all printed in the *Daily Star*, rather than, as before, in the *Star Weekly*. The trip was undertaken, however, without any specific instructions from his managing editor. The articles were written to cover the expenses and, if possible, to put him a little ahead again financially. The fact that they were used by the *Daily Star* indicates that John Bone had been impressed by his *Star Weekly* feature work— particularly, one imagines, by the most recent dispatches, those from Italy—and that he was now thoroughly conscious of Hemingway as a member of his staff.

The stories from the Black Forest, however, could not have caused Bone to think of Hemingway as anything more than a briskly entertaining writer whose greatest virtue was that he happened to be in Europe and under loose contract to the *Star*. As a group, relatively speaking, the articles were hasty and indifferent, written out of the same approach that had dominated the more commonplace of the *Star Weekly* stories Hemingway had already written both in Europe and in Canada. There was as yet little evidence that Hemingway was reacting to Miss Stein's tutoring. Some of the journalism he wrote later in 1922, when he covered the Greco-Turk fighting, and the work he did for Bone in the spring of 1923, when he was sent to the Ruhr, demonstrate a professional advance. Actually, although Hemingway saw a good deal of Gertrude Stein in the spring and summer of 1922, their most profitable association came at the end of that year and the beginning of the next. "I am going to chuck journalism I think," he wrote her from Toronto in November, 1923. "You ruined me as a journalist last winter. Have been no good since."[27] In August, 1922, however, his writing, insofar as his newspaper work is an accurate index, was comparatively pedestrian. He was still content with his natural facility and the tricks he had now acquired through experience and through his new intimacy with experienced correspondents. That the trip was exciting and instructive there can be no doubt; the articles reflect his response to the new scene, even if on the whole they don't communicate the response in a memorable way.

The most interesting element, therefore, becomes the fact that he never used this material in his fiction. To this extent it contributed to his increasing dissatisfaction with newspaper work. He discovered again that, for him, material which he used hastily for feature work was virtually useless to him for his own work. "On a newspaper," he explained later, " . . . you have to sponge your memory clean like a slate every day." Foreign correspondence differed from this only in degree. Although one did not write for quite the same oppressive deadlines, he nevertheless had to write before he had really absorbed the experience, and, in feature writing, enough of the emotion had to be written into so that the material was muddied for future use.

"In newspaper work," Hemingway declared in 1952, expanding his interpretation of working on the Kansas City *Star*, "you have to learn to forget every day what happened the day before . . . newspaper work is valuable up until the point that it forcibly begins to destroy your memory. A writer must leave it before that point." There was also another destructive ingredient in journalism. "In writing for a newspaper," Hemingway once maintained—rephrasing, as he did so often, a dictum of Miss Stein—"you told what happened and, with one trick and another, you communicated the emotion aided by the element of timeliness which gives a certain emotion to any account of something that has happened on that day."[28]

Thus the only two German articles which possessed real quality were a pair which Hemingway did not write immediately after experiencing the material. The first was mailed from Strasbourg on August 23.[29] It had been preceded by three earlier stories, datelined from the small Black Forest towns through which they were hiking. The Strasbourg article, however, dealt with the plane trip which had first brought them from Paris to Germany. Commercial flying was still an adventure in 1922, particularly in terms of its dramatic swiftness. "The trip is ten hours and a half by best express train," Hemingway pointed out, "and takes two hours and a half by plane." His exposition was precise and visual, even its sentence structure reflecting his concern with the experience he was recording.

Our suitcase was stowed aboard under a seat beside the pilot's place. We climbed up a couple of steps into a stuffy little cabin and the mechanic handed us some cotton for our ears and locked the door. The pilot climbed into his seat back of the enclosed cock-pit where we sat, a mechanic pulled down on the propeller and the engine began to roar. I looked around at the pilot. He was a short little man, his cap backwards on his head, wearing an oil stained sheepskin coat and big gloves. Then the plane began to move along the ground, bumping like a motorcycle, and then slowly rose into the air.

The second of the two superior articles was datelined from Kehl, just across the river from Strasbourg; like the description of the flight from Paris, it was written several weeks after the sequence of stories that followed their departure from the border cities.[30] It was the longest of the series, a little less than two thousand words. Hemingway's central theme was the fantasy of German inflation. He concentrated mainly, however, on the provocative tensions and griefs the situation was creating, and the shadowy, ugly types who profited from national catastrophe. The story was larded with quick vignettes of personality and attitude. Hemingway's principal episode was the gross phenomenon of the French stampeding across the Rhine each afternoon to stupify themselves on the excellent German pastry, now so cheap that it could be bought for less than the value of the smallest French coin. The limitations of space, the necessity of covering other aspects of Kehl, and the absurdity of shaping a carefully dimensioned episode at the *Star*'s rates, prevented Hemingway from making a completely successful use of the scene. It was the pastry shop, however, which stirred him; he sketched its proprietor, clients, and staff. "The place was jammed with French people of all ages and descriptions," he noticed, "all gorging cakes, while a young girl in a pink dress, silk stockings, with a pretty, weak face and pearl earrings in her ears took as many of their orders for fruit and vanilla ices as she could fill. She didn't seem to care very much whether she filled the orders or not. There were soldiers in town and she kept going over to look out of the window." Meanwhile, Hemingway saw, profiteers' cars raced by in the street, raising clouds of dust, and "inside the pastry shop young French hoodlums swallowed their last cakes and French mothers wiped the sticky mouths of their children." It was symbolically valid and powerful; "it gave you," he wrote, "a new aspect on exchange."

In the meantime the first three articles had been printed in the *Daily Star*. The stories presented the chronology of the Hemingways' movements after leaving Strasbourg and Kehl. They had been joined by Bird and his wife, and had traveled south to Freiburg. The Americans spent four days there; Hemingway's first German dispatch, datelined from Freiburg on August 17, dealt—more prosaically than in the subsequent description of the pastry shop—with Germany's financial chaos.[31] The story's looseness resulted from Hemingway's failure to make this a consistent structural quality. He padded the article carelessly with paragraphs of statistical summary and hearsay comments on other parts of Germany; he introduced a secondary theme, the current hostility to foreigners, which ran confusingly in and out of the narrative. The single most effective section was a description of Freiburg, a reminder that Miss Stein's first instruction in the spring of 1922 had concentrated on his exposition.

Freiburg seemed to be going on very well. Every room in every hotel in town was filled. There were strings of German hikers with rucksacks on their backs going through the town all day long, bound for the Black Forest. Streams of clear water flowed in the deep gutters on each side of the clean, scrubbed-looking streets. The red stone gothic spire of the red stone cathedral stuck up above the red-tiled roofs of the houses. The market place was jammed on Saturday morning with women with white handkerchiefs over their heads selling the fruit and vegetables they had brought in ox carts from the country. All the shops were open and prices were very low. It looked peaceful, happy and comfortable.

Occasionally, too, there were brief characterizations which invigorated the catch-all, Sunday supplement treatment. "We saw a girl in a coffee shop," Hemingway wrote, "eating a breakfast of ice cream and pretzels, sitting across the table from an officer in full uniform with an iron cross on his chest, his flat back even more impressive than his lean, white face, and we saw mothers feeding their rosy faced children beer out of big half litre steins." The article's essentially formless quality inhibited these strengths; as always, when he produced newspaper work merely to meet a deadline or salvage expense money, Hemingway ultimately relied on his bright precocity.

On the same day, August 17, Hemingway mailed another story, this one, if we are to believe the dateline, from Triberg, fifty miles to the northeast.[32] The article was fairly long, a little over fifteen hundred words; its principal theme was the familiar Hemingway irony of the contrast between expectation and reality. He examined the ambiguities of German sport and character with a wry vigor that was livelier than his Freiburg story, since he was at least dealing with sport, absurdities, and intrigue, but his basic treatment was the tongue-in-cheek wit that had marked his routine journalism since 1917. His disappointment in the Black Forest's lack of grandeur had been increased by the discovery that neither was it even possible to hike in solitude. " . . . you couldn't go fifteen yards along any of the wilder and more secluded roads without running into between six and eight Germans, their heads shaved, their knees bare, cock feathers in their hats, sauerkraut on their breath, the wanderlust in their eyes and a collection of aluminum cooking utensils clashing against their legs as they walked."

The third of these articles dealing with the precise sequence of their Black Forest experiences was printed in the *Daily Star* on September 5.[33] It had a visually impressive dateline, Oberprechtal-in-the-Black-Forest, fifteen miles north of Triberg. The story's eighteen hundred words, which the copy editor split into eight columns that dominated page five of the *Daily Star*, did not rise above the meager, chatty level of the two earlier tourist chronicles. The article also confirms the suspicion that Hemingway's intense hostility to the Germans was distorting his objectivity as a writer. As a feature man for the Toronto *Star*, of course, objectivity was not a prerequisite; his success had come from the personal, intimate quality of his work.

As a writer, however, his primary responsibility was to train himself in observation. An indiscriminate contempt for the German people—whom at this time he classified in conversation as Boches and Huns—would inevitably blind him to the complexities which normally allowed his subjective treatment to be so effective. His story about Kehl had been relatively free of this intemperance; he had been able to detect, as a consequence, the valid symbol of the pastry shop. The three Black Forest stories concentrated almost completely on the traditionally unattractive racial characteristics of Germans, without variety or real persuasion. The articles began to have a nagging fretfulness.

Two final stories completed the two-three-two publishing pattern of the series. Both were mailed from Cologne with an incomplete dateline; since they were printed on the same day, September 30, they were evidently sent together, probably about the middle of the month. They were an improvement over the previous three to the extent in which they exchanged the querulous complaint of the Black Forest dispatches for the more balanced, evocative treatment of the pair mailed from Strasbourg and Kehl. The Cologne article which seems to have been written first, since it dealt with the train ride from Frankfurt north to the Ruhr, had the closest resemblance to the petty antagonism of the Baden trio.[34]

Hemingway's hostility, stimulated in the Black Forest, was confirmed in the crowded railway compartments. He used a local analogy for his Toronto readers. "Traveling in Germany now," he wrote, "is exactly as much fun as strap hanging in an Avenue Road car during the crest of the rush hour." His illustrations were forceful and persuasive, better written and more graphic than his tales of the Schwartzwald peasantry. Essentially, however, they displayed the same provincialism and youthful intolerance, and a readiness to embrace any evidence that seemed to document a conventional prejudice. With relish Hemingway piled anecdote upon anecdote. The sharp, slanted vignettes are prophetic of those sections of *To Have and Have Not* in which Hemingway satirized the rich and decadent occupants of the yachts in the Key West basin in 1937. These 1922 sketches have the same crisp plausibility and expert narrative, blurred always by the easy satire of an intelligent, momentarily careless mind which is dealing with material casually explored. "You must understand," Hemingway would instruct the young writer in Key West in 1935, urging him not to judge.

His final dispatch from Germany had fewer of these subjective intensities and glib ironies. It was both the briefest of the stories and the only one printed in the *Star Weekly*.[35] Hemingway imposed restraint and professionalism which, while they sacrificed the entertaining venom of his denunciatory sarcasm, supplied a maturity that was appropriate to a temperate summary of the series. His point of view, however, remained belligerently anti-German. He launched a vignette demonstrating, he argued, "what [the German] is still capable of being." A Cologne mob had recently attempted to dislodge a huge equestrian statue of William Hohenzollern, "in a brawl that started to be a revolution and ended in a small sized riot." During the attack on the statue, Hemingway explained, a police officer appeared. "The mob," Hemingway reported, "threw the policeman into the river. In the cold, swift swirl of the Rhine against the base of the bridge the policeman hung on to one of the abutments and shouted up that he knew who was in the mob and would see that they were all punished. So the mob swarmed down and tried to push the policeman loose into the current. It meant drowning for the policeman to let go—and he hung on. Then the mob chopped his fingers loose from the stone with the hatchet with which they had been attacking the statue."

It was a monstrous anecdote. The only material comparable to it in Hemingway's early career, appropriately, was in the brutal short story called "An Alpine Idyll," first published in the 1927 *American Caravan*.[36] Here, dealing with the peasants who live in and below the Silvretta range, along the Swiss-Austrian border, Hemingway used an equally barbarous situation. His revulsion at the peasant's callous treatment of his wife's corpse was certainly an echo of the hostility which had been aroused in the Black Forest in 1922. Even the satiric title of the short story had the ironic distaste of his *Daily Star* dispatches.

### IV.

Their four-week excursion over, the Hemingways returned to Paris. The trip had enlarged the range of Hemingway's European background, even if it hadn't produced any consistently notable journalism. His hostility was fundamental and inflexible, in part the antagonism of a romantic temperament for what it conceived as a stolid, unimaginative people, in part a corollary of the anti-German indoctrination received in Italy during 1918. His point of view was to a degree a self-consciously belligerent one, a reminder that in his own mind he had seen far more of German-created tragedies than most Americans. His trip through Italy in June, only a few weeks before he went to Germany, had reminded him of the war's horror, both in its personal and national terms. He never responded to Germany, either to its terrain or its people, as he did to France or Spain or Italy. The episode nevertheless contributed to his understanding of contemporary Europe. Some years later, in an analysis of continental politics, he remembered what he had seen in 1922. "Germany," he wrote in 1934, "was never defeated in a military debacle."[37] He discussed fluently the absence of a successful German post-war revolution, indicating that the month in Germany in 1922, careless and prejudiced as it had been, was also another in the series of lessons he was receiving. One final assignment, before he completed his 1922 travels with a capable coverage of war in Asia Minor, had a symbolic relationship with the German experience.

On September 20, 1922, Hemingway was in Alsace, interviewing one of his great personal heroes. The political career of Georges Clemenceau had rested on an intense nationalism and a detestation of Germany. Hemingway had great success with the harsh old Frenchman, whose normal reticence dissolved under Hemingway's admiration and made him, Hemingway said, "for once very loquacious."[38] He was bitter and violent in what he said to the young American and in the prophecies he made for Europe. Hemingway was delighted with the interview; it was a professional triumph. Ultimately, however, it only compounded his distaste for newspaper work. The *Daily Star* would not print it. They mailed it back to him, "a great Canadian paper," Hemingway later said sardonically, and John Bone explained the rejection in a blunt note. "[Clemenceau] can say these things," the managing editor conceded, "but he cannot say them in our paper."[39] It was another useful footnote in the variety of realities Hemingway was encountering; it also pushed him one step nearer the abandonment of journalism.

# *ASIA MINOR*

"... I read everything that I could
understand [about war] and the more I
would see of it the more I could
understand."          ERNEST HEMINGWAY[1]

## *I.*

Hemingway was back in Paris from the Alsace interview
with Clemenceau by September 24, 1922, in time to attend
the murderous fight at the new Mont Rouge arena between
Siki and Carpentier. John Bone, however, permitted him
little time to enjoy a Paris autumn. A day or two after the
fight the managing editor cabled Hemingway to go to
Constantinople for the *Daily Star*. A Greek army had been
routed by the Turks; Smyrna had been burned. Lloyd
George was calling upon the Dominions to support England's deeply involved position. There was, above all, a terrible fear that the situation might at any moment produce
another world war.

Hemingway was understandably delighted. The assignment was wholly different from Bone's last commission, in
March, which had postponed his creative work and sent
him to Genoa. He was enough of a newspaperman to be
deeply curious about the dramatic struggle, raising as it did
the age-old menace of Turkey invading Europe. He was
literate and imaginative; his mind responded to the obvious
memories of other Greek armies and other Eastern expedi-
tions. The massacres and terrorism were eminently news-

worthy. His absorption in war, crystallized in 1918 and since stimulated both by reflection and by innumerable conversations with his contemporaries, was reignited by the opportunity to observe a fluid, aggressive campaign. Listening to English friends discuss Mons and the Somme, profitable as it was, and assessing his own limited experience in Italy, were academic compared to the privileged freedom of movement of a war correspondent. He packed hurriedly.

Before he left Paris there was a luncheon with Guy Hickok and Frank Mason; he discussed every aspect of the assignment with the two newspapermen. Years later Mason could remember Hemingway's excitement. He also remembered, more ruefully, that he was persuaded by Hemingway to work him onto the International News Service expense account, in return for any material he might send from Constantinople. It was purely an act of reluctant friendship on Mason's part, who had long since solved the problem of the Hearst coverage of developments in the Near East; his Paris office merely rewrote the English and French dispatches and cabled this version back to New York. Hemingway thus traveled south as the representative of a Hearst syndicate as well as a Hearst-type Canadian paper. He would have to see the war and its politics in vivid, communicable terms. It was, happily, that kind of war, and his own concern, of course, was with the men who fought it and the civilians who endured it. He would serve John Bone far better than a Balkan expert.

Bone, on the other hand, although his conception of Hemingway's role was as a feature writer, did not hesitate to endow the young reporter with considerable status. "Mr. Hemingway," the *Daily Star* announced, in a preface to his first cable, "who fought with the Italian army in the great war, is well equipped by his knowledge of the Balkans and the Near East to cover this latest assignment given him by The Star."[2] In terms of the normal complexity of a Balkan crisis, this one was relatively simple. It lent itself, journalistically, to feature treatment. Spot news breaks were rare; the assignment's news qualities were in the horror and violence which both sides had introduced, and in the large, vague clash of East and West, Moslem and Christian. The background of the situation was readily explained by most commentators as an early catastrophe of Versailles giveaways.

The cynicisms of diplomatic maneuvering made dismal reading to a generation which was bitterly realizing that it had not fought itself out of the pre-1914 entanglements. The governments of England, France, Italy, and Russia were plainly jockeying for position, offering short-term promises and some aid to the particular belligerent of their choice. English prestige and position were therefore endangered when the Greeks were badly mauled on September 7, 1922 in Anatolia, in a decisive battle begun ten days earlier. The Greeks fled across the remaining two hundred miles to the Aegean sanctuary. Civilian refugees began to crowd into Smyrna, which was penetrated by Turkish cavalry on September 9. On September 14 fire broke out in the Christian section of the panicky city. The Greeks had by this time turned the city over to the Allied commanders. Kemal Atatürk rejected all armistice proposals, persisting in his demands for the return of Adrianople and Smyrna. He threatened to invade the British mandate of Mesopotamia if his claims were not granted. Constantinople itself didn't seem altogether secure against his army.

This was the situation as Hemingway picked it up when, according to the *Daily Star*'s dramatic preface, he "succeeded in reaching Constantinople" on September 30. He promptly cabled a summary of the scene within the city.[3] His three-paragraph cable, bolstered by a triple bank of headlines and the italicized editorial description of him and his assignment, occupied the two important columns on the left hand side of the *Daily Star*'s front page. Even in the seventy-word cable he aimed for impressionism, creating it both by a string of positive adjectives—"Constantinople is noisy, hot, hilly, dirty, and beautiful"—and by a sense of tension in such familiar cabelese as "packed with uniforms and rumors" and "Foreigners . . . have booked outgoing trains for weeks ahead." His next dispatch, filed four days later, defined more clearly the approach he would use in these longer, mailed treatments.[4]

The story had as its lead the initial stages of the armistice talks at Mudania. Hemingway described the town as "a hot, dusty, badly-battered, second-rate seaport on the Sea of Marmora." He enlivened the sobriety of his basic theme with a mockery of the military which would be well received in recently demobilized Toronto, where the resentment of the English officer caste was almost a municipal characteristic. He also emphasized English and French responsibility for the war; his generation's distaste for diplomatic intrigue was evident throughout his entire coverage of the assignment. "The British wanted control in Asia Minor," he pointed out, "but Kemal did not look like a good buy to them." Hemingway moved on to what interested him much more, the fighting itself and the two armies engaged in it. His summary of the campaign was breathlessly perceptive and positive. "Kemal whipped the Greeks as every one knows. But when you realize that he was fighting a conscript army whose soldiers the barren country they were fighting to gain hated, who had been mobilized for nine years, who had no desire as men to conquer Asia Minor, and who were thoroughly fed up and becoming conscious that they were going into battle to die doing a cat's paw job, it was not the magnificent military achievement that it is made out to be."

Hemingway completed his broad definition of the several aspects of the scene with a description of Russia's role in the Near East; his aim was to provide a round-up of the backstage realities. The general tone of all his dispatches, in fact, was primarily realistic. He explored vigorously the political, diplomatic, and military aspects of the situation. His idiom, emphasis, and attitude were harsh and uncompromising. He was not the easy sensationalist, finding scare headlines and complacent cynicism in every trivial alteration of the crisis; neither was he content with the wide-eyed wonder that was the journalistic stock-in-trade of so many American correspondents during the 1920's. He did not rely on actual or imaginary first-name contacts with the great and the notorious.

The importance to Hemingway of the freedom and responsibility of his whole foreign assignment for the Star—he had now written more than thirty articles in six months—and the personal growth that occurred through the European experience, are verified by the adult quality of his war correspondence. He was troubled by the implications of the situation, by the revelations of new diplomatic ineptitude and corruption, and by the threat to world peace. John Bone, an editor of breadth and judgment, described Hemingway's European work as "a special feature in The Star."[5] Hemingway was by no means an experienced reporter. He had detoured or condensed the various journalistic drudgeries that normally preface the assignments he received or created. Because of this, and because too of the kind of training he had received in Kansas City, his reporting was never wholly conventional. The content and treatment of his dispatches, by October, 1922, were generally fresh and mature. They testified to a poise unusual in a young man of twenty-three.

On October 5 he mailed a third story—it was flown to Paris, actually, and traveled by ship from France to Canada—which indicated both his sobriety of purpose and his thoroughness in familiarizing himself with the background of this fluid situation.[6] He focused on Kemal, the most important single figure in the complex of intrigue. Although much of the material was picked up from the shop talk of his colleagues, Hemingway injected into it an imaginative vivification through analogy and characterization. He drew from contemporary politics a parallel which would be a meaningful one for the people of a Dominion city. "[Kemal] is now in something of the position Arthur Griffith and Michael Collins occupied in Ireland just before their deaths." Hemingway extended the Irish analogy. "As yet," he wrote, "his de Valera has not appeared." Hemingway argued that Mesopotamia was the critical acquisition for the Kemalists. "Whichever alliance Turkey drops clears the air very little, because the one big aim of the Kemalists, the one which they are being criticized now in their own circles for not having fulfilled, the aim which does not appear in any published pacts but that everyone in the country understands, is the possession of Mesopotamia."[7] Hemingway's final paragraph was a blunt summary and forecast.

It is oil that Kemal and company want Mesopotamia for, and it is oil that Great Britain wants to keep Mesopotamia for, so the East that is disappointed in Kemal the Saladin because he shows no inclination to plunge into a fanatical holy war, may yet get their war from Kemal the business man.

Hemingway did not limit himself to the large geopolitical issues. Remembering that his paper was being supplied each day with wire service cables, and exercising his particular gifts, he filed on October 6 a long, full-column study of Constantinople.[8] "Old timers always call it Constan," he pointed out, "just as you are a tenderfoot if you call Gibraltar anything but Gib." This careful, ingenuous accuracy was fundamental to his portrait of the city. His theme was the paradox of Constantinople's contradictory qualities; the description was an exercise in authenticity, tempered by the sensitive, romantic point of view which originally allowed him to recognize the paradox.

"In the morning," he began, "when you wake and see a mist over the Golden Horn with the minarets rising out of it slim and clean towards the sun and the Muezzin calling the faithful to prayer in a voice that soars and dips like an aria from a Russian opera, you have the magic of the east." His next paragraph smashed the illusion. "There may be," he conceded, "a happy medium between the east of Pierre Loti's stories and the east of everyday life, but it could only be found by a man who always looked with his eyes half shut, didn't care what he ate, and was immune to the bites of insects." Hemingway strengthened the paradox with a catalogue of the inhabitants whom the city now sheltered. Its population was estimated at a million and a half. "This," he declared, "does not include hundreds of battered Fords, forty thousand Russian refugees in every uniform of the Czar's army in all stages of dilapidation, and about an equal number of Kemalist troops in civilian clothes who have filtered into the city in order to make sure that Constantinople will go to Kemal no matter how the peace negotiations come out." The paragraph's last sentence had an impressive finality. "All these," Hemingway wrote, "have entered since the last estimate."

His precise catalogue of the city, as orderly and comprehensive as a large scale map, included an outline of night life of the city, where the theaters did not open until ten o'clock. "The night clubs open at two, the more respectable night clubs that is. The disreputable night clubs open at four in the morning." Hemingway mentioned discreetly the Galata settlement, as befitted a correspondent for a family paper that nonetheless granted the readability of vice. He explained that the small cluster of buildings, half way up the hill from the port, had "a district that is more unspeakably horrible than the foulest heyday of the old Barbary Coast. It festers there, trapping the soldiers and sailors of all the allies and of all nations."

Hemingway continued this personal, feature treatment in his next dispatch, despite the fact that the article was a cable, datelined October 9 from Constantinople and reaching Toronto in time to be used in the late afternoon editions that same day.[9] Hemingway had not yet dealt with the potential threat to Christians. This was one of the major news values of the situation, prominently exploited in the coverage by the New York press and the wire services. It was of particular interest to a pious, church-going community like Toronto. For the answers, Hemingway dutifully sought out Hamid Bey, "next to Kemal, perhaps," he wrote, "the most powerful man in the Angora government."

Hemingway's instinct for characterization, and his gift for the effective interviewing of celebrities—this was the primary assignment for which John Bone ultimately brought him back to Canada in the early fall of 1923—allowed him to ignore massacres for the first two paragraphs. "Bismarck," he cabled, "said all men in the Balkans who tuck their shirts into their trousers are crooks. The shirts of the peasants, of course, hang outside. At any rate, when I found Hamid Bey . . . in his Stamboul office where he directs his Kemalist government in Europe, while drawing a large salary as administrator of the Imperial Ottoman Bank, a French capitalized concern—his shirt was tucked in, for he was dressed in a grey business suit."

Hemingway's final dispatch from Constantinople—his sixth in little more than a week—was mailed the following day.[10] Mindful of his obligations as a Canadian correspondent, he located a topic of particular interest to an Empire audience. Afghanistan's borders touched almost every sore spot in the area, and its proximity to Mesopotamia was doubly significant because of Kemal's designs on the oil-rich English mandate. Hemingway's imagination responded to the proud, martial code of the Afghans. He incorporated the techniques of personal verification, political realism, and careful dialogue and vignettes. Shere Mohamet Khan, whom Hemingway had previously met in Rome, "was tall, dark-haired, hawk-faced, as straight as a lance, with the bird-of-prey eyes and the hooked nose that mark the Afghan . . . like a man out of the renaissance. . . ."

He translated the history of Afghanistan through a blend of chronology and personalities, emphasizing always the Afghan hatred of England. He told the story of the former Amir of Afghanistan—"all his life he hated the English"—who was "a great man . . . a hard man, a far-seeing man and an Afghan." The Amir spent his entire life consolidating his tribal domain into a unified nation, and in training his son. "His son," Hemingway explained, "was to carry on his work to make war on the English." The Kiplingesque quality—which Gertrude Stein had previously noted in his poetry—was more than just the coincidence of the material. The idiom and sentence structure, as well as the essential attitude and treatment, are reminders that Hemingway later recommended the Englishman's short stories, emphatically, as profitable models for a young writer.[11]

The old man died. The son, Habibullah Khan, became Amir. The English invited him to come down to India on a state visit, and he went to see what manner of people these English were. There the English got him. First, they entertained him royally. They showed him many delights and they taught him to drink. I do not say he was not an apt learner. He was no longer a man and an Afghan.

Hemingway's six Constantinople stories had touched on almost every element in the explosive, varied situation. He had defined the nature of the Turkish position, with particular emphasis on the all-important French and Russian alliances. He had attempted an analysis of the composition of the Kemalist group, and its prospects for continued unity. He had given a vivid base to the articles through the portrait of the city, and his sketch of Hamid Bey supplied a glimpse of Turkish leadership and a foreshadowing of what a Turkish occupation of Constantinople could imply. The essay on Afghanistan had reminded his readers of the fragility of European peace. He had cabled and mailed John Bone a comprehensive feature treatment of the assignment. Hemingway's reservations about newspaper work have always been sound ones, but during this entire period as a foreign correspondent in 1922 he had on the whole the sort of duties, and gave to them the kind of treatment, which reduced some of the dangers, creatively speaking, of a journalistic apprenticeship. He had, above all, done a minimum of spot news reporting.

"When you describe something that has happened that day," he wrote in 1935, "the timeliness makes people see it in their own imaginations. A month later that element of time is gone and your account would be flat and they would not see in their minds nor remember it."[12]

Hemingway, at least until he covered the Lausanne Conference late in 1922, was able to give to his journalism ingredients which to a degree replaced the false strength of timeliness. "But if you make it up instead of describe it," he continued on that same occasion in the 1930's, once again paraphrasing Miss Stein's lessons, "you can make it round and whole and solid and give it life. You create it, for good or bad. It is made; not described." Hemingway had not made up his Constantinople dispatches, but neither had he been imprisoned within the restrictions of topical reporting. He could have remained indefinitely in the city, finding other ramifications of the broad outline he had already written. Constantinople was exciting and turbulent, full of drama and romance and excess, and never more so than in October, 1922. Years later Hemingway wrote a little of it into the introspection of the writer dying in the shadow of Kilimanjaro, as Harry remembers that in Constantinople, after a night of violence and brawling, he "drove out to Rimmily Hissa along the Bosphorus."[13]

The instinct that made Hemingway a good reporter eventually eclipsed the charm of the gay, reckless life, with its echoes of 1918 moods. When he had filed his Afghanistan dispatch he left Constantinople and went after what was for him a story more important than even the political and diplomatic realities. He moved southward and followed the Greek army as it evacuated Eastern Thrace. He had missed the climactic fighting in August and September; he had no intention of missing this later phase. From Italian soldiers and officers in 1918, and from other wounded men in the Milan hospital, Hemingway had heard the stories about Caporetto; now, four years later, he was about to see his own variation of the Italian retreat.

## II.

Hemingway's reaction to the tragic spectacle of military defeat and betrayal was personal and imaginative. He datelined the first of this second set of Near East dispatches from Muradii, a small village near Lake Van, several hundred miles east of Constantinople, on October 14.[14] He was an accurate, informative reporter of this basic element of war, the withdrawal of a large body of men through hostile country. The experience illuminated everything he had read of all war, what he had heard of the American Civil War, and what he had sensed and witnessed in Italy. The things he found in Eastern Thrace told him precisely what an army looks like during an evacuation.

In their ill-fitting U.S. uniforms they are trekking across the country, cavalry patrols out ahead, the soldiers marching sullenly but occasionally grinning at us as we pass their strung-out, straggling columns. They have cut all the telegraph wires behind them; you see them dangling from the poles like Maypole ribbons. They have abandoned their thatched huts, their camouflaged gun positions, their machine gun nests, and all the heavily wired, strung out, fortified ridges where they had planned to make a last stand against the Turk. . . . Some soldiers lie on top of the mounds of baggage, while others goad the buffalo along. Ahead and behind the baggage carts are strung out the troops. This is the end of the great Greek military adventure.

Hemingway's primary concern, though he was acutely aware of the tactics and strategy of withdrawal, was with the individual Greek soldier. "Even in the evacuation," he wrote, "the Greek soldiers looked like good troops." Hemingway learned a great deal from an English captain, a cavalryman from the Indian Army. Captain Wittal was one of the two officers attached to the Greeks as an observer during the fighting around Angora in the late summer. Hemingway tried hard to put the idiom and inflection of the English officer's speech into the article's dialogue. " 'In the one show in Anatolia,' Captain Wittal said, 'the Greek infantry were doing an absolutely magnificent attack and their artillery was doing them in.' " Wittal also told Hemingway about Major Johnson, the other English observer, an experienced gunner who was so shocked by the unprofessional spectacle that he " 'cried at what those gunners were doing to their infantry.' " Years later this became another of the fragments of memory in "The Snows of Kilimanjaro"; Harry remembers "where they had made the attack with the newly arrived Constantine officers, that did not know a god-damned thing, and the artillery had fired into the troops and the British observer had cried like a child." Hemingway's last sentences in the 1922 dispatch were clear and bitter, testimony to his imaginative involvement in the scene.

All day I have been passing them, dirty, tired, unshaven, wind-bitten soldiers hiking along the trails across the brown, rolling, barren Thracian country. No bands, no relief organizations, no leave areas, nothing but lice, dirty blankets, and mosquitoes at night. They are the last of the glory that was Greece. This is the end of their second siege of Troy.

Hemingway learned other things about a retreat, things he didn't mail to Toronto but saved for the long Caporetto passages he wrote in 1929 for *A Farewell to Arms*. He had other stories, too, from Captain Wittal and from Major Johnson; the latter had become press liaison officer in Constantinople. Once again Hemingway saved them for Harry's dying monologue. "That was the day he'd first seen dead men wearing white ballet skirts and upturned shoes with pompons on them . . . he and the British observer had run . . . until his lungs ached and his mouth was full of the taste of pennies and they stopped behind some rocks and there were the Turks coming as lumpily as ever." In 1922, however, Hemingway filed no further details on the military aspects of the evacuation. He moved north toward the vast civilian exodus from Western Thrace. He stopped briefly in Constantinople,[15] and then on October 20, now many miles north of the city, he cabled from Adrianople a fine story of the refugees who were moving out of Eastern Thrace.[16] It was harsh and compressed, a vivid recapitulation of civilian tragedy. In 1922 its horror had not become a global commonplace; Hemingway saw it with a fresh, shocked awareness.

In a never-ending, staggering march the Christian population of Eastern Thrace is jamming the roads towards Macedonia. The main column crossing the Maritza River at Adrianople is twenty miles long. Twenty miles of carts drawn by cows, bullocks and muddy-flanked water buffalo, with exhausted, staggering men, women, and children, blankets over their heads, walking blindly in the rain beside their worldly goods.

This spectacle of refugee misery, beyond all the rest of what he saw in Asia Minor, left the most permanent scar on Hemingway. In his creative work he made far more use of what he learned from the military catastrophe; he told Malcolm Cowley, in fact, that he "really learned about war" in the Near East.[17] The civilian suffering, however, gave a new dimension to his determination to be a writer. He has always been generous and quick in his response to grief. His ready, decent anger had already been displayed in his indignation about Italian fascism. His susceptibilities once caused him to explain that "I cannot see a horse down in the street without having it make me feel a necessity for helping the horse, and I have spread sacking, unbuckled harness and dodged shod hoofs many times and will again if they have horses on city streets in wet and icy weather. . . ."[18] Hemingway had neither seen nor imagined such human suffering as he saw in October, 1922, along the road to Adrianople.

When he got back to France after finishing his Greco-Turk assignment, he made on the basis of it a decision about his career. "I remember," he said thirty years later, "coming home from the Near East . . . absolutely heartbroken at what was going on and in Paris trying to decide whether I would put my whole life into trying to do something about it or to be a writer." His indignation made the decision a difficult one; he had been raised, after all, in the decent world of Oak Park, with its middle-class, nineteenth-century heritage of New England humanitarianism. "I decided," he said in 1951, "cold as a snake, to be a writer and to write as truly as I could all my life."[19] The terse clarity of the Adrianople cable, which the *Daily Star* used on the first page of the second section, could not disguise what he was feeling. Once he had established the scene in the first three paragraphs, in exposition as effective as any journalism he had yet written,[20] Hemingway quickly ended the cable. His last two paragraphs, for there were only five in all, were an explicit plea for help. "At Adrianople," he cabled, "where the main stream moves through, there is no Near East relief at all. They are doing very good work at Rodosto on the coast, but can only touch the fringe."

He completed his Near East assignment three days later, with a long, two-thousand-word article which John Bone spread out across a whole page.[21] Hemingway was at last out of sight of that grim procession. He wrote the final dispatch as he rode through Bulgaria, and mailed it from Sofia on October 23. He pretended to a retrospective softening of the horror. "In a comfortable train," he declared, "with the horrors of the Thracian evacuation behind me, it was already beginning to seem unreal. That is the boon of our memories." His second paragraph was a more curt and precise appraisal of his mood. "I have described that evacuation," he said bleakly, "in a cable to The Star from Adrianople. It does no good to go over it again. The evacuation still keeps up." His memories were in reality far from sublimated.

No matter how long it takes this letter to get to Toronto, as you read this in The Star you may be sure that the same ghastly, shambling procession of people being driven from their homes is filing in unbroken line along the muddy road to Macedonia. A quarter of a million people take a long time to move.

Hemingway then supplied a detailed account of his movements and experiences during that period from which he had compressed his cable of three days earlier. "Adrianople itself," he wrote, "is not a pleasant place." He described the railway station, "a mud-hole crowded with soldiers, bundles, bed-springs, bedding, sewing machines, babies, broken carts, all in the mud and the drizzling rain." The scene was the more horrible from being lit only with kerosene flares; it was one of those "very simple things," as he explained later, which he tried in his early work to make "permanent, as, say, Goya tried to make them in *Los Desastres de la Guerra*."[22] He returned always, however, to the procession itself, particularly in a long, single sentence paragraph that reaffirmed the cable. "I walked five miles with the refugees [sic] procession along the road . . . always the slow, rain soaked, shambling, trudging Thracian peasantry plodding along in the rain, leaving their homes behind."

Hemingway ended his Near East assignment with vignettes of the tough, callous opportunism of Madame Marie, the prospering operator of Adrianople's only hotel. He carried with him a final impression of indifference toward suffering, as he traveled by train from Sofia north through Serbia and on to Trieste. Paris itself was a splendid contrast to Adrianople; the races at Anteuil were very good that year and he watched them from under a bright, blue November sky. As with Harry in "The Snows of Kilimanjaro," however, there were aspects of Paris which only aggravated his memories. "So when he got back to Paris that time he could not talk about it or stand to have it mentioned. And there in the café as he passed was that American poet with a pile of saucers in front of him and a stupid look on his potato face talking about the Dada movement with a Roumanian who said his name was Tristan Tzara, who always wore a monocle and had a headache."

### III.

The Asia Minor assignment gave Hemingway's understanding of war a depth impossible on the basis of his Italian experience alone. His education was extended by another lesson in geopolitical realities. The area of his physical background had been enlarged; a Balkan campaign had given him a wider base for the worldliness by which he illuminated so much of his early work. Few young men of twenty-three could draw on a Near East experience. Hemingway drew on it heavily. Of the sixteen brief inter-chapters in *In Our Time*, in 1925, three of the most forceful came from the Asia Minor assignment.

In 1930, when he was preparing a new edition of the short story collection, he included a prelude which he later entitled, "On the Quai at Smyrna."[23] The appalling cruelty toward their animals, by Greeks and Turks, had an almost traumatic effect on Hemingway. He used it not only in the 1930 sketch but also in "The Snows of Kilimanjaro" and—twice—in *Death in the Afternoon*. On that particular occasion, in fact, as if aware of the psychotic way in which he was returning to the scene, Hemingway allowed the Old Lady to chide him for his preoccupation. "You wrote about those mules before," she reminds him. "I know it," Hemingway replied, "and I'm sorry. Stop interrupting. I won't write about them again. I promise."[24]

He was equally absorbed by the technical possibilities of cabelese. A few weeks later, back in Europe, he showed his refugee cable to Lincoln Steffens. Steffens was impressed by the story's exposition. Hemingway protested this response. "I was seeing the scene and said so," Steffens explained subsequently. "No," Hemingway had corrected him, "read the cabelese, only the cabelese. Isn't it a great language?"[25] Most of the cabelese he sent from Asia Minor, however, had been for the International News Service rather than the *Daily Star*. None of his I.N.S. material was by-lined, nor were there any permanent records to verify his Hearst coverage. The arrangement had been a private one between Hemingway and Frank Mason.[26] More than a decade later Hemingway described the kind of material he cabled I.N.S. from Asia Minor. It was the conventional, telegraphic cabelese rather than the curt but nevertheless formed cabelese he had sent to the *Daily Star*. His output, sent at three dollars a word to, he said satirically, Monumental News Service, "would be something on this order: KEMAL INSWARDS UNBURNED SMYRNA GUILTY GREEKS . . . to appear as 'Mustapha Kemal in an exclusive interview today with the correspondent of the Monumental News Service denied vehemently that the Turkish forces had any part in the burning of Smyrna. The city, Kemal stated, was fired by incendiaries in the troops of the Greek rear guard before the first Turkish patrols entered the city.' "[27]

Hemingway's tenuous connection with the Hearst organization did not become weaker or even non-existent, as might have been expected, but stronger. He had only a few weeks of rehabilitation in Paris in November, 1922. John Bone ordered him to Lausanne to cover the conference assembling there for the diplomatic settlement of the whole Greco-Turk affair. Hemingway's coverage of the Near East assignment, however, was reversed at Lausanne. In Switzerland he did most of his writing for Universal News, the second of Hearst's overseas news agencies, rather than for the Toronto *Star*.

# *LAUSANNE*

"And at a busy typewriter outside the
door of the British press-room, cabling
hourly bulletins . . . sat . . . Ernest
Hemingway." GEORGE SLOCOMBE[1]

*1.*

Hemingway almost left the Lausanne Conference before
it was thoroughly under way. At the end of the first week,
although the meeting was of special interest to a Canadian
paper, Hemingway had made up his mind to return to
Paris. He told Henry Wales, who was in Lausanne for the
Chicago *Tribune*, that he "could not stand the expenses in
Switzerland."[2] This was always a troublesome aspect of
Hemingway's relationship with the *Star*; he paid his own
way while covering an assignment, and eventually was re-
imbursed, and his material paid for, after he had filed an
expense account.

Wales, who was then Floyd Gibbons's assistant, located
a compromise by which Hemingway could remain at Lausanne. An hour or two after talking to Hemingway, Wales
got a phone call from Charles Bertelli, the chief Hearst
correspondent in France. Bertelli, who was also in charge
of the Paris office of Hearst's Universal News Service, told
Wales that he wasn't going to be able to attend the conference himself. He asked the *Tribune* correspondent to
suggest someone who would cover the assignment for
Universal. Bertelli's principal concern was with the press

conferences and the daily communiqués. He also wanted the reporter to pick up any general news he could find and telephone it to Paris every evening; Bertelli could then write a complete story each day. Wales immediately told Hemingway to get in touch with Bertelli.

The arrangement was characteristic both of the Hearst news agencies in general and of Bertelli in particular. He himself remembered the association with Hemingway in much the same terms as Wales. "I was overwhelmed with work," Bertelli said in 1952. "[Therefore] we provided with someone over there to keep us covered and the some-one happened to be Hemingway."[3] His work for Universal, Bertelli explained, "was only short flashes and newsy stuff and nothing descriptive or long requiring the signature of a well-known writer."

Hemingway recalled the Universal assignment as a laborious one. He described it, quite accurately, as "running a twenty-four-hour wire service for an afternoon and morning news service."[4] It was journalism of a sort he had been previously spared. Almost entirely spot news, it was routine and undramatic and had a minimum of feature possibilities. As Bertelli had anticipated, virtually all of it was in the form of official hand-outs. One correspondent, Ludwell Denny, describing the first six weeks of the conference for the *Nation*, went so far as to declare that there was "an absolute control of the news sources."[5] From the beginning the newspapermen were barred from the conference sessions, which opened on November 20 in the Lausanne Casino. They were also excluded from the building to which the conference then moved, the Hôtel du Château at Ouchy. There was no point in the reporters interviewing the lesser delegates, who, according to Denny, were "as ignorant as they of what goes on up in Curzon's room." The only important delegate who held press conferences was Tchitcherin, the Soviet foreign minister. He didn't arrive at the conference until December, and his substitute, indeed, was at first refused full admission to the meetings.

Hemingway, of course, had to attend faithfully the daily ceremony at which the English secretary released the British interpretation of current activities. Inasmuch as he had to wire material both to Universal, whose stories were generally used by Hearst's morning papers, and to I.N.S., which was in a sense the afternoon agency, Hemingway also covered the other delegations in search of material. "Since each country was anxious to present its version of what had happened," Hemingway later explained, "before credence was given to any other country's account, these press conferences followed in rapid succession and you had to step very fast to get them all in."[6] Hemingway normally filed his last dispatch around three in the morning and left another story with the concierge "to open the wire with in the morning at seven." At noon he gathered with the other correspondents in the bar of the enormous Beau-Rivage Hotel, on Lake Geneva, where the British and Italian delegates were staying; later in the afternoon he went up into the town to the Palace Hotel to get the French and Turkish communiqués.

Hemingway was encountering, with the rest of the press, the same resistance he had resented in the English lieutenant colonel at the Mudania Conference in October. Secret diplomacy, official hand-outs, and the suave, high pressure tactics of Lord Curzon were another lesson in political realities. The effect of the conference on Hemingway, and its contribution to his creative production, are indicated by the poem which was accepted by the *Little Review* and published in its Exiles' Number in the spring of 1923.[7] Its title—"They All Want Peace—What Is Peace?"—summed up his contempt. Its lines and themes were forceful and precocious.

M. Stambuliski walks up the hill and down the hill. Don't
talk about M. Venizelos. He is wicked. You can see it. His
beard shows it.
Mr. Child is not wicked.
Mrs. Child has flat breasts and Mr. Child is an idealist and
wrote Harding's campaign speeches and calls Senator
Beveridge Al.

His antagonism embraced his vocation as well as diplomacy. His mockery of the newspapermen's complacent
wisdom—"Well what do you boys know this morning?
/ Oh they're shrewd. They're shrewd."—indicated that he
was once again restless with journalism. The parody of a
child's primer, coupled with the coarse realism, made the
poem an effective statement. Hemingway's obligation to
Gertrude Stein was in this case a large one. He explained
to Edmund Wilson a few months later that he had written
the verse on the train back to Lausanne from Paris, after a
lunch and afternoon of talk with Miss Stein.[8] Remembering that he had to open the Universal wire again in the
morning, Hemingway sat over a bottle of Beaune in the
dining car and tried to define the conference. "Her method
is invaluable . . . ," Hemingway told Wilson. "She has a
wonderful head."

Hemingway did not arrive at such disillusionment solely
on the basis of his previous encounters with diplomatic
parleys, as observed at Genoa and Mudania, nor solely on
his own reaction to the Lausanne Conference. The conference's deceit was all the more painful to him, of course,
because he had so recently seen its background of refugee
processions. It was also at Lausanne, however, that Hemingway received his most significant lessons in political reality, from a South African correspondent who took a liking
to him and gave him his first formal instruction.

*II.*

William Bolitho Ryall—he did not take the name William Bolitho, by which he is more widely remembered, until several years later—was representing the Manchester *Guardian* at Lausanne.[9] Both his temperament and his biography made him a persuasive mentor for Hemingway. "He had been very badly blown up in the war," Hemingway once wrote, "while commanding infantry. Afterwards he had gotten into the intelligence service and at the time of [Versailles] he had been a sort of pay-off man for the disbursing of certain sums spent by the British to subsidize and influence certain individuals and certain organs of the French press."[10]

It would be hard to imagine a man whose martial and professional backgrounds would make him more highly regarded by Hemingway in 1922. He had been wounded as a foot soldier and he had been on the inside of large, pretentious diplomatic schemes. "None of us thought of him as a genius then," Hemingway said later of the period, "and I do not think he thought of himself as one either, being too busy, too intelligent, and, then, too sardonic to go in for being a genius in a city where they were a nickel a dozen and it was much more distinguished to be hard working."[11] Bolitho had virtually every quality which would make him the first substantial non-literary influence on Hemingway since Pete Wellington and Lionel Moise in Kansas City. Later, of course, Bolitho did acquire a literary reputation. Much of his newspaper work was collected, and his *Twelve Against the Gods,* published in 1929, had for a time an enormous reputation.[12] When Hemingway knew him, however, Bolitho's force was being exerted largely through his personality. "As I was a kid then," Hemingway wrote in 1935, "he told me many things that were the beginning of whatever education I received in international politics."[13]

Walter Duranty, who saw a great deal of Bolitho during the early 1920's, gave a version of the South African which was almost identical to Hemingway's. Like Hemingway, the New York *Times* correspondent remembered Bolitho's "brilliant political insight and flair for the underlying realities of any situation"; he also declared that Bolitho "taught me . . . to think for myself."[14] Duranty, who dedicated his autobiography to Bolitho's memory, said in 1935 that "of all the people I have met in the last twenty years, and there have been some high-sounding names amongst them, I think Bolitho had the finest intellect."[15]

Bolitho later became a special writer for the New York *World*. Even in that precocious company he was a compelling figure. Those who knew him in Manhattan in 1928 and 1929 had the same response as young newspapermen like Duranty and Hemingway. "To hear Bolitho talk," said Alexander Woollcott, characteristically, "was to listen to one who himself dwelt outside of time."[16] Walter Lippmann testified to the same quality. "He was an eager guide," Lippmann wrote. "In any company he took the floor at the beginning of the evening and held it until the end, thus saving himself and the rest of the party much weariness."[17] Lippmann added that "in his company ordinary things were transfigured, acquiring the glamour of mystery and great import."

Bolitho, for Hemingway, was a more literate and informed Lionel Moise, with a self-discipline that Hemingway had missed in Moise. Hemingway's own tributes to Bolitho are explicit and personal. The characteristics which attracted Hemingway to Moise in 1918 could not possibly have had the same effect on him in 1922; he had grown beyond Moise, but he could learn from Bolitho. Even the skepticism Hemingway was feeling about journalism was shared by Bolitho, a fine columnist who nonetheless argued that newspaper work was a stepping-stone but not a career. The contempt for the trade which Hemingway had written into his poem on the Lausanne Conference—"Oh they're shrewd. They're shrewd."—was an absolute duplicate of Bolitho's own attitude toward his vocation.

"Exchange the newspaper game," Bolitho urgently advised Duranty, "for the thing we are trained to do, namely, writing. Books or plays, or what have you; in other words," he argued, " . . . capitalize your knowledge and experience and capacity for putting words on paper in a way that will interest your readers." Bolitho had a compassionate distaste for those who stayed too long in journalism. "I don't care whether it's fact or fiction," he told Duranty, "but it's got to be done somehow unless you want to end up like old 'Whiskers'—you know who I mean—as a burnt-out reporter cadging drinks and dead-dog assignments from his younger friends."

Hemingway was susceptible to such advice. Gertrude Stein had already urged him to get out of journalism. The positive assurance of such a man as Bolitho, coming as it did in the wake of Miss Stein's identical position, would have important consideration for Hemingway. "The echoes of his voice," Lippmann wrote in 1937 in his memoir about Bolitho, "are still about us." In the early winter of 1922 Hemingway was exposed continuously to that voice. He and Bolitho were together almost every night in Lausanne. When Hemingway wrote for *Esquire* in the 1930's some articles on European politics, he leaned heavily on what he had learned from Bolitho during those two months. One night Bolitho explained to him the familiar concept that power affects all men in a certain way. The South African maintained that sooner or later you could always detect the symptoms. He even persuaded Hemingway that they were evident in his personal hero, Clemenceau.

Bolitho's wit was hearty and sardonic. He quoted for Hemingway, in illustration of his power thesis, a certain Lord of the British Admiralty. It had become impossible for anyone to work with him, Bolitho explained—one of the effects of power—and the final smash came at a discussion of how to get a better class of cadets for the Royal Navy. The admiral hammered on the table, according to Bolitho, and shouted, "Gentlemen, if you do not know where to get them, by God I will make them for you!"[18] Bolitho strengthened in Hemingway his knowledgeability, his instinct for being on the inside, and his insistence that one should think for himself. Hemingway wasn't with Bolitho during the months when he was having his New York success, but he remembered him with affection and gratitude. "I never saw him after he became Bolitho," Hemingway said once, "but when he was Ryall he was a wonderful guy. He may have been even finer when he was Bolitho but I do not see how it would be possible."[19]

### III.

Lausanne thus became the kind of newspaper assignment at which a great many disreputable anecdotes about the diplomats were cynically exchanged by the journalists under very pleasant circumstances. The weather was excellent, Hemingway boxed in the mornings, usually with G. Ward Price, the London *Daily Mail*'s correspondent,[20] and, as in Constantinople, there was a good deal of alcoholic gaiety among the press. Beyond this, however, there was the discipline of continuous writing, even if it so often consisted of mere rephrasing of official communiqués, and there was the stimulant of Bolitho. At Lausanne Hemingway also saw a good deal of Lincoln Steffens, whose confidence in Hemingway's writing future was immediate and certain. The celebrated muckraker read Hemingway's "rejected manuscripts, and read short stories, since published, which made me, as they did Guy Hickok and other reporters, sure of Hemingway."[21]

The short stories could only have been "Up in Michigan" and "My Old Man," for it was just before this that a valise containing all of Hemingway's work except those two pieces was stolen from a train in the Gare du Lyons. Mrs. Hemingway, in fact, was bringing the material from Paris to Lausanne, she remembered, and in particular an unfinished novel, "because of Ernest's letters singing high praises of Lincoln Steffens, his new friend, to whom I felt certain he would want to show these . . . chapters."[22] The loss of four years' production—the suitcase held sketches that went back as far as the months in Michigan in 1919—was a shocking blow to Hemingway. His own shock was shared by his wife. "No amount of sleuthing ever brought the valise to light," she said in 1952, "and so deeply had Ernest put himself into this writing that I think he never recovered from the pain of this irreparable loss."

A Christmas holiday in Switzerland, however, was a delightful interlude, even if its prelude were a catastrophe. After ten days of skiing and bobsledding in the mountains, Hemingway returned to Lausanne in January, 1923. He continued his work for Universal, but he also wrote and mailed to Toronto two long articles about the conference. They were good dispatches, in which he again displayed his gifts as an interviewer. In effect, however, the stories were more than interviews—the one with Mussolini, the other with Tchitcherin—for in them he included detail, impressions, and evaluations of the conference as a whole. The pair of *Daily Star* articles formed a kind of two-installment assessment of the entire episode.

## IV.

The first of Hemingway's Lausanne dispatches was published in Toronto on January 27, 1923.[23] The interview with Mussolini was almost exactly two thousand words long. It appeared on the center of page eleven, its three columns fanned beneath four banks of headlines and around a good-sized photograph of the Italian politician. Before he dealt with Mussolini, however, Hemingway summed up his memories of the conference. His exposition was subjective and lively. He used analogies from his own past as well as from literature and history.

"In the Chateau de Ouchy," he began, "which is so ugly that it makes the Odd Fellows' Hall of Petoskey, Michigan look like the Parthenon, are held the sessions of the Lausanne Conference." He reminded his readers that in the nineteenth century Ouchy had been "a little fishing village of weather-stained houses, a white-painted, pleasant inn with a shady front porch where Byron used to sit resting his bad leg on a chair while he looked out across the blue of Lake Geneva and waited for the supper bell to ring, and an old ruined tower that rose out of the reeds at the edge of the lake." As always, Hemingway's ironic eye caused him to take a closer look at the contemporary Ouchy.

"The Swiss," he continued, "have torn down the fishing buildings, nailed up a tablet on the inn front porch, hustled Byron's chair into a museum, filled in the reedy shore with dirt from the excavations that cover the slope up the hill to Lausanne, and built the ugliest building in Europe around the old tower." Hemingway's sense of place, as his novels in particular indicate, is an acute one. The erasure of significant landmarks has not only pained him for the loss of beauty, but also often destroyed, in his judgment, one of the valid instruments by which a writer may retain the truth of a given period or association. He has felt this more deeply in terms of his personal typography, so to speak, than even in such a vanished symbol as Childe Harold's tower. "You need local knowledge," he once said, "and to have seen the hill before the bull-dozer hit it. You need to have fished the stream before they put in the dam for the irrigation project."[24] What has happened to Oak Park and Kansas City and New York is only slightly more offensive to him than what had been done to Lausanne since the departure of Byron. "This building . . . ," Hemingway continued for the *Daily Star*, "resembles one of the love-nests that sauerkraut kings used to build along the Rhine before the war as dream-homes for their sauerkraut queens."

He brought his impressionism closer to the conference itself. "You can tell when the Conference is in session," he wrote, "by the rows of limousines parked along the Chateau facing the lake." Hemingway dramatized the moment when the Russians left their hotel. "A taxi comes up to the door and Arrens, the Cheka man and Bolshevist press agent, comes out, his heavy, dark face sneering and his one roving eye shooting away out of control; he is followed by Rakovsky and Tchitcherin." Hemingway had talked to Tchitcherin in Genoa, ten months before, and he made a vivid estimate of the changes that had occurred in the Soviet Foreign Minister. "Tchitcherin is not as he was at Genoa when he seemed to blink at the world as a man who has come out of darkness into too strong sunlight. He is more confident now, has a new overcoat, and a better groomed look; he has been living well in Berlin, and his face is fuller, although he looks the same as ever in profile with his wispy red beard and mustache and his furtive, old clothes man slouch."

Hemingway's intention was to sketch a gallery of the conference's major personalities. The story's headlines emphasized this; one phrase, beneath several heads about Mussolini, simply promised: "OTHER CHARACTERS." Hemingway turned to the Turkish delegation. His brief, careful portrait of Turkey's chief delegate maintained the imaginative selectivity of his characterization of Tchitcherin. "Everyone wants to see Ismet Pasha, but once they have seen him they have no desire to see him again. . . . I think the solution is that Ismet has a good movie face. I have seen him, in pictures, look stern, commanding, forceful and, in a way, handsome. Anyone who has seen in real life the weak, petulant face of any one of a dozen movie stars who look beautiful on the screen, knows what I mean. Ismet's face is not weak or petulant, it is simply plain and characterless."

Ismet's final function in the dispatch was to prepare the reader for the portrait of the man who presented such a contrast to the Turk. Hemingway's sketch of Mussolini went beyond mere instinctive distaste. It was extremely hostile. He documented his hostility both by anecdote and by amateur psychoanalysis; he declared himself immediately. "Mussolini," Hemingway wrote, "is the biggest bluff in Europe." He varied his attack with a crescendo of fact, ridicule, and psychological abuse. "Get hold of a good photograph of Signor Mussolini some time," he urged, "and study it."

You will see the weakness in his mouth which forces him to scowl the famous Mussolini scowl that is imitated by every 19 year old Fascisto in Italy. Study his past record. . . . Study his genius for clothing small ideas in big words. Study his propensity for duelling. Really brave men do not have to fight duels, and many cowards duel constantly to make themselves believe they are brave. And then look at his black shirt and his white spats. There is something wrong, even histrionically, with a man who wears white spats with a black shirt.

Hemingway was skeptical of the currently fashionable comparisons between Mussolini and Napoleon. He argued, "after an intimate study of the subject," that the better parallel was with a much more ludicrous and inglorious figure. Hemingway's contemporary analogy was to Horatio Bottomley, an English financier who had been convicted in London in 1922 for the misuse of public funds and sentenced to seven years in prison.[25] Like Mussolini, Bottomley was intensely patriotic. He had once described himself as "the King's chief recruiting agent in the war." Like Mussolini, too, he had been both jingoistic politician and journalist; at the time of his conviction Bottomley was a Member of Parliament, and he had also been for many years owner and editor of *John Bull*, England's most nationalistic magazine. His reputation in Parliament was as a demagogue of extraordinary eloquence.

Hemingway, on the other hand, did not underestimate Mussolini's strength. "It isn't really Bottomley, though," he concluded. "Bottomley was a fool. Mussolini isn't a fool and he is a great organizer." As in his earlier articles on Italian fascism, Hemingway had shown a premature understanding of its quality and menace. His attitude toward Mussolini was not characteristic of most American journalists of the period.[26] The entire interview, and the position it represents in Hemingway's twenty-three-year-old evaluation of political morality, is a reminder of his indignation many years later when Archibald MacLeish cited him as one of America's literary irresponsibles. "Having fought fascism in every place that I know how," Hemingway said in 1940, "in the places where you could really fight it, I have no remorse—neither literary nor political."[27]

His response to Tchitcherin, spokesman for another totalitarianism, was less hostile, and for good reasons. The article Hemingway mailed to the *Daily Star* on January 25 made these reasons clear.[28] Tchitcherin, he felt, had none of the Italian's mean viciousness and pretense. He neither charmed nor repelled Hemingway; he interested the young reporter as he might have interested William Bolitho, as a problem in character that might be solved by independent analysis. Hemingway found the key in Tchitcherin's ironic antecedents as a Russian aristocrat. He supplemented this with one of the historical parallels by which, probably under the influence of the widely read Bolitho, he was increasingly attempting to clarify his journalism. "Tchitcherin was an old Czarist diplomat, and if Lenin is the Napoleon that made a dictatorship out of the Russian revolution, Tchitcherin is his Talleyrand."

Tchitcherin's position as foreign minister enabled Hemingway to deal comprehensively with the Soviet relationships to other nations. He enlivened with paragraphs of dialogue what could have degenerated into a dull lecture; the conversation had the lucid conviction of the professional diplomat. It was the contest between Tchitcherin and Lord Curzon, Hemingway maintained, "that made the Lausanne Conference so interesting." He spoke of it as a conflict "between the British Empire and the future Russian Empire with Curzon, a tall, cold, icicle of a man holding the whip hand with the British fleet, and Tchitcherin fighting, fighting, with arguments, historical instances, facts, statistics and impassioned pleas and finally, seeing it was hopeless, simply talking for history, registering his objections for future generations to read. . . ."

The remainder of the dispatch was a return to the intimate portraiture at which Hemingway was becoming expert. Like the Mussolini interview, this second Lausanne story was illustrated, in this case by two photographs, each one showing Tchitcherin in the gaudy uniform of a Soviet general. This was the motif of Hemingway's final paragraphs. "Tchitcherin, you must know," Hemingway explained, "has never been a soldier. He is timid personally.

He does not fear assassination, but he would turn pale if you shook your fist under his nose. Until he was twelve years old his mother kept him in dresses." Hemingway described the astonishment of a group of reporters who saw the two photographs displayed in a Lausanne shop.

"They're faked," one man said. "Why he's never had a uniform on in his life."

We all looked closely at the photographs.

"Nope. They're not faked." Some one said: "I can tell. They're not faked. Let's go and ask Slocombe."

The newspapermen found George Slocombe, "the correspondent of the London *Daily Herald*, who is Tchitcherin's very good friend and sometimes his mouthpiece," sitting in the press room of the Palace Hotel. Hemingway had known the Englishman since March, when they had covered the Genoa Conference and visited Max Beerbohm. Slocombe explained that all the Soviet commissars were automatically generals in the Red Army, and that Tchitcherin had proudly ordered the uniform in Berlin. Hemingway finished the Lausanne chapter of his Near East assignment on this ironic note. "The boy who was kept in dresses until he was twelve years old always wanted to be a soldier. And soldiers make empires, and empires make wars." The assignment as a whole, extending from Constantinople in September through the Greek retreat and the Thracian refugees in October, including as it did the close contact with the conference in November, December, and January, and embracing the personal relationships with Bolitho and Steffens, was an important episode in his European apprenticeship. He had a chance to digest and assess it and a chance also to measure his reactions against another bright, inquiring mind. He and his wife went to Rapallo and spent several days with Ezra Pound.

The atmosphere was completely different from Lausanne, save for the superficial resemblance between Pound and Bolitho. It was dominated by Pound's lively energy; it included such men as Michael Strater, the artist who had recently done the drawings for Pound's first sixteen cantos, and Robert McAlmon, whose Contact Publishing Co. had published the book. The artistic and literary intensity of the colony was enlivened by such restless expatriates as Nancy Cunard. Hemingway played tennis with Pound and Strater, and he discussed writing with McAlmon, and, McAlmon remembered later, "he talked of Sherwood Anderson, Harriet Monroe, and Gertrude Stein."[29] Hemingway explained to McAlmon that most of his manuscripts had just been lost, but that he still had some short stories. McAlmon, the most active of the expatriate publishers, told Hemingway to send them to him in Paris. This was the origin of Hemingway's first published collection, *Three Stories & Ten Poems*, which McAlmon brought out later in the year.[30] From Rapallo the Hemingways went up to the Dolomites. They stayed at Cortina d'Ampezzo for several weeks. In April their skiing was interrupted by another of John Bone's cables.

# THE RUHR

"You have to keep in touch with
[history] at the time and you can
depend on just as much as you have
actually seen and followed."

ERNEST HEMINGWAY[1]

*I.*

Hemingway's assignments from John Bone became progressively more desirable throughout his tenure as the *Star*'s staff correspondent in Europe. Now, in April, 1923, he received a particularly important one. His series of articles on the French occupation of the Ruhr was the most elaborate single undertaking of the long apprenticeship which began in Oak Park, on the *Trapeze*, in 1916, and ended in Toronto on December 31, 1923. In the scope he gave to it the Ruhr series compared creditably with his newspaper work as a mature writer in Spain in 1937, in the Orient in 1941, and in England and France in 1944.[2]

Hemingway made of the Ruhr assignment a sound piece of political reporting. He went beyond Bone's conception of him as a clever feature writer whose special forte was vivid impressionism and skeptical exposure. The series was tangible evidence of his personal growth and of his responsive debt to such disparate influences as Gertrude Stein and William Bolitho. His approach and treatment retained few remnants of the provincialism that had limited the breadth of certain *Star Weekly* stories and of his report on the

Black Forest trip in August, 1922. He did more than rise
to the serious requirements of the new assignment; he had
developed sufficiently to give it dimensions John Bone had
not visualized. The managing editor, indeed, took advantage of his pre-publication reading of the first three articles
to insert some publicity in the *Star Weekly* about the forthcoming *Daily Star* series. On the same day the first dispatch
was printed there appeared in the weekend supplement a
full column called "Something About Ernest M. Hemingway, Who Is Taking the Lid Off Europe."[3] The column
included more than a dozen paragraphs, some of them dealing with the series, others discussing Hemingway's colorful
biography. Readers were urged to follow "these intensely
interesting articles."

The occupation of the Ruhr was a melancholy spectacle,
one further testimonial to the waste and failure of the war
and its treaties. Hemingway was able to make good use of
the political instruction and experience he had received at
Lausanne. He was compelled to translate Bolitho's lectures
into a working pattern of expository analysis. His basic
approach was a measure of the thoughtfulness with which
he was attempting to communicate a catastrophe whose
ramifications extended beyond the German frontiers. Hemingway did not merely catch the first train for Cologne.
He wrote in Paris three introductory articles defining the
situation and its antecedents. He explained his premise in
the opening paragraphs of his first story, datelined from the
French capital on April 3 and printed in Toronto eleven
days later.[4]

"To write about Germany," he began, "you must begin
by writing about France." This was a reminder of a quality
Miss Stein detected in him the previous year; she found him
a studious young man. His series of articles on the Franco-
German situation, as it was billed in the *Daily Star*, demonstrated a thorough, investigative quality. His first European

correspondence, in early 1922, was not unlike the material enterprising American undergraduates used to send back to their home-town newspaper during a summer trip. He was more gifted than most of the young string correspondents who wandered across the Continent in the decades between the wars, but his initial strength, like theirs, had been the ingenuous transcription of the novelties he was encountering. Now, at only twenty-three, he had become sufficiently literate to expand his facility into a larger vision without losing the freshness and without becoming ponderous in his new knowledge. "There is a magic in the name France," Hemingway continued in the opening paragraph. "It is a magic like the smell of the sea or the sight of blue hills or of soldiers marching by. It is a very old magic." His idiom and point of view were personal and imaginative. His new skills had not yet made him a journalistic hack. "France," he wrote, "is a broad and lovely country." He did not hesitate to use emotionalism. "The loveliest country that I know. It is impossible to write impartially about a country when you love it."

His tone established, Hemingway shifted to his principal theme. "But it is possible," he said, "to write impartially about the government of that country." He stated his undertaking and its genesis. "France refused in 1917 to make a peace without victory. Now she finds that she has a victory without peace. To understand why this is so we must take a look at the French government." It was in this way that Hemingway launched the series, with a few lines of evocative prose, an epigrammatic summary of the central events of the recent past, and a touch of journalistically useful didacticism. The rest of the article was a lucid resumé of the contemporary alignment of French political parties. Hemingway ended this first installment with a promise of exciting revelations. " . . . the sinister tale that is unfolding day by day in the French chamber of deputies about how Poincaré was forced into the Ruhr, against his own will and judgment, [and] the strange story of the rise of the royalists in France and their influence on the present government will be told in the next article."

The initial dispatch, like all the articles in the series, had been long and detailed, but Hemingway gave his summary of essentially stale material an illusion of fresh exposure. Less expert and glossy, it had nevertheless a kind of pre-*Time* flow and vigor, with the same oversimplification of political complexities. Its two thousand words were spread out by the *Daily Star* beneath a four-column double banner and three banks of smaller headlines. It was illustrated with a panel of five of the politicians Hemingway discussed. It was further dignified by an editorial paragraph announcing it as the first of a series and by a note at the end in which the editor paraphrased Hemingway's own last paragraph. "In the next article," the reader was told, "to be published on Wednesday next, Mr. Hemingway will describe the amazing growth and power of the Royalist party in France."

John Bone intended to handle the series as in every way a feature of his newspaper. The second article was run in the paper's most prominent position, as the lead story in page one's seventh and eighth columns.[5] Hemingway's essentially romantic temperament had responded to the apparent drama of this republican paradox of a modern royalist party. Its famous names, mysterious power, and its echoes of past glories had for expatriates something of the more remote glamor of the Stuart dynasty. Hemingway's romanticism, however, which had made the Black Forest such a disappointment to him, was in this series rarely more than one of the contributive elements in his point of view. His sense of realism allowed him to detect the uglier aspects of the royalist group. Stylistically, to be sure, his quickened sensibility was reflected in the brisk, colloquial idiom, livelier and more dramatic than the measured, academic exposition of the first article, but his systematic debunking included an attack on the royalist leader, Léon Daudet, and an implicitly hostile description of their papist coloration.

Hemingway's profile of the duc d'Orléans was less frankly unfriendly, but there was nothing in his description of the royalist claimant that made Philippe seem a well qualified candidate. "Philippe," Hemingway wrote drily, "lives in England, is a big, good looking man and rides very well to hounds." It was in his paragraphs about the party's hoodlums that Hemingway thoroughly destroyed the illusion of a gallant noble cause.

There is a royal fascisti called the Camelots du Roi. They carry black, loaded canes with salmon colored handles and at twilight you can see them in Montmartre swaggering along the streets with their canes, a little way ahead and behind a newsboy who is crying *L'Action Française* in the radical quarter of the old Butte.

Hemingway reminded his readers that French politics were unlike those of any other nation. "It is a very intimate politics, a politics of scandal." The long article, illustrated with photographs of Daudet and Philippe, and a facsimile of *L'Action Française*'s masthead, ended with Hemingway's blunt citation of a 1922 interview in which Poincaré had assured the press that France would never occupy the Ruhr. "Meantime," Hemingway concluded, without interpretive comment, "the French government has spent 160 million francs (official) on the occupation and Ruhr coal is costing France $200 a ton." Again the editor précised the next dispatch. "In the next article Mr. Hemingway will deal with the French press, telling how the papers are paid to print only what the government wants."

The third article was a natural sequel to the analysis of

the royalists, for Hemingway now made it clear that subscribers to *L'Action Française* were at least getting more than official hand-outs.[6] This was not the case with the average reader of a French paper. "What," Hemingway asked in his lead, "do the French people think about the Ruhr and the whole German question? You will not find out by reading the French press." This anomaly, by Toronto standards, was the theme of the third dispatch, which continued the bi-weekly schedule of the series; the first article had been published on a Saturday, the second on the following Wednesday, and now the discussion of the French press appeared three days later, on Saturday, April 21. Like its predecessor, it had been the subject of advance comment in the *Star Weekly*. "Did you know," a paragraph of advertisement had run, "that all European governments have a special fund for newspaper publicity that does not have to be accounted for?"[7] Like its predecessor, too, it was again the front page feature.

Hemingway's revelation for his Toronto audience was as blunt as possible. "French newspapers," he declared, "sell their news columns just as they do their advertising space." He tried to be detached in his exposition, but some cynicism was inevitable. "As a matter of fact," he wrote, "it is not considered very chic to advertise in the small advertising section of a French daily. The news item is supposed to be the only real way of advertising." Hemingway explained the process of subsidy and emphasized that the reader of every metropolitan daily found only such governmental news as the government chose to print. He applied this situation to the Ruhr occupation. "When the government has any special news . . . it pays the papers extra. If any of these enormously circulated daily papers refuses to print the government news or criticizes the government standpoint, the government withdraws their subsidy—and the paper loses its biggest advertiser. Consequently the big

Paris dailies are always for the government, any government that happens to be in."

The resumé of France's position had demonstrated his capacity for assessing and communicating a large block of material. The writing itself had never equaled the terse artistry of some of his Near East dispatches, which for the moment remained the best instances of his journalism as a technical transition toward fiction. Neither, on the other hand, had there been in these three Paris dispatches any of the excess of some of the work that preceded the Constantinople assignment. The articles indicate that he was achieving a maturity of attitude and self-control without which he would have remained merely one more talented young reporter.

Above all the articles demonstrated his understanding of and identification with a nation not his own. *The Sun Also Rises*, begun two years later, would display a calm utilization of the European background, more effective than the heady, artistically confusing sense of exoticism that blurred many American treatments of an expatriate experience. The extent of his feeling for Paris, implicit in these three articles, permitted Hemingway to write of it in his novel without a labored crescendo of repetitive discovery. Paris, he said later, "was a fine place to be quite young in and it is a necessary part of a man's education."[8] In April, 1923, his Paris education already allowed him to write of the city with restraint.

The material itself had been neither profound nor revolutionary; it was available to any observant newspaperman. The consistent fusing of observation and interest and studiousness into a well-balanced support of his talent was nevertheless an important progression. The progression was particularly noticeable when Hemingway in the subsequent installments returned to the same scenes from which eight months earlier had come the indifferent Black Forest reports.

## II.

The seven articles dealing with Germany got off to an inauspicious start. The *Daily Star* mishandled the sequence, breaking the pattern Hemingway was building. His plan had been to begin his survey of Germany with Offenburg, the southernmost limit of the French occupation. He himself followed the scheme, and his first two dispatches, the fourth and fifth of the series, were datelined from the Baden railroad town. The *Daily Star*, however, jumbled the first three German dispatches in such a way that the second Offenburg story, chronologically speaking, was printed on April 25, a story from Frankfurt appeared on the following Saturday, and the first Offenburg article, describing the trip from Paris to Strasbourg and ending as Hemingway boarded the train for Offenburg, was printed on Wednesday, May 2. The paper offered on that date a partial apology which confirms Hemingway's deliberate sequential intent.

It was merely one further professional vexation, of a kind that had been anticipated by the paper's cavalier treatment of his interviews with Mussolini and Clemenceau, and by its complaints, on another occasion, when he wrote prophetically and pessimistically about the German post-war currency.[9] The copy desk's carelessness broke the functional plan by which Hemingway was going to follow the international railway line from Offenburg to Karlsruhe to Frankfurt, on to Cologne and Düsseldorf. The plan had a neat simplicity, for the route not only carried the reader through the heart of the occupied region, but it also automatically clarified the occupation's failure. France's inability to keep the transportation artery flowing was a measure of her inability to make the occupation fruitful. Rearranged into their intended pattern, the two Offenburg dispatches give an effective picture of the process of getting to Germany and of the initial German scene.

The fourth article, indeed, employed a treatment different from the one Hemingway used in his three introductory dispatches.[10] His first responsibility had been to inform; the treatment had been objective and undramatic. Now, however, his goal was mood and atmosphere. His treatment became scenic and dramatic. It was excellent training for a fictionalist; it was an exercise in the relationship between theme and style. The article also demonstrated a narrative control which permitted Hemingway to increase the story pace toward an episodic climax whose implications remained in the reader's mind without anticlimax as the dispatch ended. Even the carefully contrived gerunds are reminders that these had been the months of his increasing association with Gertrude Stein. "In the cold, grey, street-washing, milk-delivering, shutters-coming-off-the-shops, early morning," he wrote, "the midnight train from Paris arrived in Strasbourg."

In the border town Hemingway had his first glimpse of the effects of the occupation. There were no trains running from Strasbourg into Germany. He took the tram, observing closely the pictorial quality of the scene. "There is a great deal of description," Miss Stein had said of his early work, "and not very good description." Now his description was much improved, its composition linear and immediate. "There were sharp peaked plastered houses criss-crossed with great wooden beams, the river wound and rewound through the town and each time we crossed it there were fishermen on the banks, there was the wide modern street with modern German shops with big glass show windows and new French names over their doors . . . a long stream of carts was coming in to market from the country, streets were being flushed and washed." Hemingway was trying to see each composition with a painter's vision; each new paragraph contained a central object for the eye. To this he was beginning to add tonal quality of sensation and statement.

In the stretch of country that lies between Strasbourg and the Rhine the tram track runs along a canal and a big blunt nosed barge with LUSITANIA painted on its stern was being dragged smoothly along by two horses ridden by the bargeman's two children while breakfast smoke came out of the galley chimney and the bargeman leaned against the sweep. It was a nice morning.

Hemingway was cleared by the customs inspector and walked down the road to the Kehl station. He wandered out to the track and discovered four French soldiers, "of the 170th Infantry Regiment, with full kit and fixed bayonets." The indirect dialogue was a prophecy of the slick finish he gave to *The Sun Also Rises* in 1926 through precisely the same device. "One of them told me there would be a train at 11:15 for Offenburg, a military tram; it was about half an hour to Offenburg, but this droll train would get there about two o'clock. He grinned. Monsieur was from Paris? What did monsieur think about the match Criqui-Zjawnny Kilbane? Ah. He had thought very much the same. He had always had the idea he was no fool, this Kilbane. The military service? Well, it was all the same. It made no difference where one did it. In two months now he would be through. It was a shame he was not free, perhaps we could have a talk together. Monsieur had seen this Kilbane box? The new wine was not bad at the buffet. But after all he was on guard. The buffet is straight down the corridor. If monsieur leaves the baggage here it will be all right."

Hemingway made the buffet the story's climax. Everything in the dispatch had been a preparation for this. There was a neat balance by which the waiter became the major character, supplemented by the tableau-like figures who drifted in and out of the restaurant. Hemingway did not reproduce with dull fidelity all the scene or its speech; his selective condensation was completely a device of the short story rather than the conventional feature article. It is the technique as well as the milieu which remind us of so many of the episodes and structures of his early fiction.

In the buffet was a sad-looking waiter in a dirty shirt . . . a long bar and two forty-year-old French second lieutenants sitting at a table in the corner. I bowed as I entered, and they both saluted.

"No," the waiter said, "there is no milk. You can have black coffee, but it is ersatz coffee. The beer is good."

The waiter sat down at the table. "No, there is no one here now," he said. "All the people you say you saw in July cannot come now. The French will not give them passports to come into Germany."

"How do they get along with the French here in town?"

"No trouble. They are good people. Just like us. Some of them are nasty sometimes, but they are good people. Nobody hates, except profiteers. They had something to lose. We haven't had any fun since 1914. If you make any money it gets no good, and there is only to spend it. That is what we do. Some day it will be over. I don't know how. Last year I had enough money saved up to buy a gasthaus in Hernberg; now that money wouldn't buy four bottles of champagne."

Hemingway preserved the scene's strength by ending the dispatch quickly, but without an abruptness that would have thrown the buffet vignette out of focus. "There was a shrill peep of a whistle outside. I paid and shook hands with the waiter, saluted the two forty-year-old second lieutenants, who were now playing checkers at their table, and went out to take the military train to Offenburg."

The fifth article picked up this narrative thread with easy consistency.[11] "Offenburg," his lead began, "is the southern limit of the French occupation of Germany. It is a clean, neat little town with the hills of the Black Forest rising on one side and the Rhine plain stretching off on the other." Hemingway was impressed by the calm solidarity of the German resistance. He had talked to many natives; he reproduced these conversations in his dispatches without any of the earlier, Black Forest series' arch references to his awkward German. They had all told him of their personal debt to the government, which supported the unemployed with public funds. He hitch-hiked from Offenburg to Ortenberg, where there was a north-bound train service. The article's final passage was an account of the ride he got on a motor truck.

His treatment here had the same forcefully creative quality that had distinguished the initial Offenburg dispatch. Detached from the long expository introduction about the railroad problem, these paragraphs were a self-sufficient sketch, five or six hundred words of the narrative and portraiture he later achieved in such early published vignettes as "The Revolutionist." The opening paragraph was blunt and careful, wholly in the structural idiom of his later fiction. "The driver was a short, blonde German with sunken cheeks and faded blue eyes. He had been badly gassed at the Somme. We were riding along a white, dusty road through green fields forested with hop poles, their tangled wires flopping. We crossed a wide, swift, clearly pebbled stream with a flock of geese resting on a gravel island. A manure spreader was busily clicking in the field. In the distance were the blue Schwartzwald hills." There was no break between these opening lines of the sketch and its immediate extension by authentic, stylized paragraphs of unadorned, functional dialogue.

"My brother," said the driver, guiding the big wheel with one arm half wrapped around it. "He had hard luck."

"So?"

"Ja. He never had no luck, my brother."

"What was he doing?"

"He was signal man on the railroad from Kehl. The French put him out. All the signal men. The day they came to Offenburg, they gave them all twenty-four hours."

"But the government pays him, doesn't it?"

"Oh yes. They pay him. But he can't live on it."

"What's the matter?"

"Well, he's got seven kids. . . . They pay him what he got, but the prices are up and where he was signal man he had a little garden. It makes a difference when you got a garden."

"What's he do now?" I asked.

"He tried working in the sawmill at Hausach, but he can't work good inside. He's got the gas like me. Ja. He's got no luck, my brother."

Taken together in this way, with the sketches and vignettes isolated from the firm but conventional exposition, the two Offenburg articles represented a new creativity in Hemingway's journalism. His apprenticeship was nearly completed; certainly it was entering its final phase. He was beginning to be able to do occasionally, even under the inhibitions of his journalistic medium, what he would soon do with regularity in the steady production of short stories during the first few years of his professional career.

That his apprenticeship was not wholly completed, however, was demonstrated by the sixth German dispatch.[12] Datelined from Frankfurt-on-Main, and designed to follow the second Offenburg article, it was not in any way the equal of its pair of predecessors. The *Trapeze*-style wit was full of condescension for his audience, his talent, and his material. The tone itself was in many ways a return to the juvenile belligerence of his 1922 Black Forest series. The idiom and point of view, as well as the careless style and structure, had the same glib facility and the broad, spoiled wit.

Then we talked about the war. I asked the [brave Belgian] lady if she had been in Belgium during the occupation.

"Yes," she said.

"How was it? Pretty bad?" I asked.

The B.B. lady snorted, her most powerful Belgian snort. "I did not suffer at all."

I believe her. In fact, having traveled with the brave Belgian lady, I am greatly surprised and unable to understand how the Germans ever got into Belgium at all.

The seventh dispatch, mailed from Mainz on April 22, was more reassuring.[13] It established that the quality of the Offenburg articles had not been a fluke. The opening section was mainly expository. Hemingway used a cross-section survey to vivify and document the impact of inflation upon the German people. He described the night he spent in a luxury hotel, in order to "investigate how the profiteers lived," and he recounted too the fluctuations of prices from town to town along his route. During the previous week, "investigating the actual living conditions," he had talked to a small factory owner, several workmen, a hotel keeper, and a high school professor. He recorded a long paragraph of dialogue from the first three citizen-groups, but his strongest emphasis was on the teacher.

There were three paragraphs of detailed and informative

speech by the white collar representative, paralleling those by the other witnesses; then, in the closing lines of the dispatch, Hemingway once again became the creative writer rather than the journalist. The final section was another of the notable internal sketches he began in Kehl.

"But how will it all come out?" I asked him.

"We can only trust in God," he said. Then he smiled. "We used to trust in God and the government, we Germans. Now I no longer trust the government."

"I heard you playing very beautifully on the flute when I came to the door," I said, rising to go.

"You know the flute? You like the flute? I will play for you."

So we sat in the dusk in the ugly little parlor and the schoolmaster played very beautifully on the flute. Outside people were going by in the main street of the town. The children came in silently and sat down. After a time the schoolmaster stopped and stood up very embarrassedly.

"It is a very nice instrument, the flute," he said.

Hemingway mailed his next dispatch from Cologne, five days later.[14] The *Daily Star* printed it on May 9, still maintaining the Wednesday-Saturday cycle of publication. The article contained none of the careful, semi-fictional vignettes that were making the series so clearly a transitional step toward his creative work, but, at the same time, it was an expository enlargement of the sketch about the high school professor. There was real distress in Hemingway's reaction to the acute suffering which accompanied inflation; it reaffirmed the fact that a basis of the evocative sketches was his new capacity to respond without restrictive prejudice.

"There are no beggars," he wrote. "No horrible examples on view. No visible famine sufferers nor hungry children that besiege the railway stations." Hemingway stressed this paradox of national well being. "The tourist leaves Germany," he maintained, "wondering what all this starving business is about. The country looks prosperous." He bluntly stated the reality. "For every ten professional beggars in Italy," he wrote bitterly, "there are a hundred amateur starvers in Germany." He defined this poignant conception. "An amateur starver does not starve in public." As the dispatch ended, the briefest of the series, Hemingway's newly powerful impulse toward artistic composition displayed itself tentatively. "In the evening," he noted, "the brilliant red or the dark blue of the officer's formal mess kit that is compulsory for those officers who dine in Cologne, colors the drab civilian crowds. Outside in the street German children dance on the pavement to the music that comes from the windows of the ball room of the officers' club."

This vestige of the Offenburg and Mainz sketches was the final appearance of any memorable writing in the series. As always during his newspaper career, Hemingway's best effects depended on the extent of his response to his material; the response was given with increasing reluctance, and it invariably perished quickly. His ninth article illustrated this process.[15] His instinct for a provocative approach was shown by his resumption of the theme of hatred in the occupied zone; his artistic numbness restricted him to an expository investigation of the tension. The lead was a promise of further vignettes. "You feel the hate in the Ruhr," he began, "as an actual concrete thing. It is as definite as the unswept, cinder-covered sidewalks of Düsseldorf or the long rows of grimy brick cottages, each one exactly like the next, where the workmen of Essen live." He never clothed this theme, however, with anything but straightforward documentation through standard, undramatized anecdote and political analysis. Once, briefly, when he had been describing the momentary German unity in the first days of the French occupation, he seemed on the verge of something creative.

"It was most uplifting," an old German woman told me. "You should have been here. Never have I been so uplifted since the great days of the victories. Oh, how they sang. Ach, it was wonderful."

Hemingway stopped there, returning to his conventional account of the large outlines of the situation. He could visualize sketches and vignettes in the material, as it were, but he lacked the impulse to attempt any more creative fragments. He was already anticipating and preparing for the end of the series. He began to curve the material back toward France and the themes of his three introductory articles. "The end of the Ruhr venture," he concluded, "looks very near."

The final dispatch of the series, as well as the manner of its publication, testified with painful clarity to Hemingway's loss of interest in the assignment.[16] John Bone had been able to promise and maintain the Wednesday-Saturday cycle of publication only as long as Hemingway mailed the articles regularly. When the managing editor printed the ninth dispatch, however, on Saturday, May 12, he could not pledge, as before, that its sequel would appear on the following Wednesday. He hadn't received it. Bone could merely assert that "the tenth will be published in a few days."[17] When the tenth article did arrive in Toronto, date-lined from Düsseldorf on May 5, Bone printed it promptly and was able to preserve the bi-weekly sequence. Again, however, he had no assurance to its successor, for the prefatory note on May 16 simply said once more that "the next will be published in a few days."[18] At this point Hemingway suddenly wound up the assignment; no further articles were printed, although Bone clearly anticipated at least an eleventh story.

The last dispatch, therefore, was not a clear-cut terminal article. It had the same aura of imminent completion as the first Düsseldorf story, but there was no deliberate summation. As before, Hemingway continued to see the material in terms of dramatic sketches; as before, he never permitted them to materialize. Some of his paragraphs, as he left the Ruhr assignment, were virtually a first draft of what he was visualizing, reminders again that his apprenticeship was ending, and containing all the elements of brief, effective vignettes save final execution.

Hiking along the road that runs through the dreary brick outskirts of Düsseldorf out into the pleasant open country that rolls in green swells patched with timber between the smoky towns of the Ruhr, you pass slow-moving French ammunition carts, the horses led by short, blue-uniformed, quiet-faced Chinamen, their tin hats on the back of their heads. . . . French cavalry patrols ride by. Two broad-faced Westphalian iron puddlers who are sitting under a tree and drawing their unemployment pay watch the cavalry out of sight around a bend of the road.

I borrowed a match from one of the iron puddlers. They are Westphalians, hard-headed, hard-muscled, uncivil and friendly. They want to go snipe shooting. The snipe have just come with the spring, but they haven't any shot guns. They laugh at the little Indo-Chinamen with their ridiculous big, blue helmets on the back of their heads and they applaud one little Annamite who has gotten way behind the column and is trotting along to catch up, holding his horse's bridle, sweat running down his face, his helmet joggling down over his eyes. The little Annamite smiles happily.

*III.*

Hemingway left Germany as soon as he had mailed that tenth dispatch. He had spent six weeks on the assignment and written almost twenty thousand words. As journalism, his treatment had been invariably competent, occasionally excellent; as prose, the treatment had been frequently provocative and in several instances so good as to make certain dispatches memorable. He had shown genuine vocational dexterity, handling with poise an assignment that could have developed in a cheap and hackneyed pattern.

For the first time, too, his newspaper writing could be accurately described as an undeniable indication of his talent and development as a creative writer. In spite of its ambiguous conclusion, the series confirmed and enlarged the managing editor's regard for him. "An important addition even to the Lloyd George articles," one of the blurbs had said, referring to a current series by the former prime minister, "are those by Hemingway, who is well known to thousands of *Daily Star* readers. His close-up pictures of Mussolini and Tchitcherin, his despatches from Genoa, Constantinople, and Rapallo, where he was sent by The *Star*, were followed by [sic] intense interest."[19]

John Bone had printed six of the ten articles on the front page of the *Daily Star*. Three of the remaining four appeared on the important page one of the second section, and the other, the initial dispatch of the series, was published on page four of the first section. None of the stories had been buried in the back pages. Most of them were illustrated, and they had all been both by-lined and copyrighted. The material had been consistently featured during a six-week period by a metropolitan daily. The advertisements had stressed the reporter and his talents as much as the contents of the series itself. "Hemingway," according to one of *Star Weekly*'s paragraphs, "has not only a genius for newspaper work, but for the short story as well. He is an extraordinarily gifted and picturesque writer." The next line was ironic in its implication that Hemingway preferred to reserve his energy for his Toronto journalism. "Besides his despatches for The *Star*, he writes very little else, only two or three stories a year."[20]

The *Star Weekly* might have added, however, that the material profit from the German series would now enable Hemingway to write more fiction than had been previously possible. A month generally elapsed between the time when the young American filed an expense account and the moment when the *Star*'s check arrived in Paris. By the middle of June, 1923, therefore, Hemingway was sufficiently secure so that he did no further journalism that summer. He went from Germany directly back to the Dolomites, where he had left his wife, and they returned together to Paris. Hemingway spent the next ten weeks on his own work. The writing which he resumed and completed during June and July of 1923, particularly the second project he undertook, was wholly natural in the light of what he had occasionally experimented with in the German dispatches. While he was correcting the proofs of *Three Stories & Ten Poems*, he prepared for publication the vignettes of *in our time*.

# CHAPTER

## XI

# *PARIS*

"Fame was what they wanted in that town."
ARCHIBALD MACLEISH[1]

*I.*

Hemingway encountered most of the significant experiences of his personal and professional life before he was twenty-five years old. None of these experiences was unique in a man so young; as a cluster of episodes, however, they were premature, and pertinent in terms of the early maturity of his style and literary attitudes. He was barely eighteen when he began his vocation. He was not yet nineteen when he was severely wounded in the war. At nineteen he was the victim of an acutely unhappy love affair. He was married at twenty-two, a father two years later. He was a foreign correspondent when he was twenty-two, and a month after his twenty-fourth birthday, in August, 1923, he received his first major publication as a creative writer.

For Hemingway publication had a significance beyond the conventional connotations of acceptance and recognition. It hastened the abandonment of intrusive journalism. It confirmed his talent; this was of special importance to a temperament as competitive as his. Most important of all, publication allowed Hemingway to complete his apprenticeship and initiate the proper beginnings of his artistic career. "I am glad to have it out," he wrote Edmund Wilson in November, 1923, three months after the appearance of *Three Stories & Ten Poems*, "and once it is published it is back of you."[2]

The comment was precociously acute. Hemingway's life and work have been deliberately and severely compartmentalized, displaying a chapter-like development that has required the specific emergence from one period as a prelude to entrance into its successor. "In writing," he said many years later, during what he regarded as just such a completion and inaugural, "I have moved through arithmetic, through plane geometry and algebra, and now I am in calculus."[3] He could not commence the phase of his work which began in the summer of 1925 with the writing of *The Sun Also Rises* until he had completed the material which had its origins in his journalism and in his associations with Anderson, Gertrude Stein, and Ezra Pound. This material, the finale of his newspaper career and the initial compartment of his formal artistic life, included *Three Stories & Ten Poems*, *in our time*, *In Our Time*, and *The Torrents of Spring*. Hemingway himself has dated his work as beginning with *Three Stories & Ten Poems*. "The only work of mine that I endorse or sign as my true work," he said in 1951, "is what I have published since *Three Stories & Ten Poems* and the first *In Our Time*." It was an auspicious beginning.

The sequence of these two expatriate pamphlets, however, was not as had been planned. *in our time*, which differed from the 1925 *In Our Time* in that it contained only the brief vignettes which function as inter-chapters between the short stories of *In Our Time*, was originally scheduled to be published before the stories and verse, "but," Hemingway once explained, "being hand printed at Bill Bird's press and he having plenty of other things to do, it was delayed until 1924."[4] *Three Stories & Ten Poems* therefore became Hemingway's first volume.[5] Advance copies were ready by the middle of August, 1923, printed in Dijon and published by Robert McAlmon's Contact Publishing Company. Hemingway was pleased to be part of a series of books by such expatriates as Marsden Hartley, Mina Loy, and William Carlos Williams. He sent a copy to his family in Oak Park and another to Bill Horne, and when he got to Toronto in September, 1923, he gave several to his friends on the *Star*. The copy he presented to Gertrude Stein and Alice Toklas was inscribed to them "with love from Hemingway." Miss Stein told Hemingway in the fall of 1923 that she had written a review of *Three Stories & Ten Poems*, but the notice never appeared.[6]

Edmund Wilson, however, published a joint review of it and *in our time* in the *Dial* the next year.[7] Hemingway thus had the good fortune to receive his first American comment from a critic who continued to be one of his most sensitive interpreters. Wilson felt that *in our time* was "the more important book." Most of his review was devoted to its vignettes and sketches. He had little to say about the three short stories in *Three Stories & Ten Poems*, save to outline the relationship between Anderson, Hemingway, and Gertrude Stein. As for the verse, Wilson concluded that "Mr. Hemingway's poems are not particularly important."[8]

Hemingway himself said nothing about the poetry in his correspondence with Wilson in the fall of 1923, nor has he ever commented in detail on his own verse or on poetry in general. He has written many introductions to volumes of prose, but never to a book of verse. On the basis of casual statements his attitude seems to be the responsible, Poundian one that good poetry is as important as good prose, but even more rare, and that on the whole most poetry is written without the concentration it requires, and whose absence is more easily detectable in prose. Hemingway has enunciated his own taste in contemporary verse by his positive response to the verse of T.S. Eliot and Ezra Pound. "All of Eliot's poems are perfect," Hemingway wrote in 1925, "and there are very few of them. He has a very fine talent and he is very careful of it. He never takes chances with it and it is doing very well thank you."[9] He went on to declare that Pound, on the other hand, was a major poet. "A damned good poet," Hemingway said of Eliot, many years later, "and a fair critic, but he would not have existed except for dear old Ezra, the lovely poet and stupid traitor."[10]

It was from Ezra Pound's edicts about imagism, in fact, and from their application to his own verse, that Hemingway profited most strongly from the exercise of writing poetry.[11] He employed the same intensely concentrated pattern that he would use in the more important prose exercises of *in our time*. If Hemingway lacked a capacity for deeply sustained, original poetic expression, there was no doubt of his gift for the forceful enunciation of emotion and, above all, absorbing narrative. The best of the poems in *Three Stories & Ten Poems*[12]—particularly "Along with Youth," "Oklahoma," and "Montparnasse"—were sharp and focused, with everything emerging from a minutely examined object. His poems, like the vignettes and sketches of *in our time*, were a final exercise in the completion of an apprenticeship that was rooted in journalism but was now growing beyond it.

## II.

It was *in our time*—done, after all, in the prose medium for which its author had been training—that demonstrated most clearly Hemingway's progress as a writer. Although the book was not published until the next year, in March, 1924, *in our time* was written, like the poems and the three short stories, during the first European period of 1922 and

1923.[13] The vignettes were a blueprint of what Hemingway was attempting stylistically and a definition of the attitudes he was forming about his experiences. There has frequently been an attempt to endow the vignettes either with a biographical sequence or with a sketch-by-sketch relationship to the short stories among which they were ultimately placed in *In Our Time* in 1925. The effect of these distortions is to belittle Hemingway's intention and achievement in the vignettes.

The sketches do not preserve an accurate chronology of Hemingway's personal life. Their only chronology is the chronology in which they were written. A vignette derived from Kansas City is placed after vignettes drawn from the war and from European newspaper work; bullfighting sketches, based upon episodes observed in Spain in 1922 and 1923, precede the sketch of Nick Adams being wounded in Italy in 1918. When Louis Cohn was preparing the first substantial Hemingway bibliography, in 1931, he discussed a number of such questions with his friend. "The chapters [i.e., vignettes]," Cohn reported, "are to be considered as separate entities."[14] When Hemingway wrote them in Europe in 1923 he was using them as tools of self-instruction. "I was trying to write then," he said in 1932, "and I found the greatest difficulty, aside from knowing truly what you felt, rather than what you were supposed to feel, and had been taught to feel, was to put down what really happened in action; what the actual things were which produced the emotion that you experienced."[15] He also declared, on that same occasion, that he had been interested in "life and death . . . commencing with the simplest things." Hemingway cited specific illustrations of what he meant by "these very simple things": " . . . in the case of an execution by a firing squad," he explained, "or a hanging. . . ."

When he discussed his apprenticeship in *Death in the*

*Afternoon* in 1932, in other words, he was talking explicitly about the vignettes of *in our time*. The vignettes were, quite literally, composed, and with painful, artistically instructive care. Furthermore, rearranged into basic groups—war, bullfighting, journalism—they simultaneously demonstrate the development of Hemingway's fundamental themes and attitudes. The balance between the three sets of experience was an exact one: six sketches dealt with war, six with bullfighting, and six with newspaper experiences. The latter are in certain ways the most significant of the sketches. In two instances Hemingway's initial treatment of the material is available as a Toronto *Star* dispatch. The cycle of his compositional process can thus be followed through three drafts: newspaper dispatch; publication in the *Little Review* in April, 1923[16]; and final revision in the summer of 1923 for *in our time*.

### III.

The first version of "chapter 3" of *in our time* was cabled to Toronto from Adrianople on October 20, 1922.[17] A revision was published as the third of the *Little Review* series in April, 1923. The final draft which Hemingway gave to Bill Bird for *in our time* was completely declarative.

Minarets stuck up in the rain out of Adrianople across the mud flats. The carts were jammed for thirty miles along the Karagatch road. Water buffalo and cattle were hauling carts through the mud. No end and no beginning. Just carts loaded with everything they owned. The old men and women, soaked through, walked along keeping the cattle moving. The Maritza was running yellow almost up to the bridge. Carts were jammed solid on the bridge with camels bobbing along through them. Greek cavalry herded along the procession. Women and kids were in the carts crouched with mattresses, mirrors, sewing machines, bundles. There was a woman having a kid with a young girl holding a blanket over her and crying. Scared sick looking at it. It rained all through the evacuation.

The 1922 cable, although it had many points of likeness with the finished vignette, differed from it in several important respects. Its last two paragraphs were general ones, describing the relief agencies that were operating in Thrace. These paragraphs had no validity for the re-drafting of the dispatch into the vignette; none of the material appears in the second, *Little Review* draft, or in the final, *in our time* version. The cable's first three paragraphs, however, do constitute that first draft.

In a never-ending, staggering march the Christian population of Eastern Thrace is jamming the roads towards Macedonia. The main column crossing the Maritza River at Adrianople is twenty miles long. Twenty miles of carts drawn by cows, bullocks and muddy-flanked water buffalo, with exhausted, staggering men, women and children, blankets over their heads, walking blindly in the rain beside their worldly goods.

This main stream is being swelled from all the back country. They don't know where they are going. They left their farms, villages and ripe, brown fields and joined the main stream of refugees when they heard the Turk was coming. Now they can only keep their places in the ghastly procession while mud-splashed Greek cavalry herd them along like cow-punchers driving steers.

It is a silent procession. Nobody even grunts. It is all they can do to keep moving. Their brilliant peasant costumes are soaked and draggled. Chickens dangle by their feet from the carts. Calves nuzzle at the draught cattle wherever a jam halts the stream. An old man marches bent under a young pig, a scythe and a gun, with a chicken tied to his scythe. A husband spreads a blanket over a woman in labor in one of the carts to keep off the driving rain. She is the only person making a sound. Her little daughter looks at her in horror and begins to cry. And the procession keeps moving.

The three paragraphs for the *Daily Star* were more than competent journalism. They were well-written by any standards. This was the cable which so impressed Lincoln Steffens, when Hemingway showed it to him at Lausanne in December, 1922. When Steffens wrote about the incident almost ten years later, in his autobiography, he even used some of Hemingway's own words. Steffens remembered the story as "a short but vivid, detailed picture of what [Hemingway] had seen in that miserable stream of hungry, frightened, uprooted people."[18] Steffens inevitably recalled the story in terms of adjectives; Hemingway had used a variety of modifiers in the cable. The process of redrafting began here.

Save for such virtually corporate words as "thirty," "mud," and "Greek," the *in our time* vignette contained only ten legitimate adjectives: *no*, used twice, *loaded*, *old*, *yellow*, *soaked*, *solid*, *young*, *scared*, and *sick*. Three were participles, and the twice-employed "no" was not a conventional descriptive adjective. Hemingway relied in the final draft on four basic modifiers, *old*, *yellow*, *young*, and *sick*. This was in sharp contrast to the cabled first draft, where, sharp and clear as he made it, he nevertheless used almost thirty adjectives. He relied there on compound modifiers such as "never-ending," "muddy-flanked," and "mud-splashed." He used such adjectival sequences as "exhausted, staggering," and "ripe, brown." He used such familiar modifiers as "worldly goods," and pejorative adjectives like "ghastly." This was one of the devices Hemingway had in mind when he spoke later of the limitations of journalism. "In writing for a newspaper," he declared in 1932, "you told what happened and, with one trick and another, you communicated the emotion aided by the element of timeliness which gives a certain emotion to any account of something that has happened on that day."[19]

There were other tricks which the necessities of deadlines and hasty readers compelled a reporter to rely on. Hemingway's best journalism, of which the Adrianople cable was an example, used the tricks sparingly, but they could not be concealed. "If a writer of prose knows enough about what he is writing about," Hemingway said in 1932, "he may omit things that he knows and the reader, if the writer is writing truly enough, will have a feeling of those things as strongly as though the writer had stated them. The dignity of movement of an ice-berg is due to only one-eighth of it being above water."[20] In newspaper writing, however, most of the effects had to be well above the surface; none of them could be totally submerged.

The 1922 cable, for example, was directed for the reader by a series of comments from the author. "They don't know where they are going," Hemingway had written of the refugees. He was deliberately shaping the reader's response as a supplement to the overt impact of the scene he was describing. He continued the prodding when he told his Toronto audience that "now they can only keep their places." "It is all they can do to keep moving," he added later. Even the most obtuse reader would sense the tragedy, but the dimension which Hemingway later termed the architectural element of writing was necessarily lost by this reportorial steering. There was additional, less direct commentary to guide the newspaper reader. When Hemingway wrote of the "brilliant peasant costumes," now become "soaked and draggled," he was also pushing his audience toward a reaction. Phrases such as "to keep off the driving rain" and "in horror" were equally pejorative, designed to get through quickly to readers who ran while they read.

All of this relatively heavy shaping was cleansed from the vignettes. The ultimate effect became proportionately more forceful by virtue of the new understatement and compression. In the *in our time* draft the reader's horror was far greater because he seemed to be reaching his own conclusions. The sketch was also made more evocative, at a subtler level, by the new image Hemingway introduced. The metaphor of the cable was both strong and familiar. Hemingway had enforced it by the most direct exposition. "Now they can only keep their places in the ghastly procession," he cabled, "while mud-splashed Greek cavalry herd them along like cow-punchers driving steers." The grim likeness between the procession and a cattle drive is retained in the vignette, but it has ceased to be the central image. In a direct way it survives only in the verb of the ninth sentence. In the second draft, in fact, for the *Little Review*, Hemingway eliminated "herded" altogether. His substitution of "rode hard on" did not satisfy him. It was too explicit.

That momentary choice, however, did contain an element of the new image—driftwood, or, even more precise, the log floats Hemingway had seen all through his boyhood in northern Michigan. He re-emphasized the verb "jammed," used only once in the cable. The reference to the camels is an entirely new one, particularly important because it permitted the introduction of the gerund "bobbing." Gerunds, indeed, had a new importance in the vignette. The form, with all its utility for the communication of movement and flow, occurs ten times in the sketch. Approximately one out of every thirteen words was now a gerund. Not content with this emphasis, nor with the exhaustive revision as a whole, Hemingway inserted an additional, eleventh gerund when the vignette was republished in 1925 in *In Our Time;* in the sixth sentence he changed "walked" to "walking."[21]

The effect of the driftwood image was to vivify the paragraph. The equation with a log jam is fresher and more denotative than the cattle metaphor. The procession is still moving forward, as in the cable, but its progress is even more sluggish; it is resisted, as a log jam is resisted, by its own pressure. The frame within which the scene is held has been altered to fit the new image. An artist in the best of his journalism, Hemingway had bound the cable by the procession metaphor. "In a never-ending, staggering march," he had cabled in the first line, "the Christian population of Eastern Thrace is jamming the roads towards Macedonia." The last sentence of the first draft had knotted the image. "And the procession," he concluded in 1922, "keeps moving."

For the second, *Little Review* draft, the frame was completely remade. The first line of the vignette not only states the image and introduces the frame, as had been done in the cable, but also initiates the affirmation of the image. "Minarets," the sketch begins, "stuck up in the rain out of Adrianople across the mud flats." As the reader moves into the paragraph, the minarets become the long poles which are scattered upright along the path of a log run. Throughout the body of the sketch there is a constant emphasis and restatement of the saturated, almost submerged quality of the scene. The water-logged immobility is in every line. "It rained," the vignette ends, "all through the evaluation."

This was not the last step in the process of revision. The compositional structure of the cable had been primarily one of paragraphs and cumulative effect. The second and third drafts became exercises in directional composition, more subtle than the adjectival steering of the cable. It was a prelude of the pictorial device that would be tested in an occasional Ruhr dispatch in April and May of 1923. "Chapter 3" of *in our time* is dominated by two figures who had been merely part of the crowded scene in the *Daily Star* cable. The woman in labor, and her weeping daughter, are no longer details in the panoramic sweep of cavalry, an old man, cows, water buffalo, carts, a husband, men, women, children, calves, a young pig. Hemingway has drawn the woman and her child out of the procession and made them the central object. Were the vignette an etching, they would be in a lower corner, the procession behind and around them, illuminated by the story which is told in the faces and positions of these two victims. This was the Goya-like quality Hemingway deliberately sought to inject into the vignettes of *in our time;* a large, incomprehensible human tragedy was vivified by the episode within it. The husband did not survive the rewriting. Now the weight of our response falls upon the young girl, and the horror of her situation is thereby magnified. There is not even a father to shield her.

Such a deletion was a functional pruning of the same kind which persuaded Hemingway to rearrange in each draft the pitiful list of possessions the refugees clutched. In the cable he used the phrase "worldly goods," stale and unevocative, supplemented by the entire third paragraph's precise catalogue. For the *Little Review* all this excessive clutter was reduced to a single sentence. "Women and kids were in the carts crouched with mattresses, mirrors, sewing machines, bundles, sacks of things." In the final draft for *in our time*, still anxious to eliminate the unspecific, Hemingway erased "sacks of things." The possessions were the more poignant by their specific meagerness.[22]

The transformation of experience into final draft had been a complicated process, extending over a period of several months and marked by absorption so scrupulous that as late as 1930, when Scribner's republished *In Our Time*, Hemingway continued to make revisions in the vignette. At that time he repressed the surviving cabelese by inserting "There was" in the fourth sentence. He added a comma in the tenth line after "carts," and, still preoccupied with pictorial composition, he described the woman in labor as having a "baby" rather than a "kid."

This concern with precision was much more than a characteristic of youthful intensity or expatriate craftsmanship. It has continued all through Hemingway's mature work, a persistent reflex dictated by his own artistic demands. A Hemingway manuscript is a facsimile of the three drafts of "chapter 3" of *in our time*, adjectives crossed out, more precise modifiers inserted above the erasures, punctuation meticulously altered to give weight to key words, good verbs replaced by better ones. The vignettes of *in our time*, made possible by both the demands and the inadequacies of newspaper work, are the solid base of Hemingway's work.

*IV.*

None of the other five newspaper vignettes is as compositionally instructive as the sketch of the refugee procession. Each of them, however, reaffirms the debt to journalism and to Paris tutorials. The scenes Hemingway chose were characteristic of the world into which he had thrust himself as a police reporter and war correspondent, violent and brutish, but invariably made complex and significant by some private gesture or act within the scene.

"Chapter 6" was the last of the six *Little Review* vignettes. It was also the only one which survived intact the transcription from magazine to book. Hemingway made no revisions in it either in the summer of 1923 or later when he was preparing it for *In Our Time* in 1924. It was a flawless rendition into a creative paragraph of the cabelese he had so admired in journalism and of the blunt declaration he had been absorbing from Sherwood Anderson and Gertrude Stein. Its limitation derived from this same rigidity of syntax. The paragraph is without variation of rhetoric or level; verb followed subject in each of the eleven sentences with the dull perfection of a military ritual.

They shot the six cabinet ministers at half-past six in the morning against the wall of a hospital. There were pools of water in the courtyard. There were wet dead leaves on the paving of the courtyard. It rained hard. All the shutters of the hospital were nailed shut. One of the ministers was sick with typhoid. Two soldiers carried him downstairs and out into the rain. They tried to hold him up against the wall but he sat down in a puddle of water. The other five stood very quietly against the wall. Finally the officer told the soldiers it was no good trying to make him stand up. When they fired the first volley he was sitting down in the water with his head on his knees.

Like the refugee vignette, "chapter 6" derived from Hemingway's 1922 assignment in the Near East. It had not been observed, however, nor had it been sifted through the draft of a dispatch to the *Daily Star*. Hemingway had been back in Europe for a month by the time the six Greek ministers were shot in Athens on November 28, 1922. In Paris, however, Hemingway again encountered an American movie cameraman whom he first met at Madame Marie's in Adrianople in October. Shorty Wornall brought him up to date on what took place after Hemingway's departure from the area. Hemingway was attempting in "chapter 6" to reproduce not only the execution scene which Shorty described to him, but also the film operator's idiom. There is a distinct parallel between the diction of the vignette and the lines Shorty had spoken in one of Hemingway's *Daily Star* dispatches.

"Got some swell shots of a burning village to-day."
Shorty pulled off a boot. "Good show—a burning village.
Like kickin' over an ant hill. Shorty pulled off the other
boot. "Shoot it from two or three directions and it looks
like a regular town on fire. Gee I'm tired. This refugee
business is hell all right. Man sure sees some awful things
in this country." In two minutes he was snoring.[23]

Such a dialogue utilization of the vignette was completely consistent. Hemingway employed several of the *in
our time* sketches for that kind of exercise in capturing a
particular voice. The two Mons vignettes, "chapter 4" and
"chapter 5," were drawn directly from post-war conversations with his friend Dorman-Smith, the professional English soldier whom he had first met in Milan in November,
1918. The clipped, upper-class diction of Sandhurst was
unmistakable and deliberate. A similar emphasis on a specific idiom occurred in "chapter 2." Hemingway clearly
intended the idiom of its narrator to be a vulgar, relatively
unliterate one. The vocabulary is as limited as that of an
English regular army officer, but in an entirely different
way. It is the colloquial one of an American city dweller.
The language has the alternating vagueness and clarity of
urban, lower-class speech. The matador "got" the horn
through his sword hand; he holds one hand "tight" against
the "place"; badly injured, the matador is said to get up
"like crazy drunk," and tries to "slug" the men. The bullfighter is a "kid." The narrator's language is functionally
ungrammatical; the bullfighter "couldn't hardly" lift his
arm. In the last line of the *Little Review* version the narrator
says that "the crowd come down the barrera into the bull
ring." One of the first fluent interpreters of bullfighting
whom Hemingway encountered in Spain, in fact, was just
such an American as the idiom of "chapter 2" characterized.
He sat next to Hemingway and Mike Strater all afternoon,

and they listened to him again that night in a little Madrid restaurant. Hemingway described him and his idiom in a 1923 article for the *Star Weekly*.[24]

Most of the vignettes, however, were primarily concerned with the compositional reproduction of scene and emotion. The voice of the narrator was generally more anonymous than in such sketches as the Mons paragraphs and "chapter 2" and "chapter 6." A more characteristic treatment, in which Hemingway practiced declarative narration and ironic omission of comment, occurred in "chapter 17." The scene was an American version of the execution of the Greek ministers. Unlike the source of "chapter 6," it had been closely observed by Hemingway in Kansas City five years earlier. Sam Cardinella was hung in 1918 in the old Jackson County jail at the corner of Missouri Avenue and Oak Street. Hemingway's description of the jail and its execution routine was scrupulously accurate. Like the vignette of the Greek firing squad, this one has a bleak aura of human triviality which is as reminiscent of Goya as the violent scenes themselves. The anti-clerical quality is particularly noticeable; Goya's Spanish priests seldom have less dignity than the American priest whom Hemingway deflates with the single verb, "skipped." When he revised the vignette in 1924 for *In Our Time*, Hemingway inserted another ironic, Goya-like detail. To the next to the last sentence, after "chair," he added the sardonic phrase, "holding up a little crucifix."

"Chapter 18," the last vignette of *in our time*, provides a different sequence of manuscript drafts. In "chapter 3" the chronology of revision had led in a normal way from Adrianople cable to magazine publication to book form. Here the process was reversed. In September, 1923, several months after he had completed the manuscript of *in our time*, Hemingway was back in Toronto, hard pushed to manufacture feature material for the *Star Weekly*. His first articles, quite naturally, drew heavily upon the expatriate experience he had so recently, and regretfully, left. One of the earliest of these articles, published in Toronto on September 15, 1923, was a long account of European royalty, partially derived, once again, from conversations in Paris with Shorty, the American movie cameraman.[25]

In these paragraphs of 1923 journalism Hemingway did little more than reproduce with accuracy and wit the actual conversation in Paris between himself and the American cameraman. A good feature writer, he was content to exploit the easy possibilities of a situation which was tailored for Sunday supplement treatment. His only deliberate manipulation of the structure, aside from the vaudeville-like exchanges, was to emphasize the heavy Americanisms of Shorty and the lugubrious, basically un-British quality of Greek royalty. Both these elements would be well received in the provincial atmosphere of Toronto; after all, he was back at the old stand, expressing once again "the Canadian point of view." The vignette, on the other hand, had been a careful, frugal treatment which shaped the situation toward a specific effect.

The king was working in the garden. He seemed very glad to see me. We walked through the garden. This is the queen, he said. She was clipping a rose bush. Oh how do you do, she said. We sat down at a table under a big tree and the king ordered whiskey and soda. We have good whiskey anyway, he said. The revolutionary committee, he told me, would not allow him to go outside the palace grounds. Plastiras is a very good man I believe, he said, but frightfully difficult. I think he did right though shooting those chaps. If Kerensky had shot a few men things might have been altogether different. Of course the great thing in this sort of an affair is not to be shot oneself!

It was very jolly. We talked for a long time. Like all Greeks he wanted to go to America.

Hemingway's creative concern was with George. This was the final vignette; it would become the epilogue of *In Our Time*. Its statement, in terms of the previous seventeen sketches, was explicit. Here, in a garden in Athens, was the ultimate irony of a contemporary experience. The leader of an ancient nation, whose people had recently fought and lost a painful, costly war, out of which had come the catastrophic Thracian refugee processions, was discovered to be an amiable, inept facsimile of an English gentleman. George did not equate with the inherited, accepted concepts of divine leadership and the romantic principles of monarchial glory. George equated with any Greek short order cook in Oak Park or Kansas City or Chicago.

The final vignette, controlled and professional, was an appropriate climax to this thin book which Edmund Wilson would soon call "the soundest" written by an American about the war.[26] Small wonder that Hemingway was not jubilant about his forthcoming return to Canada. He was abruptly halting his literary career at the moment of ignition, exchanging the stimulating world of Europe for one about which he had no illusions; he knew Toronto too well, in several variations. Such a detour as this, however, could be only momentary. He had acquired too much momentum both from his European newspaper work and from his progress and position as a young writer. His departure from Europe on August 17, 1923 was neither the end of one period nor the beginning of a new one. It was no more than a temporary suspension of the narrative.

The publication of *Three Stories & Ten Poems*, and the assurance that *in our time* would soon appear, were the virtual epitaph on his apprenticeship. Now there remained only the actual separation from journalism. Toronto was the ideal scene for such a separation.

# *TORONTO*

"Hemingway seems very much not to
have liked Canada."

GERTRUDE STEIN[1]

## I.

Scrutinized dispassionately, with the hindsight of thirty years, Hemingway's final Toronto period in the autumn of 1923 has all the elements of swiftly paced catastrophe. Its chronology and actors provide the outline of a vivid melodrama. All the components were present: hero, villain, dilemma and choice, suspense, theme, and explosive resolution. The four months' narrative had a neat unity of time and place. There was even off-stage comic relief in the person of Ezra Pound, who sent Hemingway mocking letters from Paris, derisively addressed to "Tomato, Can."

Hemingway talked seriously, in fact, of using the experience as fiction. He discussed on several occasions the possibilities of a satiric novel to be called *The Son-in-Law*. Its principal character was to have been Harry C. Hindmarsh, the assistant managing editor of the *Daily Star*. Ultimately, however, Hemingway rejected the scenario. He explained to a Toronto colleague, after reflection, that a novelist should not write a book whose main character was someone he detested; the emotion distorted your perspective, Hemingway explained.

If Hemingway's transformation from journalist to writer still required confirmation, this episode of the abandoned

novel about Harry Hindmarsh may be regarded as pro-
nouncing it complete. The principle Hemingway enunciated, and by virtue of which Hindmarsh was spared a
savage fictional portrait, may have been false or question-
able; the fact that Hemingway was assessing prospective
material in such terms was the significant element. His apprenticeship was over. Journalism had been the most important single factor, supplemented by travel, the shocks
of war and peace, and personal and literary associations,
but by September, 1923, its utility was ended. Hemingway's
firm and expanding psychology as a writer indicated that
an extension of journalism, particularly under the incessant
pressures of a city room schedule, could result only in chaos
and rebellion. The whole episode had a classic finality of
doom.

The decision to return to Canada for two years, to be
sure, was in many ways a sound one. Occasioned by his
wife's pregnancy and the necessity of providing their child
with a stable infancy, it was the sort of behavior which
would be taken for granted in the sober world of, say, Oak
Park. It was also, on the other hand, a notable gesture of
private fortitude in a twenty-four-year-old writer who had
been living with pleasure and professional profit in a milieu
where such decisions are almost unique. Given this kind of
mature responsibility on Hemingway's part, the plan might
conceivably have worked, despite inevitable personal stress
and possible artistic inhibition, had all the surrounding factors been ideal. The mechanism of the Toronto drama,
however, contained only the most hostile elements.

At first there was a falsely benign aura to the enterprise.
It was, after all, a kind of homecoming. Some of Heming-
way's distaste was removed by the warmth with which
Gregory Clark, the *Star Weekly*'s feature editor, greeted
him, and by the affection which developed between the
Clarks and Mrs. Hemingway. Clark noticed that Heming-

way spoke easily and familiarly, without bravado, of Gertrude Stein, and Pound, and James Joyce. In his reminiscence there was none of the swagger that might have been legitimately expected. Clark felt easier about the elaborate build-up he had given down at the *Star* in preparation for the prodigal's return.

The *Star*, as always, had had a large turnover. Hemingway had to be introduced to most of the staff. Clark's prefatory enthusiasm, however, had been substantiated by Hemingway's own achievement as a correspondent. They had all read his European dispatches, particularly those from the Near East. He came back to Toronto as a veteran reporter of some stature. He now belonged to John Bone and the *Daily Star*, on the other hand, rather than to Cranston and the more leisurely, semi-literary *Star Weekly* with which he had been primarily associated in 1920 and 1921. Although Cranston had reservations about the American's temperamental capacity to adjust to the demands of a daily paper, he was pleased with Hemingway's success. It was a good job, one hundred and twenty-five dollars a week and, it was assumed, a permanent assignment interviewing local and visiting celebrities. Soon, however, like the rest of the *Star*'s staff, Cranston became aware that Hemingway was receiving the celebrated Hindmarsh treatment. An important agent in the final dissolution of Hemingway as a journalist had appeared.

Harry Comfort Hindmarsh remains today a bleak and ambiguous individual. It is no exaggeration to say that he is one of the half dozen most important men in North American journalism. His papers have no particular place in the consciousness of the American public, although most American newspapermen are familiar with both the *Daily Star* and the *Star Weekly*, but they dominate the highly competitive Canadian newspaper scene. Hindmarsh, an important contributor to the emergence of this Toronto

empire, has for forty years puzzled and enraged his colleagues and employees. Today, as president of The Toronto
Star Limited, he is the object of vast gossip and calumny,
and occasional deep loyalty. Both he and the *Star* are the
targets of continuous published and private speculation.[2]

In September, 1923, when Hemingway returned to
Toronto, Hindmarsh, after a decade with the *Star*, was its
assistant managing editor. He had succeeded Cranston
when the latter became editor of the *Star Weekly*. Although
he was married to the publisher's daughter—hence the title
of Hemingway's abortive novel—Hindmarsh himself was
harassed by his own immediate superior, John Bone. Hindmarsh was also attempting the difficult job of simultaneously boosting circulation and ridding the *Daily Star* of
the raffish young men whose talents frequently made the
circulation possible. He has lived to see a time when he
need hire none but sober university graduates like himself.
Shortly after World War II he declared with relish: "The
cult of the prima donna [in journalism] is dead."[3]

In 1923, however, the cult was very much alive, both in
Toronto and throughout the American newspaper world.
Hindmarsh concluded automatically that Hemingway, fresh
from the undisciplined routine of overseas work, was a
member of that school. Between September 10, 1923, when
he went on the *Star*'s payroll, and September 25, Hemingway was not assigned a single story of sufficient importance
to rate the paper's lavishly given by-line. He was sent to
the city hall with vague instructions to see what was going
on. He covered concerts at Massey Hall, and he was sum-
moned from bed at four in the morning to cover one-alarm
fires. The routine was a stereotype with a certain kind of
newspaper executive of the period; it is preserved in the
anachronistic behavior of Hollywood's city editors. Few
*Star* reporters of any duration escaped it. Almost all of
them have memories of front-page glory and sudden descent

to the woman's page. Hemingway, however, didn't even have the consolation of being removed from journalistic privilege; he began at the bottom. His degradation was observed with resentment by another young reporter.

Morley Callaghan, several years younger than Hemingway, was in 1923 a part-time member of the *Star*'s editorial staff. He was just completing his undergraduate work at the University of Toronto, and beginning to write the short stories which were to make him so significant a literary force in the 1920's and 1930's. Like so many young men of talent in Toronto, he had almost necessarily gravitated toward the *Star Weekly*. One of the legends to which he responded most actively was the picture Greg Clark and Jimmy Cowan and Frise, the cartoonist, had created for him that summer of their friend Hemingway. Callaghan's first glimpse of Hemingway did not increase his own precarious adjustment to the perverse world of Hindmarsh's city room.

"One morning that fall," Callaghan recalled in 1952, "I went over to check the assignment book." Callaghan, an articulate man, has a precise and ready memory. "I looked down the list and I saw Hemingway's name, and then his name again, and finally, down at the bottom, I saw it a third time." The young Canadian, who thought of Hemingway as one whose literary career had been firmly launched, was naturally curious about what kinds of assignments he was being given, and why he should receive so many of them. He was appalled at what he saw. "They were all piddling," Callaghan remembered, "just junk assignments." At this moment Callaghan first saw Hemingway, whom he recognized from Jimmy Cowan's description. Hemingway walked over and studied the book himself. "Jesus Christ," he muttered.

Callaghan and Hemingway, inevitably, became close friends that autumn. Their friendship survived into the late

1920's, when Callaghan moved to Paris for a time; finally it dissolved in the meaningless acrimony of New York literary gossip. Callaghan never concealed his admiration for certain aspects of Hemingway's work, nor did he ever belittle his own early debt to the American. "I'll always be grateful to Hemingway," said Callaghan, thirty years after that first meeting in the Toronto city room, "because at a time when I needed encouragement he told me I was going to be a great writer."[4]

In the fall of 1923 Callaghan's serious writing had scarcely incubated. Hemingway, a published writer and the friend of legendary Paris figures, was an important experience for him. Their relationship in Toronto verifies from another direction the solidity of Hemingway's projection of himself at this time as a writer rather than a newspaper man. Callaghan was astonished to discover later, in Paris, that he and Hemingway were virtually contemporaries. The latter's air of maturity in Toronto came from more than his involvement in the war, or the fact that he was married. It stemmed directly from his professional concept of writing as an intensely worthy craft. His deep seriousness—about writing—endowed Hemingway with adulthood and sobriety. His affinity for Callaghan was a symptom of this. There were other reporters whom Hemingway might have cultivated with more profit to himself. Callaghan was not only an obscure member of the staff, he was also, in his own memory of the period, "very, very green." Hemingway, however, was drawn instinctively to his transparent intensity about writing.

The editorial staff as a whole was literate and intelligent; many of them had the conventional newspaperman's ambitions to write fiction. None of them had the rigidity of purpose which Hemingway and Callaghan shared. It is significant that when Gregory Clark tried to sort out his memories of this period, in 1950, he persistently confused

Callaghan with Hemingway, and vice versa. The average would-be writer on the *Star*, as on most newspapers, rarely looked beyond the *Saturday Evening Post*, and seldom that high. They were more impressed, indeed, by Hemingway's success as a foreign correspondent than by the beginnings of his literary career; Callaghan thought of him as a writer who was temporarily and unfortunately a reporter. The two had in common their unsolemn dedication to art.

Hemingway urged Callaghan to commit himself totally to serious writing. Callaghan remembered the American as being "bishop-like" in his severity and urgency. They read each other's work and talked about "all other living writers," and in particular of Sherwood Anderson, whom Callaghan admired immensely. Callaghan was shown the proofs of *in our time* when they arrived from Paris. Thus Hemingway created the illusion of a transplanted Latin Quarter, introducing an air of deep resolve into the limited world of the Toronto arts. He was a figure of substance to the young reporters of his own age. Once or twice they feted him in their fraternity house at the university. Hemingway's comment after one of these salons indicated again the kind of milieu with which he had enveloped himself. "They made me feel like Anatole France," he told a colleague.

Hemingway's confidante on that occasion was Mary Lowry, an intelligent, witty Canadian who was emancipating herself from much the same genteel background Hemingway had known in Oak Park. Later she published a number of deftly written short stories and established herself as a successful free lance. In 1923, however, she was merely another rebellious *Star* reporter, thoroughly familiar with the Hindmarsh treatment. Her small office became a refuge for Hemingway. "He would storm in there," she said many years later, "and rave and rant about that so and so."[5] She found him an engaging fellow sufferer, and even in his frustration an amiable and entertaining prisoner. "Hemingway," she remembered, "was always lots of fun." With several others from the paper they used to gather after work or between assignments at Child's for coffee, or at Angelo's, where chianti was served in the thick china cups of a dry town.

Prohibition and its indignities were but another of the elements which menaced Hemingway's plan to remain in journalism for an additional two years. Toronto was a caricature of puritanism, notorious for its blue laws and its Sabbath solemnity. Hemingway's response to such personal restrictions was characteristic of Americans who had lived abroad. He and Mary Lowry were sent to cover a conclave of Toronto clergymen discussing the necessity for legal censorship of the movies. As an attitude this was for Hemingway merely a variation of prohibition. He slouched down in his chair, feet up on the bench in front of him, grumbling and cursing. "Goddamn," he told the girl loudly, "I hate refinement."

Had he deliberately sought an area of organized refinement, Hemingway could not have selected a better locale than Toronto. Even the countryside repelled him. His first substantial assignment, on September 24, took him to the mining towns west of Toronto. The landscape was not very different from what he had seen, unappalled, in the Ruhr that spring. He was as temporarily unreasonable as most reluctant repatriates. "Driving through it," he wrote for the *Daily Star*, "was like going through some desolate early illustration of Pilgrim's Progress."[6] He might have used the same metaphor to describe the sequence of six-day working weeks he was spending in the desolate routine of Toronto journalism. This was a vocational morass he had been previously spared. The Toronto *Daily Star* was as different from the Kansas City *Star* as is the New York *Journal*

*American* different from the *Herald Tribune* or the late Boston *Transcript*.

*II.*

In 1923, under the energetic leadership of Hindmarsh's father-in-law, the late Joseph E. Atkinson,[7] the *Star* was emerging as the colossus of Canadian journalism. Sensational headlines, red type, comic strips, eyewitness and flamboyant reportage, basic English, and many photographs were the fundamental tools. In the bible-belt atmosphere of southern Ontario the *Star*'s management also uncovered in religion an appeal which Hearst, for example, though he frequently attempted it, was never able to exploit fully in the United States. Atkinson's nickname in the trade was an indication of the pious hypocrisy his contemporaries felt they detected in the contradictory components of his papers. They called him Holy Joe.[8]

There was no style book on the *Star*, and no editor with the scrupulous regard for prose that had distinguished Pete Wellington. Both Hindmarsh and the managing editor, John Bone, were hard-working editors with genuine talents for discovering news and merchandising it profitably, but there was no exchange department here, nor was there the camaraderie of a group of young reporters determined to write fiction. The staff was intelligent, cynical, and wholly insecure. The paper was racked by alternate spasms of free spending and hangovers of harsh economy. It was a provincial paper run in a big-town way. On the whole it exhibited most of the flaws and few of the virtues of both categories. Veteran Toronto newsmen recall the existence of only one prose directive in the *Star*'s city room. On the bulletin board was an admonishment to "Put a Punch in Every Paragraph." Beyond this the *Star* did not venture in matters of rhetoric.

Hemingway's vocational reaction to this atmosphere was

a natural one. He manufactured, by and large, the kind of material that was required. His first story was published on September 15, by the *Star Weekly*[9]; Cranston bought it to tide Hemingway over until he went on the *Daily Star* payroll. The article established the pattern of much of the work he would do during the next three and a half months. In it he exploited the sort of gossip a working newspaperman acquires almost unconsciously. Assessing his audience with cynical shrewdness, Hemingway prepared a Sunday supplement treatment of contemporary European royalty. It was written with a minimum of organization and re-drafting; Hemingway's reservoir of intimate anecdote, and the engaging background of personal reminiscence, provided readability and movement.

Hemingway's work continued to demonstrate this expert, angry facility. Late in October he managed to get himself transferred to the *Star Weekly* staff, removing himself to a degree from Hindmarsh's tyranny.[10] He was unquestionably one of the magazine's principal attractions.[11] He shared the featured columns with Fred Griffin and Gregory Clark. Occasionally, as in two excellent installments on bullfighting, Hemingway laid aside his facility and attempted to transcribe the kind of emotion and narrative he had already achieved in the stories and vignettes of his two Paris volumes.[12] In the second of these Spanish articles, indeed, he spilled out his restless longing for a reprieve from Toronto and from journalism. "That was just three months ago," he wrote bitterly, after a buoyant description of the Pamplona fiesta. "It seems in a different century now, working in an office. . . . But it is only fourteen days by water to Spain and there is no need for a castle. There is always that room at 5 Calle de Eslava. . . ."

For the moment, however, he could only sublimate his distress with the dubious release of *Star Weekly* freedom as opposed to *Daily Star* oppression. He turned frequently to his European memories, for stories about continental hunting, fishing, and skiing.[13] His nostalgia even permitted him to make a new assessment of his Black Forest experience of two summers before. A Toronto exile had cleansed the original dispatches of their querulous prejudice; to that extent the Canadian banishment was a purge.

. . . we fished all through the Black Forest. With rucksacks and fly-rods, we hiked across country, sticking to the high ridges and the rolling crests of the hills, sometimes through deep pine timber, sometimes coming out into a clearing and farmyards and again going for miles without seeing a soul except occasional wild looking berry pickers. We never knew where we were. But we were never lost because at any time we could cut down from the high country into a valley and know we could hit a stream. Sooner or later every stream flowed into a river and a river meant a town. . . . We cut across the high, bare country, dipping down into valleys and walking through the woods, cool and dim as a cathedral on the August hot day.[14]

There were paragraphs as effective as these in almost all the material he wrote in Toronto during the last months of 1923. Hemingway, after all, was now a relatively finished writer; inevitably his journalism occasionally displayed thoughtful or instinctive craft. These were isolated paragraphs, however, frequently buried in a soggy, journeyman treatment. The general tone of his articles became increasingly pedestrian. By early November he was writing two long articles for almost every issue of the *Star Weekly*. "Pretty soon," he told another reporter bitterly, "I'll be writing the whole damn magazine." It even became necessary to mask part of his productivity behind the decent cloak of a pseudonym; the most flagrant of his hack work began to appear under the by-line of John Hadley.[15] Frequently, whether they were signed with his own or Hadley's name, his stories were little more than extensions of news items briefly used by the *Daily Star* or turned over to the *Star Weekly* by the city desk for feature treatment. Hemingway-Hadley wrote at length of the possibilities of flood in the Great Lakes, of General Wolfe's diaries, of an experiment for introducing iodine into the Toronto reservoirs, and of the impregnability of Ontario bank vaults.[16]

It was sorry material on which to waste the time that even such synthetic stories required. It was impossible for him to turn to his own work. "I write slowly," he told Ernest Walsh in 1925, "and with a great deal of difficulty and my head has to be clear to do it. While I write the stuff I have to live it in my head."[17] There wasn't room in his head for cops and robbers stories, a six-day week, and serious writing. Even to his journalism he brought standards that were personally exacting. "Don't talk about it before you write it," he warned Mary Lowry once, as they walked back to the *Star* after a provocative interview with the survivors of a Japanese earthquake. "You mustn't talk about it," Hemingway insisted. "You'll spoil it."[18]

Sometimes, of course, Hemingway found material to which he responded. On November 24 he printed in the *Star Weekly*, without a by-line, a highly personal statement on contemporary literature.[19] The article, whose sharp brevity was more characteristic of his fiction than of his usually wordy stories for Cranston, was occasioned by the award of the Nobel Prize to William Butler Yeats. The point of view was forceful and informed, written in the sardonic idiom with which he has customarily delivered his literary opinions; it would have been more suitably placed in the columns of *Poetry* or the *Little Review*. "William Butler Yeats has written, with the exception of a few poems by Ezra Pound, the very finest poetry of our time. This is a statement that will be instantly challenged by the admirers of Alfred Noyes, John Masefield, Bliss Carman, and Robert Service. Let them read what they like. There is little use in attempting to convert a lover of coca-cola to vintage champagne."[20]

By mid-November Hemingway had decided to go back to Europe with the new year. Stimulated by his decision, and acting upon Cranston's friendly agreement to help finance the trip through the purchase of extra *Star Weekly* stories, Hemingway poured out a torrent of copy so large that the magazine was still using his material after he had left Toronto. He wrote a hasty but provocative description of a confidence man selling worthless European currency to hungry vagrants,[21] and he assembled an exhaustive chronicle of anecdote about European night life.[22] A long story published on December 22 was slickly tailored for the Christmas season.[23] Its three separate episodes, each of them illustrating the holiday as celebrated in Switzerland, Italy, and Paris, indicated once again that he was instinctively working in fiction patterns. The material of these vignettes was generally mawkish and careless, but the sketches themselves were presented in terms of situation and dialogue, with a well-paced narrative and a certain amount of climax and resolution. On the whole, however, Hemingway displayed himself to better immediate advantage in less personal material, in articles about Toronto bookies, legendary New Year's Eves, the world's great imposters, and memories of Chicago.[24] The final fruit of the Toronto misadventure was published on January 19, 1924, a derisive sneer in which Hemingway could no longer suppress his contempt for the New World and his jubilation about his European prospects. In a trolley two girls had giggled about his felt hat.

"Say," said a gentleman in a cap, who had been observing me truculently for some blocks, "what do you mean getting fresh with a couple of girls?"

"I'm very sorry, sir, but I cannot detain you longer." I bowed. "But I must leave the street car here. I have an appointment with the new mayor."

"For two bits I'd give you a sock on the jaw," observed the gentleman in the cap.

"I couldn't think of it for a moment," I said. "My dear fellow, it would be quite impossible. I could not think of accepting a piece of hosiery from a chance acquaintance, no matter how pleasant."

I bowed again and descended from the car. The gentleman in the cap was comforting the two young ladies.

"I'd have poked him a minute," said the gentleman.

"He had no right to talk to a decent working girl like that," sobbed one of the girls.

"I'd have poked him," comforted the gentleman in the cap.[25]

*III.*

The friction between Hemingway and the assistant managing editor had not been dissolved by the former's transference to the staff of the *Star Weekly*. Cranston's men were always at the disposal of Hindmarsh, either for regular city desk assignments or for special chores. Hemingway's attitude toward the *Daily Star* editor had been openly hostile since early October. At that time Hindmarsh sent him to New York to cover the arrival of Lloyd George, despite the young American's plea that his wife would almost certainly be delivered in Toronto during those few days.[26]

One of Hemingway's colleagues remembered that the latter's single comment, on another occasion, when Hindmarsh ordered him to a municipal park to get a nature story,

had been: "Let's go back to the office and beat the hell out
of Hindmarsh." The circumstances of Hemingway's ultimate resignation from the *Star* are obscure, clouded by
conflicting testimony and the reticence that has often
muzzled witnesses to many such episodes on the paper.
Hemingway, however, was never reticent about the *Star*.
His own version of the final break, written years later in
a letter to Cranston—at a time when the retired editor was
preparing a volume of reminiscences—was precise and psychologically plausible.

Hemingway told Cranston in 1951 that he had been
assigned to do an interview with Count Aponyi, the Hungarian diplomat. The Hungarian gave Hemingway a number of official documents which would clarify his mission,
and "extracted a promise that they would be returned later
in the day." Hemingway sent the papers to Hindmarsh,
with a note requesting him to put the papers in the office
safe until he could take them back to the Count. Hindmarsh,
according to Hemingway, read the note and threw the
documents in the wastebasket. Later that day, in the normal
routine of office-cleaning procedure, they were burned in
the furnace. Hemingway resigned as soon as he learned of
the destruction of the papers.

Even the bookkeeping records of the *Star* do not clarify
the episode. They merely indicate that Hemingway resigned
some time in December and drew his final pay on the last
day of the month. It was an explosive separation; around
it there developed extravagant details that have made it one
of the legendary city room tales. Many years later Hemingway's venom toward Hindmarsh was sufficiently alive so
that he responded aggressively to a Toronto Newspaper
Guild plea for contributions with which to organize the
*Star*. He sent the Guild a check for one hundred dollars,
"to beat Hindmarsh."[27] After four pages of eloquent comment on his former editor, he changed his mind. "On sec-

ond thought," Hemingway wrote, "I'm making it $200. I welcome the opportunity to take a swing at that . . . Hindmarsh."

In January, 1924, Hemingway and his small family left Toronto, their proposed two years in Canada reduced to four months. Hemingway never went back, although one of the ingredients of his Toronto legend is that he appeared triumphantly in person in the *Star* city room to distribute copies of his first novel. He did continue to write Greg Clark and Morley Callaghan. Once in a mood of depression years later he speculated to Clark about a fishing trip to northern Ontario, where he felt one could escape entirely from society. He remembered Cranston with affection, and when the latter took his family abroad in 1925 it was Hemingway who guided them around Paris. "I never enjoyed myself so much," he told Cranston early in 1951, "as working under you and with Greg Clark and Jimmy Frise. It was why I was sad to quit newspaper work. Working under Hindmarsh was like being in the German army with a poor commander." He saw a good deal of Morley Callaghan during the next few years in Paris, but on the whole Toronto held for him the bitter memories which equate with any suspension of forward movement.

That the period was no more than a suspension had been made clear by the occasional real quality of his journalism that fall, as well as by the genuine professional aura which such interested young writers as Callaghan, Mary Lowry, and Jimmy Cowan detected in him. Within these final exercises of his literary apprenticeship are the tangible evidences of his five years of training. He had perfected the narrative talent which would be a characteristic of all his fiction, and which has enabled him to reach more varieties of readers than any other serious writer of his generation. His instinct for narrative had always been a strong one. Journalism altered the instinct from gift to craft. The kind of newspaper writing he did between 1920 and 1923, and the basic lessons he received in Kansas City in 1917 and 1918, required that he tell stories rather than report events.

The rather special pattern of Hemingway's employers had also permitted and encouraged the development of such an important instrument of his fiction as dialogue. The conventional inhibitions of spot news reporting, with its insistence on the merely factual and expository, were replaced for Hemingway by a medium which facilitated his training as a fictionalist through its appetite for human interest material. Even in the hasty structures of his 1923 journalism Hemingway erupted into passages of vivid, careful speech which confirmed his obligation to the *Star Weekly*'s flexibility.

He was an old man, with a face like a leather water bottle.
"Well, Papa, no fish today," I said.
"Not for you," he said solemnly.
"Why not for me? For you, maybe?" I said.
"Oh, yes," he said, not smiling. "For me trout always. Not for you. You don't know how to fish with worms." And spat into the stream.
"You're so rich you know everything. You are probably a rich man from your knowledge of fishworms," I said.[28]

The necessity to communicate people rather than events, and the stylistic freedom both the *Star Weekly* and the *Daily Star* extended to their reporters, enabled Hemingway to exercise the lucid exposition which would in three years vivify *The Sun Also Rises*. His coverage of the Lloyd George assignment in October, 1923, was an uneven one, made more exasperating than usual by the amount of copy that was required of him and by his separation from his wife during the last weeks of her pregnancy. The highly personal diction of his serious writing, nevertheless, could be practiced without reprimand for such a paper. Hemingway attempted a definition of the English politician's oratory. "It is his wonderful voice," he wrote, "combined with his Gaelic gift of prophecy that strikes one. When he talks, you feel he is a prophet, and prophets have a way of their own. He talks much as Peter the Hermit must have talked about the crusades."[29] The sharply etched lines of portraiture were equal testimony to Hemingway's debt to the freedoms of *Star* journalism. "With his silvery hair and keen face," Hemingway explained in another Lloyd George dispatch, "he looked in the big cape like some retired medieval fencing master."[30]

Journalism had also encouraged, in this same area, Hemingway's persistent and usually legitimate air of vast knowledgeability. It was part of a newspaperman's necessity for and opportunities of being on the inside of a situation. Authenticity is above all a reporter's virtue. Journalism encouraged Hemingway to throw himself responsively into whatever atmosphere he was exploring. It required him to know just a shade more than the layman about any given situation. An inevitable extension of this vocational knowledgeability, of course, was a sardonic recognition of human frailty and a skepticism about large truths. Hemingway's sense of humor had always been a highly developed one. The hearty nature of his adolescent burlesque was encouraged by the *Star Weekly;* as the scope of his journalism extended into politics and diplomacy, his wit became more subtle and ironic.

"Although Lloyd George is universally popular with Americans," Hemingway wrote characteristically on October 8, 1923, just before he finished that particular assignment, "some of them seem just a bit confused as to who he is. One New Yorker said to The Star: 'I guess there wasn't anybody else could take the helm the way he did. I have just finished reading his book, *Men Like Gods*. I guess things would be pretty good all right if we had that Utopia, eh?' "[31] In December, 1923, writing about European night life, Hemingway remembered a conversation at Florence's in Paris, where the proprietress and staff were American Negroes.

"Miss Flawnce she ain't a niggah no mo. No suh. She done tell customahs mammy's an Indian lady fum Canada," a waiter explained. "Ah'm luhnin' to talk that English way, too. Ah'm goin' tuh tell people my mammy's an Indian lady fuhm Noble Scotia. Yes, suh. We'll all be Indiums this tahm nex' yeah. Yes, suh."[32]

Of all the tangible professional profits that came to Hemingway through his apprenticeship in newspaper work, this knowledgeability and its sardonic derivation of wit were the most immediately apparent. His style matured to a degree in the discipline of cabelese; after his association with Gertrude Stein he began to introduce the harsh, declarative structure of his mature prose into his feature material. On the whole, however, his newspaper rhetoric could seldom be more economical than was appropriate to a reporter who was usually paid by the word. The interludes of buoyant humor and ironic wit were basic to his success as a correspondent; he exercised them constantly. In the months immediately after his abandonment of newspaper work, in fact, Hemingway was inclined to think of himself at least in part as a humorist.

This attitude was stimulated by his friendship with Donald Ogden Stewart, whom he had first met in Europe in 1923, and of whom he saw a great deal in 1924 and 1925. He was much impressed by the satirist's work—and its success—and particularly by *Mr. and Mrs. Haddocks Abroad*. One of the last pieces of journalism Hemingway attempted at this time, indeed, was a humorous account of bullfighting which Stewart rejected in 1924 for *Vanity Fair*. Hemingway thought of "Mr. and Mrs. Elliot" as a funny story, and as late as July, 1925, when he was working on the first draft of *The Sun Also Rises*, he regarded that manuscript as in part a humorous one. In the fall of 1925, as an interlude between drafts of the novel, Hemingway wrote the satiric *The Torrents of Spring*. Here, in the parody and irony of literary denunciation, Hemingway displayed among other qualities the fluency and ease of newspaper training. The book was written, its author claimed, in ten days. To the degree that it was hasty and, according to some versions, written solely to make money, it derived directly from his journalism. It was also, however, a very funny book, which it was meant to be, and occasionally a very thoughtful book, professionally, which it was also meant to be; in the sense that it was a blend of haste and talent, *The Torrents of Spring* was his journalistic epitaph.

Between late 1925, however, when he wrote the satire, and January, 1924, when he formally abandoned journalism, Hemingway wrote a number of excellent short stories and the first draft of his novel. Journalism was completely thrust aside in its inhibitory sense on January 19, 1924, when the Hemingways sailed from New York on the Cunard liner *Antonia*. "Toronto," Hemingway told his friends from the *Star* in ironic farewell, "has taken five years off my life." His sense of humor and general maturity allowed him to recover rapidly from the disaster of those final four months of newspaper work; 1924 would be a year of intensive serious writing. His bitterness about the Toronto episode, however, never completely healed. Even the manner in which Cranston was discarded by the *Star* in 1932 enraged him. "He was as badly treated by the Toronto *Star*," Hemingway declared in 1952, not long before the editor's death, "as a man could be and that is almost as far as a man can get in being badly treated."

Journalism had been laborious and frequently exasperating. It had also been financial security of a sort, and the virtually certain guarantee of an increasingly profitable future. It required considerable artistic intensity to abandon a vocation in which he was a professional, with good credentials, and to turn instead to the insecurity of creative writing. He was in 1924 merely one of a number of promising young American writers. The compulsion could not be resisted. "Ernest," his wife said many years later, "felt if we did not get away from that atmosphere quickly, his soul, which means his own creative writing, would dry up within him."

Hemingway's debt to journalism was a large one, and he always acknowledged it. Unlike many ex-newspapermen, however, he neither sentimentalized the profession nor misunderstood its essential threat to creative writing. "In newspaper work," he explained later, "you have to learn to forget every day what happened the day before." He always felt a parallel between journalism and war. Each, he maintained, is valuable to a writer "up until the point that it forcibly begins to destroy your memory." His views on this are emphatic. "A writer must leave it before that point. But he will always have scars from it."

The last days in Toronto evaporated in farewell parties, the determined drudgery by which he flooded Cranston with *Star Weekly* articles, and a wedding in their apartment at which Hemingway was best man for Jimmy Cowan. Mary Lowry saw them off at the station, and an awkward, partly unhappy, occasionally profitable episode was over. He had embedded himself in the legend of the Toronto newspaper world. Younger men who joined the *Star* were entertained and instructed by the tales of his fury and his skill and his ironic wit. The paper became distantly vain of his association with it; the morgue accumulated a substantial Hemingway folder. In occasional items which the *Star* printed about his books, its reporters sometimes referred to him as "a former Torontonian." It must have made him laugh. He was no more a former Torontonian, Chicagoan, or Kansas Citian, than he was a former newspaperman. He had lived in all those places, and in many others, and he had been a newspaperman, but he had become a writer.

# *NOTES*

Complete documentation of this study, so much of whose material was assembled through correspondence and interview, would have required, quite literally, almost one hundred footnotes for each twenty-five pages of text. In order to avoid such a repetitive apparatus, and yet at the same time maintain some decencies of responsible documentation, footnotes have been attached, in the main, only to those statements whose entire text is readily available to the general reader. This has not been a fixed principle; whenever a chapter's footnoting seemed to allow a moderate amount of extension, without becoming an unwieldy catalogue, I have included full citation of this research by correspondence and interview. Unless a specific declaration is made in the footnote, all the correspondence is unpublished. Hemingway's short stories are in all cases cited from their first magazine or book appearance, since the date and nature of original publication are generally relevant to the theme of apprenticeship.

The following abbreviations are used throughout the notes:

| | |
|---|---|
| *Baker* | Carlos Baker, *Hemingway: The Writer as Artist* (Princeton University Press, 1952). |
| *Brumback* | Theodore Brumback, "With Hemingway before *A Farewell to Arms*," Kansas City *Star* (December 6, 1936), 1C, 2C. |
| CAF | Charles A. Fenton. |
| *Cohn* | Louis H. Cohn, *A Bibliography of the Works of Ernest Hemingway* (Random House, 1931). |
| *DITA* | Ernest Hemingway, *Death in the Afternoon* (Scribner's, 1932). |
| DS | Toronto *Daily Star*. |
| EH | Ernest Hemingway. |
| (Int.) | Indicates that the material was obtained by interview with the particular source on the specified date: *i.e.*, J. C. Edgar to CAF, March 15, 1952 (Int.). |
| "Malady of Power" | Ernest Hemingway, "The Malady of Power," *Esquire*, IV (November, 1935), 31, 198-199. |
| "Monologue to the Maestro" | Ernest Hemingway, "Monologue to the Maestro," *Esquire*, III (October, 1935), 21, 174A, 174B. |
| "Old Newsman" | Ernest Hemingway, "Old Newsman Writes," *Esquire*, II (December, 1934), 25-26. |
| SW | Toronto *Star Weekly*. |
| *Toklas* | Gertrude Stein, *Autobiography of Alice B. Toklas*, (Harcourt, Brace, 1933). |

## CHAPTER ONE

Hemingway's high school fiction and journalism have never been reprinted or collected. His position, legitimate and understandable in a writer of his exacting personal standards, is that juvenilia belongs to the author and his wastebasket. There is a file of the *Trapeze* in the school library. Most private Hemingway collections, and many major American libraries, possess those issues of the *Tabula* containing Hemingway's fiction and poetry. I am deeply indebted to the following individuals for the patience and generosity with which they endured and clarified my questions: Miss Fannie Biggs; the late Arthur Bobbitt; Colonel Wayne Brandstadt; Mrs. Kenneth W. Carr; Mrs. Margaret Adams Charnals; Lewis A. Clarahan; Chester B. Clifford; Mrs. Robert Craig Corlett; Richard A. Craig; Miss Jean Crawford; Albert W. Dungan; Mrs. Elsbeth Eric; John Gehlmann; Mrs. Charles E. Goodell; Mrs. Olga F. Gray; Mrs. F. L. Gjesdahl; Paul F. Haase; Tom H. Hildebrand; Mrs. Carl Howe, Jr.; Mrs. Carl R. Kesler; Miss Elizabeth G. Kimball; Mrs. George C. Kindred; Mrs. J. J. Lowitz; Roswell H. Maveety; Mrs. Avery A. Morton; Frank J. Platt; Hale Printup; Gordon D. Shorney; Elliott Smeeth; Mrs. Richard Wilson Steele; Arthur L. Thexton; Professor Edward Wagenknecht; Miss Ruth Wagenknecht; Philip M. White; Mrs. Mildred B. Wilcox; The Reverend Edward W. Willcox; Mrs. Janet Lewis Winters; Lyman Worthington; Miss Margaret Wright; Miss Mignon Wright; Deb Wylder; and Dr. Eugene Youngert.

1. Janet Lewis Winters to CAF, May 8, 1952. Mrs. Winters, wife of the critic and poet, Yvor Winters, and herself a well-known poet and university teacher, graduated from Oak Park High School in 1916.

2. There is a harsher picture of both Oak Park and its high school, as experienced by one of the few lower middle-class members of the overwhelmingly middle-class student body, in the autobiography of Robert St. John, *This Was My World* (Doubleday, 1953). St. John's comments are a realistic antidote to the consistently mellow recollections of the majority group to which Hemingway belonged, but as a distinct minority report they do not alter the general picture of secure and prosperous suburbia.

3. Samuel Putnam, *Paris Was Our Mistress* (Viking, 1947), 128-29. Solemn literary pronouncements of this kind are generally ironic on Hemingway's part. The statement itself, however, is well authenticated; Putnam made immediate notes on the con-

versation, which took place in Paris shortly after the publication of *The Sun Also Rises* in 1926.

4. *Senior Tabula* (Publishing Board of the Oak Park and River Forest Township High School, 1917), 105. The final issue of the *Tabula* was annually entitled *Senior Tabula*, fulfilling the function of a Class Book for the graduating class. Hereafter cited as *Senior Tabula*.

5. "Monologue to the Maestro," 174B.

6. *Senior Tabula*, 23.

7. Ernest Hemingway, "Judgment of Manitou," *Tabula*, XXII (February, 1916), 9-10. Both the *Tabula* and the *Trapeze* were indifferently proofread. Mistakes in punctuation and spelling have been silently corrected.

8. Ernest Hemingway, "A Matter of Colour," *Tabula*, XXIII (April, 1916), 16-17.

9. Ernest Hemingway, "Sepi Jingan," *Tabula*, XXIII (November, 1916), 8-9.

10. Ernest Hemingway, "How Ballad Writing Affects Our Seniors," *Tabula*, XXIII (November, 1916), 41.

11. Ernest Hemingway, "The Inexpressible," *Tabula*, XXIII (March, 1917), 46; *ibid.*, "The Worker," 22.

12. Ernest Hemingway and Fred Wilcoxen, "Athletic Verse," *Tabula*, XXIII (March, 1917), 39.

13. EH to CAF, September 23, 1951. Hemingway had forgotten a vivid description of football's tedious horrors in *The Torrents of Spring* (Scribner's, 1926), 85-6.

14. *Trapeze*, VI (March 2, 1917), [1].

15. "Ring Lardner Returns," *Trapeze*, VI (May 4, 1917), [3].

16. "Some Space Filled by Ernest Macnamara Hemingway," *Trapeze*, XXV (May 11, 1917), [3]. The volume numbering of the paper shifts unaccountably in several issues of this period. The bound volume, however, is labeled without variation as Volume VI.

17. "High Lights and Low Lights," *Trapeze*, XXV (May 25, 1917), [4].

18. *Trapeze*, XXV (May 25, 1917), [2].

19. *Ibid.*, [1]. This was an unsigned article listing the college plans of the class of 1917.

20. Ernest Hemingway, "Class Prophecy," *Senior Tabula*, 57-62.

21. Ernest Hemingway, "Defense of Dirty Words," *Esquire*, II (September, 1934), 158D.

22. *Idem.*

## CHAPTER TWO

This chapter, like its predecessor, could not have been written without the patient assistance of a number of generous people. The reliance upon their testimony is necessarily heavy, since no material comparable to Hemingway's high school writing is available to the student of his Kansas City period. Save for the single exception noted in the text, it is impossible to identify with real assurance the stories written by Hemingway for the *Star* in 1917 and 1918. I am irreparably indebted to the following individuals for their many kindnesses: Charles I. Blood; Sumner Blossom; George T. Bye; Marvin H. Creager; Russel Crouse; Clyde Brion Davis; J. N. Darling; J. Charles Edgar; Paul W. Fisher; E. B. Garnett; Norman Greer; the late Henry J. Haskell; Wilson Hicks; Clifford Knight; Landon Laird; Frances and Richard Lockridge; the late Lionel C. Moise; William B. Moorhead; William M. Reddig; Robert H. Reed; T. Murray Reed; John Selby; Wesley W. Stout; E. H. Taylor; Harry Van Brunt; Marcel Wallenstein; C. G. Wellington; Paul I. Wellman; Dale Wilson; and Montgomery Wright.

1. Maxwell Perkins, "Ernest Hemingway," *Book-of-the-Month Club News* (October, 1940), 4. This brief sketch by Hemingway's editor and friend was written on the occasion of the publication of *For Whom the Bell Tolls*.
2. Tyler Hemingway died in Kansas City in 1922. Henry J. Haskell died on August 20, 1952, after fifty-four years on the staff of the *Star*. He had been its editor since 1928. He was twice awarded a Pulitzer Prize.
3. Courtney Ryley Cooper, "Star Man," *Saturday Evening Post*, CCIX (December 19, 1936), 56.
4. Henry J. Haskell to CAF, February 8, 1952.
5. Kansas City *Times*, November 26, 1940, 1. Hemingway gave this interview, published in the morning edition of the *Star*, in Kansas City. The interview, an excellent one, and itself a good illustration of Pete Wellington's tutelage, had neither by-line nor initials. Its author was Paul W. Fisher, at the time a reporter on the *Star*, and later director of public relations for United Aircraft.
6. *Idem.*
7. Mr. Moise died on August 7, 1952, at Desert Hot Springs, California. At the time of his death, at the age of sixty-three, he was on sick leave from his position—a responsible one—as editor of the Hearst predate service. Even his obituaries did

not include a full list of the papers where he had worked, in addition to the *Star*, during his forty years in American journalism: the Chicago *Tribune*, Boston *Record*, New York *Daily News*, New Orleans *Times-Picayune*, *Rocky Mountain News*, Milwaukee *Sentinel*, New Orleans *Item*, Los Angeles *Examiner*, and the Los Angeles *Express*, of which he was for a time city editor. During the 1930's Moise was both city editor and, later, an editorial writer on the *Wisconsin News*.

8. Paul W. Fisher to CAF, April 2, 1952. Mr. Fisher was the reporter who interviewed Hemingway for the Kansas City *Times* in November, 1940. See footnote 5, above.

9. Kansas City *Star*, March 1, 1918, 1.

10. These two sketches were first published among the other untitled vignettes of Hemingway's second expatriate volume, *in our time* (Three Mountains Press, 1924), chapters 10-11. See Chapter Eleven for a more complete discussion of the *in our time* vignettes. Hereafter cited as *in our time*.

11. Kansas City *Star*, July 17, 1917, 8.

12. *Idem.*

13. *in our time*, 17.

14. *Ibid.*, 28-9.

15. *Brumback, IC.*

16. *Idem.*

17. There are a number of other forceful, less extended uses of his Kansas City experience throughout Hemingway's mature work, additional evidence that the importance of the period to him cannot be measured accurately by its relative brevity.

18. See Chapter Nine for a description of this episode.


## CHAPTER THREE

In the preparation of this chapter I became obligated to the following individuals for help and advice: Professor Charles M. Bakewell; J. Charles Edgar; Mrs. Charles W. Fyfe; William D. Horne, Jr.; Charles P. LeMieux, Regional Director, American Red Cross; Mrs. Dorothy R. McGlone; Marguerite M. Schwarz; Zalmon G. Simmons, Jr.; William B. Smith; and Frederick W. Spiegel.

1. *Brumback*, 1C.

2. Kansas City *Star*, May 13, 1918, 4.

3. For a more complete history of the American Field Service, see Charles A. Fenton, "Ambulance Drivers in France and Italy: 1914-1918," *American Quarterly*, III (Winter, 1951), 326-43.

4. Charles M. Bakewell, *The Story of the American Red Cross in Italy* (Macmillan, 1920), 223-24. Professor Bakewell, Sheldon Clark Professor Emeritus of Philosophy at Yale University, was a member of the Public Information Department of the Red Cross in Italy in 1918. His volume is the only complete account of Red Cross activities in Italy in World War I, although it should be supplemented by Red Cross bulletins and reports.

5. Ernest Hemingway, *Green Hills of Africa* (Scribner's, 1935), 70.

6. *Brumback*, 1C. The remainder of the account of the trip to Europe and the events in Paris is based upon this article.

7. Kansas City *Star*, July 14, 1918, 5A. Hereafter cited as *Star*.

8. Ernest Hemingway, "A Natural History of the Dead," *Winner Take Nothing* (Scribner's, 1933), 140. The story, which had no magazine publication, originally appeared the year before as part of one of the dialogues with the old lady of *DITA*.

9. *Star*.

10. *Ciao* (June, 1918), [1].

11. *Ibid.*, [3].

12. *Brumback*, 2C.

13. *Star*.

14. *Oak Leaves*, August 10, 1918, 56. Brumback's letter to Doctor Hemingway was reprinted in the Oak Park weekly newspaper as part of an article about Hemingway.

15. *Idem*.

16. *Current Biography: 1948* (H. W. Wilson Co., 1949), 409.

17. *Oak Leaves*, October 5, 1918, 12.

18. *Ibid.*, August 10, 1918, 56.

19. Ernest Hemingway to Maxwell Perkins, December 21, 1926. *Baker*, 4n.

20. Frederic Manning, *The Middle Parts of Fortune* (Piazza Press, 1929). The novel, one of the most memorable of World War I, was published anonymously. Manning was a member of London and Paris avant garde groups. He died in 1935. There was only one edition of the original version. In 1930 there appeared another edition, "with certain prunings and excisions," under the title, *Her Privates We*, this time with Private 19022 listed as its author.

21. Ernest Hemingway, "Introduction," *Men at War* (Crown, 1942), xvi.

22. *Ibid.*, xiv.

23. *Ibid.*, xiii-xiv.

24. *Oak Leaves*, October 5, 1918, 12.

25. *Ibid.*, 13.
26. Dorothy Vandercook, "For Whom the Bell Tolled," Chicago *Tribune,* December 3, 1940, 14. This letter by a grammar school classmate was sent to the reporter then writing the *Tribune*'s famous "Line o' Type" column. It was occasioned by the columnist's erroneous reflection, a few days earlier, that Hemingway had never used his Chicago background in any of his fiction.
27. Ernest Hemingway, "Soldier's Home," *Contact Collection of Contemporary Writers* (Contact Publishing Company, 1925), 86.
28. *Brumback,* 2C.
29. Ernest Hemingway, "Up in Michigan," *Three Stories & Ten Poems* (Contact Publishing Company, 1923), 3-10. See Chapter Seven for additional comment on this story.

## CHAPTER FOUR

The testimony of Gregory Clark and the late J. Herbert Cranston is drawn from the author's correspondence and/or interviews with them, from Mr. Cranston's posthumous autobiography, *Ink On My Fingers* (Ryerson Press, 1953), and from three articles: Herbert Cranston, "Hemingway's Early Days," Midland (Ont.) *Free Press Herald* (October 17, 1945), 2, and "When Hemingway Earned Half a Cent a Word on the Toronto Star," New York *Herald Tribune Book Review* (January 13, 1952), 6; and Gregory Clark, "Hemingway Slept Here," Montreal *Standard* (November 4, 1950), 13-14. In addition to my debts to Mr. Clark and Mr. Cranston, as well as to Mr. W. H. Cranston for permission to quote from his father's correspondence, I am also obligated to the following individuals: Nathaniel A. Benson; Arthur S. Bourinot; the late Augustus Bridle; Ralph B. Cowan; Alan Creighton; William Arthur Deacon; Merrill Denison; Grant Dexter; Wilfred Eggleston; Robert A. Farquharson; Edward M. Gundy; Wellington J. Jeffers; Professor Fred Landon; J. V. McAree; D. C. McArthur; W. L. McGeary; Professor Kenneth MacLean; Carlton McNaught; J. A. McNeil; Keith Munro; Mark E. Nichols; Lorne Pierce; Gillis Purcell; Emerson B. Reid; David B. Rogers; Bernard K. Sandwell; Charles Vining; Claire Wallace; Clifford Wallace; and John Winterbottom.

1. J. Herbert Cranston to CAF, August 7, 1951. Mr. Cranston was assistant managing editor of the Toronto *DS* when the weekend edition, the Toronto *SW*, was launched in 1910. In

1911 he was transferred to the new publication as its editor. He remained in charge until his resignation in 1932. He died in Midland, Ontario, in December, 1952.

2. Gregory Clark to CAF, June 19, 1952 (Int.). Gregory Clark was not only the *SW*'s feature editor in 1920, but also one of its outstanding staff writers. He has become widely known and respected as a Canadian newspaperman, war correspondent, and radio writer. In Toronto he is regarded as the unofficial keeper of the narrative and legends of Hemingway's Canadian period.

3. *SW*, February 14, 1920, 7. Verification of this article as Hemingway's comes from the *Star*'s pay records. The indifferent proofreading of both the *DS* and the *SW*—particularly the former—is a convincing symptom of their casual professional standards. Spelling mistakes have been silently corrected, although English-Canadian variations of American spellings are retained. The punctuation has not been altered save in the case of extreme and confusing errors.

4. *Ibid.*, March 6, 1920, 13.

5. *Ibid.*, March 13, 1920, 11.

6. *Ibid.*, April 10, 1920, 17.

7. *Ibid.*, March 13, 1920, 10.

8. *Ibid.*, April 24, 1920, 13.

9. For the student of Hemingway's metaphor there are significant parallels between this section of the 1920 *SW* article and the long, provocative short story written in 1924, "Big Two-Hearted River," particularly in terms of the ritualistic therapy so important to the story's theme.

10. *SW*, June 26, 1920, 17; *ibid.*, August 5, 1920, 11.

11. *Ibid.*, August 28, 1920, 24.

12. *Ibid.*, November 20, 1920, 25-26.

13. *Ibid.*, April 10, 1920, 12.

14. *Ibid.*, April 24, 1920, 11.

15. Lionel Moise was a bona fide expert on the hobo world. A veteran of the Kansas City *Star*, who watched his local arrivals and departures for fifteen years, remembered that Moise "had visited probably every hobo jungle between the Pacific Coast and Kansas City." Once when a tramp came to the *Star* with an intriguing but fantastic story, he was automatically turned over to Moise for interrogation. Moise and the bum conversed in a dialect of jungle language, entirely unintelligible to the other reporters. After a few minutes Moise pronounced the story authentic and it was used in the next edition.

16. *SW*, April 3, 1920, 9, 12.

17. *Ibid.*, June 5, 1920, 1 (General Section).

18. *Ibid.*, December 11, 1920, 25-26.

19. Cranston said in an article describing his association with Hemingway that the American "wrote some twenty-four pieces" for the *SW* in 1920. Cranston kept his own books during this period; he derived the figures from these records and from the payment entries in the *Star's* own accounts. If Hemingway did sell nine additional articles to the *SW* in 1920 they were either brief ones, without by-lines—which is unlikely, since by-lines were lavishly given—or were bought but never printed. The second alternative is more probable; it would have been consistent with Cranston's generosity toward his contributors. The discrepancy may also arise in part, on the other hand, from the inclusion in Cranston's figures of some or all of the seven by-lined articles the *SW* bought from Hemingway in 1921. See Chapter Five.

20. In January, 1952, in his *Herald Tribune* article, Cranston cited half a cent a word as "our regular rate on the *SW* in those early days." In a letter of August 7, 1951 to the author, he said, "I think I paid him about ¾ a cent a word to begin with, which later reached one cent."

CHAPTER FIVE

It is both a pleasure and an embarrassment to acknowledge—in several cases for the second or third time—the generous help I received from the following individuals in the preparation of this chapter: Gregory Clark; the late J. Herbert Cranston; Roy Dickey; William D. Horne, Jr.; Professor Norman F. Maclean; Florence E. Parker, Specialist on Cooperatives, Bureau of Labor Statistics, U. S. Department of Labor; William B. Smith; Y. K. Smith; Jerry Voorhis, Executive Secretary, Cooperative League of the United States of America; Dr. James Peter Warbasse; Professor Colston E. Warne, Department of Economics, Amherst College; and Donald M. Wright.

1. H. Rappaport, "False Cooperatives and a $15,000,000 Shell-Game," *Nation*, CXIII (October 19, 1921), 447. Hereafter cited as *Nation*.

2. During the 1940's Harrison Parker emerged from retirement as the self-styled hereditary chancellor of The Puritan Church. He was reported to have taken in over $230,000 through a puzzle contest to raise a "building fund." The Appellate Court of Illinois ruled that "no Puritan Church, no theology, congregation or services existed," and that Parker, his wife, and

sister constituted the "governing body." The court ordered Parker to return the contributions of five complainants. The federal government thereupon filed an income tax lien for $39,184.24 against The Puritan Church for taxes allegedly due on its income between 1945 and 1948.

3. "The Co-operative Society of America," *Co-operation*, VII (July, 1921), 118. *Co-operation*, a monthly publication of the Cooperative League of the United States of America, was edited by Dr. James P. Warbasse, an effective enemy of spurious co-operatives.

4. *Nation*, 447.

5. Y. K. Smith was at this time about forty years old. He has had an extensive career in the advertising business, and was for many years copy chief of the New York office of D'Arcy Advertising Company, a St. Louis agency, one of the larger American advertising organizations.

6. [Donald M. Wright], "A Mid-Western Ad Man Remembers," *Advertising & Selling*, XXVIII (March 25, 1937), 54. Donald Wright is now a free-lance writer. Hereafter cited as "Mid-Western Ad Man."

7. Ernest M. Hemingway, "A Divine Gesture," *Double-Dealer*, III (May, 1922), 267-68. Almost thirty years later Hemingway returned briefly to this genre with two fables, "The Good Lion" and "The Faithful Bull," *Holiday*, IX (March, 1951), [50-51]. "The Good Lion" is reprinted in *The Hemingway Reader*, ed. Charles Poore (Scribner's, 1953), 611-14.

8. Ernest M. Hemingway, "Ultimately," *Double-Dealer*, III (June, 1922), 337.

9. Sherwood Anderson, *Sherwood Anderson's Memoirs* (Harcourt, Brace, 1942), 474-75. Hereafter cited as *Memoirs*.

10. *Co-operative Commonwealth*, II (September, 1920), 3.

11. "Mid-Western Ad Man," 54, 58.

12. *SW*, May 21, 1921, 21; *ibid.*, August 20, 1921, 22; *ibid.*, December 17, 1921, 15.

13. *Ibid.*, July 2, 1921, 21.

14. *Ibid.*, February 19, 1921, 13.

15. The misspelling occurred in the articles of February 19, May 21, July 2, August 20, and December 7—in the five articles, in other words, which were set up as columns.

16. *SW*, May 21, 1921, 21.

17. *Ibid.*, February 19, 1921, 13.

18. *Ibid.*, July 2, 1921, 21.

19. *Ibid.*, February 19, 1921, 13.

20. *Ibid.*, November 12, 1921, 11.

21. *Ibid.*, May 28, 1921, 21.

22. *Ibid.*, December 17, 1921, 15.
23. The Toronto Star Reference Library.
24. John Bone died in 1928. He had some of Pete Wellington's qualities—dedication to the paper, absorption in his profession, rigid insistence on a responsible level of performance—but he lacked the Kansas City editor's consuming regard for good writing. Although Bone was invariably astute in the recognition of talent, his primary concerns were the expansion of the *Star*'s circulation and the solidification of his own personal position. There is no evidence that he ever attempted to influence Hemingway's style or treatment of material, or that he regarded Hemingway as a promising creative writer. He simply saw in the young American's lively gifts an inexpensive way of making the *Star* more readable.
25. Harvey Breit, "Talk with Ernest Hemingway," *New York Times Book Review* (September 7, 1952), 20.
26. *Memoirs*, 473.

## CHAPTER SIX

1. Sherwood Anderson to Lewis Galantière, November 28, 1921. *Letters of Sherwood Anderson,* ed. Howard Mumford Jones & Walter B. Rideout (Little, Brown, 1953), 82-3.
2. EH to Sherwood Anderson, no date. The letter was written from Paris, shortly before Christmas, 1921.
3. Carlton McNaught, *Canada Gets the News* (Ryerson Press, 1940), 145-46.
4. *SW*, February 18, 1922, 15.
5. *Ibid.*, February 4, 1922, 3.
6. *Ibid.*, March 4, 1922, 25.
7. *Ibid.*, March 25, 1922, 15.
8. Robert McAlmon to Norman Holmes Pearson, February 28, 1952.
9. EH to Sherwood Anderson, March 9, 1922.
10. *SW*, March 18, 1922, 12; *ibid.*, March 4, 1922, 3.
11. *Ibid.*, March 11, 1922, 12.
12. *Ibid.*, 13.
13. *Ibid.*, March 18, 1922, 15.
14. *Ibid.*, March 25, 1922, 22.
15. *Ibid.*, 3.
16. *Ibid.*, April 15, 1922, 29.
17. *DS*, April 13, 1922, 17.
18. *Ibid.*, April 10, 1922, 1.
19. *Ibid.*, April 24, 1922, 1, 2

20. *Ibid.*, 2.
21. *Ibid.*, April 18, 1922, 1.
22. *Ibid.*, June 10, 1922, 5.
23. *Ibid.*, June 24, 1922, 16; *SW*, June 24, 1922, 5.
24. See Chapter Nine.
25. See Chapter Eleven.
26. *SW*, August 12, 1922, 11.

## CHAPTER SEVEN

Many people contributed immeasurably to this and the previous chapter, including Louis Henry Cohn; Max Eastman; Wilbur Forrest; Otis L. Guernsey, Jr.; Mrs. Guy Hickok; Thayer Jaccaci; Harold Loeb; Frank Mason; and Professor Carl F. Schreiber. I am also indebted to Stanley Pargellis and the staff of The Newberry Library for their kindnesses, and to Mr. Pargellis for permission to quote from the Library's unpublished correspondence between Hemingway and Sherwood Anderson. I am similarly obligated to Carl Van Vechten as executor of the Gertrude Stein papers in the Yale Collection of American Literature, and to Donald Gallup and Alfred A. Knopf as editor and publisher of letters written to Miss Stein; and to Edmund Wilson for permission to quote from the Hemingway correspondence printed in Mr. Wilson's *The Shores of Light*. My greatest debt is to Professor Norman Holmes Pearson for the patience with which he shared and clarified his ideas about Stein's work; the general pattern and treatment of her literary relationship with Hemingway, and some details I have cited, I owe to "Gertrude Stein and Writing on Writing," a lecture given by Professor Pearson on November 7, 1952 as a Peters Rushton Seminar at the University of Virginia.

1. John Peale Bishop, "Homage to Hemingway," *New Republic*, LXXXIX (November 11, 1936), 40. Bishop quoted Hemingway directly: "Ezra [Pound] was right half the time, and when he was wrong, he was so wrong you were never in any doubt about it. Gertrude was always right."
2. EH to Sherwood Anderson, May 23, 1922.
3. *In Our Time* was published in New York in September, 1925. The finished manuscript had been sent to New York, to Donald Ogden Stewart, in September, 1924. The five European stories therefore become, in terms of acquiring the experience, largely the product of 1922, the first six months of 1923—the Hemingways returned to Canada in August, 1923—and part of 1924. During 1922, in other words, Hemingway

accumulated at least the outlines of the material for such stories as "Mr. and Mrs. Elliot," which dealt with an expatriate poet; "Cat in the Rain," with its portrait of a young American couple in Italy; the Tyrolese story, "Out of Season," which included another aspect of expatriation; the sketch of expatriate response to a return to the United States, "Cross Country Snow"; and "My Old Man," the long narrative about an expatriate American jockey and his son.

4. EH to Sherwood Anderson, March 9, 1922.

5. Gertrude Stein to Sherwood Anderson, undated letter [spring, 1922]. "[Hemingway] is a delightful fellow," Miss Stein told Anderson, "and I like his talk. . . ."

6. *Toklas*, 260.

7. William L. Phillips, "How Sherwood Anderson Wrote *Winesburg, Ohio*," *American Literature*, XXIII (March, 1951), [7]-30.

8. Frank Mason to CAF, September 17, 1952 (Int.). Mason remained in charge of the Paris office of I.N.S. until 1926. He is regarded by survivors of the period, including himself, as the original of the American newspaperman named Krum who appears briefly in Chapter Five of *The Sun Also Rises*.

9. Guy Hickok died in 1951. It was with Hickok that Hemingway made, in the former's Ford, the trip through Italy that resulted in the 1927 short story, "Che Ti Dice La Patria?" Mr. Hickok was associated with the Voice of America at the time of his death. Prior to this he had been Program Director of NBC's International Division.

10. EH to Edmund Wilson, November 25, 1923. Edmund Wilson, *The Shores of Light* (Farrar, Straus and Young, 1952), 117.

11. *Ibid.*, 118.

12. Gertrude Stein, "How Writing Is Written," *The Oxford Anthology of American Literature*, II, ed. William Rose Benét and Norman Holmes Pearson (Oxford University Press, 1938), 1451. Hereafter cited as *Oxford*.

13. EH to Sherwood Anderson, May 23, 1922.

14. *Oxford*, 1447.

15. *Toklas*, 266.

16. *Idem*.

17. *Idem*.

18. Ernest Hemingway, "Mr. and Mrs. Elliot," *In Our Time* (Boni & Liveright, 1925), 109.

19. "Monologue to the Maestro," 174B.

20. *Oxford*, 1449.

21. EH to Gertrude Stein, August 15 [1924]. *The Flowers of Friendship: Letters Written to Gertrude Stein*, ed. Donald

Gallup (Alfred A. Knopf, 1953), 165. Hereafter cited as *Gallup*.

22. "Monologue to the Maestro," 21.
23. *Toklas*, 265.
24. EH to Gertrude Stein, August 15 [1924]. *Gallup*, 164.
25. Gertrude Stein, *Narration* (Chicago University Press, 1933), 35.
26. William Bird was at this time European manager of the Consolidated Press. He was also publishing expatriate work in Paris; in 1924 he printed Hemingway's *in our time*.
27. EH to Gertrude Stein, November 9, 1923.
28. *DITA*, 2.
29. *DS*, September 9, 1922, 8.
30. *Ibid.*, September 19, 1922, 4.
31. *Ibid.*, September 1, 1922, 23.
32. *Ibid.*, September 2, 1922, 28.
33. *Ibid.*, September 5, 1922, 5.
34. *Ibid.*, September 30, 1922, 9.
35. *SW*, September 30, 1922, 16.
36. Ernest Hemingway, "An Alpine Idyll," *American Caravan*, ed. Van Wyck Brooks *et al.* (Macaulay, 1927), 46-51.
37. "Old Newsman Writes," 26.
38. Ernest Hemingway, "a.d. Southern Style," *Esquire*, III (May, 1935), 25.
39. *Idem.*

## CHAPTER EIGHT

1. EH to CAF, September 23, 1951.
2. *DS*, September 30, 1922, 1.
3. *Idem.*
4. *Ibid.*, October 23, 1922, 1 (Second Section).
5. *Ibid.*, September 30, 1922, 1.
6. *Ibid.*, October 24, 1922, 1 (Second Section).
7. At this point in the article, in verification of Hemingway's foresight, the *DS* news editor inserted a note pointing out that on the previous day, almost three weeks after Hemingway wrote his story, a wire service cable had revealed that the Turks would indeed claim Mesopotamia at the forthcoming peace conference.
8. *DS*, October 28, 1922, 1 (Second Section).
9. *Ibid.*, October 9, 1922, 1.
10. *Ibid.*, October 31, 1922, 5.
11. "Monologue to the Maestro," 174B. The first line of Hemingway's October 9 cable was itself a variation of the opening

sentence of Kipling's short story about an earlier Russian threat to Afghanistan, "The Man Who Was": "Let it be clearly understood," Kipling had begun, "that the Russian is a delightful person till he tucks in his shirt."

12. *Ibid.*, 21.
13. Ernest Hemingway, "The Snows of Kilimanjaro," *Esquire*, VI (August, 1936), 197.
14. *DS*, November 3, 1922, 10.
15. Hemingway mailed from Constantinople on October 18 a long article which was the least impressive of his Near East dispatches. It was published in the *DS* on November 10, on page 12, but in treatment it was an uncharacteristic return to his loose, *SW* approach. He presented a grab bag of material whose various sections were held together only by their common connection with naval episodes in the Bosphorus. Its appeal for a Canadian audience was in its obvious admiration for the Royal Navy. Its paragraphs were hearty and British, and a reminder that Hemingway was accustomed to being paid by the word. It was also mildly corrupt as a piece of journalism, since at no point did he fulfill in any complete way his avowed, censor-free exposure of naval activities.
16. *DS*, October 20, 1922, 1 (Second Section).
17. Malcolm Cowley, "A Portrait of Mister Papa," *Ernest Hemingway: The Man and His Work*, ed. John K. M. McCaffery (World, 1950), 49.
18. *DITA*, 4.
19. EH to CAF, September 23, 1951. In 1934, in an angry denunciation of the complacent indignation of literary critics about the depression, Hemingway defined his position similarly when he declared that "things were in just as bad shape, and worse, as far as vileness, injustice and rottenness are concerned, in 1921, '22 and '23 as they are now. . . ." "Old Newsman Writes," 25.
20. See Chapter Eleven for a more complete discussion of this 1922 dispatch and its relationship to the vignettes of *in our time*.
21. *DS*, November 14, 1922, 7.
22. *DITA*, 3.
23. Ernest Hemingway, "Introduction by the Author," *In Our Time* (Scribner's, 1930), 9-12. The sketch was retitled "On the Quai at Smyrna" in the 1938 collection of all Hemingway's short stories through that date [Ernest Hemingway, *The Fifth Column and the First Forty-Nine Stories* (Scribner's, 1938), 185-86], and retains this title in subsequent publication.
24. *DITA*, 2, 135.

25. Lincoln Steffens, *Autobiography of Lincoln Steffens* (Harcourt, Brace, 1931), 834.
26. Frank Mason's recollection thirty years later was that Hemingway cabled him relatively little material; most of it, he added, was of no particular use to a syndicate primarily interested in spot news. Mason felt that he did remember one eloquent paragraph dealing with a refugee scene.
27. "Old Newsman Writes," 25.


CHAPTER NINE

The help of the following individuals was generously available to me in the preparation of the two chapters—Eight and Nine—on the Near East Assignment: Charles F. Bertelli; Constantine Brown; Robert McAlmon; Frank Mason; Mrs. Paul Scott Mowrer; G. Ward Price; Henry Wales; and Basil Woon.

1. George Slocombe, *The Tumult and the Shouting* (Macmillan, 1936), 191-92. Slocombe represented the London *Daily Herald* at Lausanne. In 1946 he became literary editor of the European edition of the New York *Herald Tribune*.
2. Henry Wales to CAF, August 7, 1952. Mr. Wales succeeded Floyd Gibbons as the Chicago *Tribune*'s chief European correspondent.
3. Charles F. Bertelli to CAF, August 19, 1952.
4. "Malady of Power," 31.
5. Ludwell Denny, "Up in Curzon's Room," *Nation*, CXVI (January 10, 1923), 40.
6. "Malady of Power," 31.
7. Ernest Hemingway, "They All Want Peace—What Is Peace?" *Little Review*, IX (Spring, 1923), 20-21.
8. EH to Edmund Wilson, November 25, 1923. Edmund Wilson, *The Shores of Light* (Farrar, Straus and Young, 1952), 118.
9. Bolitho's obituary in the New York *Herald Tribune* two days after his death in France on June 2, 1930 was a full column long. It discussed in some detail not only his colorful career but also his work and personality. The obituary quoted from his journalism to illustrate his "knack for polishing off a person with a single, compact . . . epigrammatic phrase." Bolitho's style, in other words, was a journalistic rendition of the sort of thing Gertrude Stein was doing and teaching in a more literary way. Hemingway's Lausanne poem echoes such Ryallisms as, "Hoover will make a good President because he does

not know how to enjoy himself," and "Ramsay MacDonald is a swell political barytone."

10. "Malady of Power," 31.
11. *Idem.*
12. William Bolitho, *Twelve Against the Gods* (Simon and Schuster, 1929). This collection of studies of a variety of historical figures, ranging from Alexander the Great through Casanova, Isadora Duncan, and Woodrow Wilson, was Bolitho's greatest success. His theme was that the adventurer is an outlaw. "Adventure," he wrote in his Introduction, "must start with running away from home." For a portrait of Bolitho which confirms and extends the kind of personal influence he exerted, see Sisley Huddleston, *Back to Montparnasse* (Lippincott, 1931), 250-54.
13. "Malady of Power," 31.
14. Walter Duranty, *I Write as I Please* (Simon and Schuster, 1935), 95, 169.
15. *Ibid.*, 95.
16. William Bolitho, *Twelve Against the Gods* (Readers Club, 1941), ix.
17. *Ibid.* (Modern Age Books, 1937), viii.
18. "Malady of Power," 199.
19. *Ibid.*, 31.
20. *Ibid.*, 31, 198. Also, G. Ward Price to CAF, August 30, 1952. Mr. Price is still a featured correspondent for the *Daily Mail*.
21. Lincoln Steffens, *Autobiography of Lincoln Steffens* (Harcourt, Brace, 1931), 834.
22. Hadley R. Mowrer to CAF, March 25, 1952. Hemingway said in 1951 that he "felt so badly about the loss that [I] would almost have resorted to surgery in order to forget it." *Baker*, 12. See also Hemingway's preface to Lee Samuels, *A Hemingway Check List* (Scribner's, 1951).
23. DS, January 27, 1923, 11.
24. EH to CAF, July 29, 1952.
25. Hemingway had mentioned Bottomley earlier in 1922, briefly, in the article on Rhone Canal fishing, *DS*, June 10, 5. Hemingway there explained that he was carrying a copy of the London *Daily Mail* to wrap the fish in. At sundown, he wrote, the moment arrived at which "to rewrap the trout in Lord Northcliffe's latest speech . . . and, saving the Bottomley case to read on the train going home, put the trout filled paper in your jacket pocket."
26. The majority of American estimates of Mussolini, with the notable exception of a New York *World* series by Bolitho, were distinctly enthusiastic and admiring.

27. *Time*, XXXV (June 24, 1940), 92.
28. *DS*, February 10, 1923, 2.
29. Robert McAlmon to Norman Holmes Pearson, February 28, 1952.
30. See Chapter Eleven.


## CHAPTER TEN

1. "Old Newsman Writes," 25.
2. For a check list of this material, as well as a comprehensive description and analysis of the Spanish Civil War period, see *Baker*.
3. *SW*, April 14, 1923, 2.
4. *DS*, April 14, 1923, 4.
5. *Ibid.*, April 18, 1923, 1, 4.
6. *Ibid.*, April 21, 1923, 1, 7.
7. *SW*, April 14, 1923, 2.
8. Ernest Hemingway, "A Paris Letter," *Esquire*, I (February, 1934), 156.
9. Ernest Hemingway, "a.d. Southern Style: A Key West Letter," *Esquire*, III (May, 1935), 25.
10. *DS*, May 1, 1923, 1, 28.
11. *Ibid.*, April 25, 1923, 1, 2.
12. *Ibid.*, April 28, 1923, 1, 2.
13. *Ibid.*, May 5, 1923, 1, 34.
14. *Ibid.*, May 9, 1923, 1 (Second Section).
15. *Ibid.*, May 12, 1923, 1 (Second Section).
16. *Ibid.*, May 16, 1923, 1 (Second Section).
17. *Ibid.*, May 12, 1923, 1 (Second Section).
18. *Ibid.*, May 16, 1923, 1 (Second Section).
19. *SW*, April 14, 1923, 2.
20. *Idem.*


## CHAPTER ELEVEN

1. Archibald MacLeish, "Years of the Dog," *ACT FIVE and Other Poems* (Random House, 1948), 53.
2. EH to Edmund Wilson, November 25, 1923. Edmund Wilson, *The Shores of Light* (Farrar, Straus and Young, 1952), 117.
3. Harvey Breit, "Talk with Mr. Hemingway," *New York Times Book Review*, LV (September 17, 1950), 14.
4. *Cohn*, 16.

5. Ernest Hemingway, *Three Stories & Ten Poems* (Contact Publishing Company, 1923). The stories were "Up in Michigan," "Out of Season," and "My Old Man." Six of the ten poems had been published in *Poetry*, XXI (January, 1923), 193-95. The pamphlet was originally advertised in the spring of 1923 as *2 Stories & 10 Poems*. McAlmon described the series as a whole as "dedicated to the idea that artists need not please either money-making publishers, or a main street public." There were three hundred copies printed, many of which Hemingway distributed himself; the pamphlet was also on sale at Sylvia Beach's Paris bookstore.

6. The critical reception of *Three Stories & Ten Poems*, in fact, was characteristic of the fate of most expatriate volumes of the period. The only public recognition the pamphlet received in 1923 was a short paragraph by Burton Rascoe in his New York *Tribune* column, "A Bookman's Daybook," in which he mentioned having received a copy from Lewis Galantière, adding that he had "not yet gotten around to reading it."

7. Edmund Wilson, "Mr. Hemingway's Dry-Points," *Dial*, LXXVII (October, 1924), 340-41. Hereafter cited as *Dial*.

8. *Ibid.*, 340.

9. Ernest Hemingway, "Homage to Ezra," *This Quarter*, I (May, 1925), 222.

10. Harvey Breit, "Talk with Mr. Hemingway," *New York Times Book Review*, LV (September 17, 1950), 14.

11. Like several of his contemporaries—Fitzgerald, for example, as well as Faulkner and Dos Passos—Hemingway wrote a moderate amount of verse in the process of becoming a prose writer. In 1923 he was thinking of his own work in such terms that *Poetry* could describe him as "a young Chicago poet now abroad," who would "soon issue in Paris his first book of verse." Until the publication of the first six vignettes of *in our time* by the *Little Review* in April, 1923, in fact, Hemingway's published creative work had been almost exclusively verse. His response to the variety of Paris associations, to Ezra Pound, to Miss Stein, and to the imagists as a school, is apparent in the changing contours of his poetry.

By and large, the poems were least successful when they seemed to derive most self-consciously from Hemingway's fidelity to the imagist doctrine. When he applied the ideology to a deeply felt, rather than a literary experience—as, for example, in the brief "Captives," where the metaphor was the Thracian refugee procession—his use of the discipline was more forceful. The gerunds, at least, are reminders that whether he was writing prose or poetry he was working in the aura of Gertrude Stein; for her, as for Pound, the two mediums had essentially the same objective. "Do not tell in mediocre verse," Pound had said, "what has already been done in good prose." The better poems also have the lucidity, as well as the meter and rhyme sometimes, of a Kipling or Housman refrain. The least flabby were those whose material dealt with the themes which would emerge so forcefully in his early fiction; his sketches and short stories existed in miniature in the verses about war, politics, and boyhood.

12. These poems are particularly interesting as an early introduction of the motif which would dominate most of the fiction of Hemingway's first period. This was the thesis which appeared in *In Our Time* in 1925, where a Michigan boyhood is seen to equate with adult crime and violence and pain. The two components of experience, the past and the present, lacked the subtlety of balanced restraint that made *In Our Time*'s counterpoint so strong, but the poems had a slick finish of technical glitter, as well as the idiomatic strength of his short stories.

13. Like *Three Stories & Ten Poems*, *in our time* was part of a series of uniform volumes. In this case it was a more formal sequence, an "Inquest into the state of contemporary English prose," edited by Ezra Pound. Hemingway's was the sixth and final volume. Six of the eighteen vignettes were evidently written between December, 1922, when Hemingway's early work was lost in Paris, and April, 1923, when this initial *in our time* material was printed in the *Little Review*. The remaining twelve were written prior to the middle of July, 1923, when Hemingway delivered the manuscript of *in our time*.

14. *Cohn*, 21.

15. *DITA*, 2.

16. Ernest Hemingway, "In Our Time," *Little Review*, IX (April, 1923), 3-5.

17. *DS*, October 20, 1922, 1 (Second Section).

18. Lincoln Steffens, *Autobiography of Lincoln Steffens* (Harcourt, Brace, 1931), 834.

19. *DITA*, 2.

20. *Ibid.*, 192.

21. The gerund was retained in the Scribner 1927 edition of *In Our Time*. The 1930 edition reverted to the *in our time* form, as have subsequent editions.

22. This particular revision actually went through four drafts rather than three. On October 23, 1922, three days after sending the cable from Adrianople, Hemingway mailed from Sofia a long dispatch about the refugee procession. In it he began

the condensation of detail. "I walked five miles with the refugees [sic] procession along the road, dodging camels, that swayed and grunted along, past flat wheeled ox carts piled high with bedding, mirrors, furniture, pigs tied flat, mothers huddled under blankets with their babies, old men and women. . . ." *DS*, November 14, 1922, 7.

23. *Idem.*
24. *SW*, October 20, 1923, 1 (Magazine Section).
25. *Ibid.*, September 15, 1923, 1 (Magazine Section).
26. *Dial*, 341.

## CHAPTER TWELVE

My thanks to Morley Callaghan, Gregory Clark, and the late J. Herbert Cranston must be renewed at this point, even before I make grateful acknowledgment of the generous help of Clifton W. Barrett; Ralph Foster; Peter B. Kyne; O. E. McGillicuddy; Vernon McKenzie; Mrs. Paul Scott Mowrer; Donald and Mary Ross; and Allan Wade.

1. Gertrude Stein to Sherwood Anderson, undated letter (early 1924).
2. The most accurate published estimate of Mr. Hindmarsh is Pierre Berton, "Hindmarsh of The Star," *Maclean's*, LXV (April 1, 1952), 16-17, 37-40, 42.
3. *Ibid.*, 42.
4. Morley Callaghan to CAF, June 19, 1952 (Int.). Callaghan was never a disciple of Hemingway in the patronizing sense with which most literary criticism has belittled the Canadian. His talent was wholly different, celtic and imaginative, and his style has grown steadily in individuality. The critical dismissal of him as no more than a Hemingway imitator derived largely from the fact that his early material was often drawn from a reporter's world; like Hemingway, he frequently wrote about whores and cops and athletes. For an account of the quarrel between Hemingway and Callaghan, see Arthur Mizener, *The Far Side of Paradise* (Houghton, Mifflin, 1951), 212-13. See also, for Callaghan's version, Jock Carroll, "I Never Knocked Out Hemingway," Montreal *Standard* (March 31, 1951), 9, 25.
5. Mary Lowry Ross to CAF, June 20, 1952 (Int.). Much of Mrs. Ross's work for the *Star* in 1923 was feature material for the *SW*, but she also covered—sometimes with Hemingway as her partner—straight news assignments for the *DS*.

6. *DS*, September 25, 1923, 4.
7. Joseph Atkinson died in Toronto in 1948. Although Harry Hindmarsh succeeded him as President, Atkinson willed the material assets of The Toronto Star Limited to a group of trustees, with a number of Ontario charities as beneficiaries of the trust. See Pierre Berton, "The Greatest Three-Cent Show on Earth," *Maclean's*, LXV (March 15, 1952), 7-9, 57-60.
8. The circulation techniques of the *Star* were lampooned about this time by two Toronto newspapermen, during a period when the *Star* was publishing, with a lavish advertising budget, Dickens's *Life of Christ*, a *Life of Edith Cavell*, Dickens's *Love Letters*, and gruesome photographs of French battle-fields.

> To Hindmarsh and Knowles
>     Mr. Atkinson spoke,
> If we don't sell more papers the *Star*
>     will go broke;
> I've three super-salesmen who say
>     they can sell,
> They're Jesus and Dickens and Edith
>     Cavell.
>
> Come fill up our columns with sob-stuff
>     and sex,
> Shed tears by the gallons and slush
>     by the pecks,
> Let the presses revolve like the
>     mill-tails of Hell
> For Jesus and Dickens and Edith
>     Cavell.
>
> Then hey for the paper that strives
>     for the best.
> (If Jesus makes good we'll put over
>     Mae West)
> With cuties and comics and corpses
>     and smell.
> And Jesus and Dickens and Edith
>     Cavell.

9. *SW*, September 14, 1923, 1 (Magazine Section).
10. On October 4, a few days after Hemingway's story about the Sudbury coal fields, the *DS* used, unsigned, his interview in Toronto with Lord Birkenhead. Hemingway's theme was that

"Lord Birkenhead, the austere, unapproachable, super-cynical, and supercilious Earl of Birkenhead, is a myth." He then demonstrated the invariably successful illusion, journalistically speaking, that the Lord High Chancellor was in reality just like the *DS*'s readers, only more so. "In fact," Hemingway wrote knowledgeably, "in his flannels and striped tie he looked not unlike one of the Leander rowing men, except, of course, for a slight discrepancy at the waist." *DS*, October 4, 1923, 12.

11. Dr. Lorne Pierce, editor since 1920 of the distinguished Toronto publishing house, The Ryerson Press, recalls that "I read [Hemingway] regularly. . . . I was interested in what he had to say, and in the way he said it. . . ."

12. *SW*, October 20, 1923, 1 (Magazine Section); *ibid*, October 27, 1923, 1 (Magazine Section).

13. *Ibid.*, November 3, 1923, 20; *ibid.*, November 17, 1923, 19; *ibid.*, January 12, 1924, 20.

14. *Ibid.*, November 17, 1923, 19.

15. John Hadley was the Christian name of the Hemingways' son, born in Toronto on October 10, 1923.

16. *SW*, November 17, 1923, 18; *ibid.*, November 24, 1923, 19; *ibid.*, December 15, 1923, 1 (Magazine Section); *ibid.*, December 1, 1923, 1 (Magazine Section).

17. EH to Ernest Walsh and Ethel Morehead, undated letter (1925). Mr. Walsh and Miss Morehead were the editors of *This Quarter*, which published such early Hemingway stories as "The Undefeated" and "Big Two-Hearted River."

18. Mr. O. E. McGillicuddy, a reporter on the *DS* in 1923, and later an editor of the Toronto *Globe and Mail*, said in 1952, in this same connection, that Hemingway "heartily disliked routine assignments, but could really write a good colour or feature article when given the time he felt he required."

19. *SW*, November 24, 1923, 35.

20. Excellent as it was, the Yeats article had a darker side. Several weeks later Hemingway wrote another story about the Irish poet. It had none of the clarity of its predecessor; it was cheap and vulgar, with no more validity than the paragraphs of a gossip columnist. Its derisive tone was keyed to his audience's prejudices; Hemingway portrayed Yeats as an untidy buffoon who—during a lecture tour—kept his Toronto host up all night with his garrulous eccentricities. "He told literary anecdotes. He chanted his own poems. He crooned Erse sagas." *SW*, December 22, 1923, 35.

   On only one occasion, out of the score or more articles he wrote that fall, did Hemingway match the intensity of the first Yeats story. An article published under his own by-line on December 8 was an expert instrument of controlled satire. The sustained narrative about the pawnshop market for second-hand medals was supported by excellent dialogue and brief, fresh snatches of exposition. *SW*, December 8, 1923, 21.

21. *Ibid.*, 18.

22. *Ibid.*, December 15, 1923, 21.

23. *Ibid.*, December 22, 1923, 1 (Magazine Section).

24. *Ibid.*, December 29, 1923, 1 (Magazine Section); *ibid.*, 20; *ibid.*, 20, 21; *ibid.*, January 19, 1924, 19.

25. *Ibid.*, January 19, 1924, 1 (Magazine Section).

26. Hemingway's coverage of the arrival of Lloyd George in New York and the subsequent official train journey to Montreal was his largest single assignment during the four months in Toronto. Hindmarsh's original plan had been to send three correspondents to Manhattan: Hemingway, Mary Lowry, and Robert Reade, one of the *DS*'s top reporters and a favorite of Mr. Atkinson. At the last moment Hemingway was informed that he would be handling the assignment alone. This was itself a shock, since the *Star* always required a great deal of copy, from all angles, on such a story. Coupled with the fact of his wife's imminent delivery, it encouraged Hemingway to regard the entire episode as a deliberately conceived tactic of personal torment. He did the job competently, however. Exploiting his previous observation of Lloyd George at Genoa the year before, he filed seven prominently featured stories between October 3 and October 6; three of them were long and detailed, and all but one were by-lined. It was an exhausting assignment in every way; Lloyd George's first day in New York required Hemingway to be with the story from early morning at the harbor, through a round of speeches, lunch, and receptions, and on to the theater that night. Hemingway turned the assignment over to another *DS* correspondent in Montreal—the latter noted in his first dispatch that Lloyd George's New York program "would wear out any man"—but he wasn't able to get back to Toronto for the birth of his son; his wife was delivered on October 10, two weeks prematurely, while Hemingway was on the train from Montreal. See *DS*, October 5, 1923, 1; *ibid.*, October 6, 1923, 1; *idem; idem; SW*, October 6, 1923, 2; *ibid.*, 3; *DS*, October 8, 1923, 14.

27. The occasion of Hemingway's letter to the Toronto Newspaper Guild was a personal appeal to him by the late Allen May, an employee of the *Star* who had met Hemingway in Spain, where May served during the Civil War in Dr. Nor-

man Bethune's blood bank unit. See also, Pierre Berton, "Hind-marsh of The Star," *Maclean's*, LXV (April 1, 1952), 38.

28. *SW*, November 17, 1923, 19.
29. *DS*, October 6, 1923, 1.
30. *SW*, October 6, 1923, 2.
31. *DS*, October 8, 1923, 14. H. G. Wells's *Men Like Gods* was published in 1923.
32. *SW*, December 15, 1923, 21.

# INDEX

## A

Adrianople: 172, 182, 183, 184, 185, 229, 232

*Advertising & Selling*: 108, 275

Afghanistan: 178, 179, 180

Aigle: 141

Aldis, Mrs. Dorothy: 99

Alps: 62

Alsace: 53, 168

A.E.F.: 85

*American Caravan*: 167

American Civil War: 180

American Field Service: 48, 51, 52-53

American Red Cross: 48, 51, 52

American Red Cross, Ambulance Corps: 52-55, 59, 61, 62

American Red Cross, Ambulance Corps, Section IV: 54, 58, 60, 61, 62, 66

American Red Cross, Canteen: 62-63

American Red Cross Hospital, Milan: 60, 67, 68, 72

*American Volunteer Motor-Ambulance Corps in France*: 52

Anatolia: 181

Anderson, Sherwood: 100, 103-105, 107, 116-120, 122, 126, 145-150, 156, 203, 225, 226, 236, 248

Anderson, Tennessee: 119

Anglo-American Press Association: 126

Anteuil: 185

*Antonia* (Cunard Line): 261

Aosta: 142

Aponyi, Count: 256

*Argosy*: 113

Arrens,  : 198

Asia Minor. *See* Greco-Turk War.

Associated Press: 120

Athens: 237

Atkinson, Joseph E.: 76, 78, 120, 250, 287

*Autobiography of Alice B. Toklas*: 266

## B

Baden: 211

Baker, Carlos: 266

Bakewell, Charles M.: 271

*Batouala*: 132-133

Baudelaire, Charles: 124

*Beau Brummell*: 10

Beerbohm, Max: 138, 141, 202

Belgium: 217

Bellaria: 130

Berlin: 202

Bertelli, Charles F.: 188-189

*Bibliography of the Works of Ernest Hemingway, A*: 266

Biggs, Fannie: 6-10, 31, 47, 157

Bird, William: 159, 225, 229

Birkenhead, 1st Earl of: 287-288

Bismarck, von, Prince Otto: 177

Black Forest: 217, 252

Bobbitt, Arthur: 20-24, 26

Bolitho, William: 151, 192-195, 201-205, 281, 282

Bone, John: 116, 133, 142, 160, 169, 170, 171, 174, 177, 184, 187, 203, 204, 205, 207, 220, 222, 244, 245, 250, 276

*Book-of-the-Month Club News*: 269

Boston *Transcript*: 250

Bottomley, Horatio: 200, 282